ROUTLEDGE LIBRARY EDITIONS:
POLITICAL THOUGHT AND
POLITICAL PHILOSOPHY

Volume 4

TROTSKY, TROTSKYISM AND THE TRANSITION TO SOCIALISM

TROTSKY, TROTSKYISM AND THE TRANSITION TO SOCIALISM

PETER BEILHARZ

Routledge
Taylor & Francis Group

LONDON AND NEW YORK

First published in 1987 by Croom Helm Ltd

This edition first published in 2020
by Routledge
2 Park Square, Milton Park, Abingdon, Oxon OX14 4RN

and by Routledge
52 Vanderbilt Avenue, New York, NY 10017

Routledge is an imprint of the Taylor & Francis Group, an informa business

British Library Cataloguing in Publication Data
A catalogue record for this book is available from the British Library

ISBN: 978-0-367-21961-1 (Set)
ISBN: 978-0-429-35434-2 (Set) (ebk)
ISBN: 978-0-367-23058-6 (Volume 4) (hbk)
ISBN: 978-0-367-23062-3 (Volume 4) (pbk)
ISBN: 978-0-429-27816-7 (Volume 4) (ebk)

Publisher's Note
The publisher has gone to great lengths to ensure the quality of this reprint but points out that some imperfections in the original copies may be apparent.

Disclaimer
The publisher has made every effort to trace copyright holders and would welcome correspondence from those they have been unable to trace.

TROTSKY, TROTSKYISM AND THE TRANSITION TO SOCIALISM

PETER BEILHARZ

CROOM HELM
London & Sydney

© 1987 Peter Beilharz
Croom Helm Ltd, Provident House, Burrell Row,
Beckenham, Kent BR3 1AT
Croom Helm Australia, 44-50 Waterloo Road,
North Ryde, 2113, New South Wales

British Library Cataloguing in Publication Data
Beilharz, Peter
    Trotsky, Trotskyism and the transition
    to socialism.
    1. Communism — History — 20th century
    I. Title
    335.43'3   HX40
    ISBN 0-7099-3995-7

Phototypeset by Sunrise Setting, Torquay, Devon
Printed and bound in Great Britain by Mackays of Chatham Ltd, Kent

Contents

Preface

Castoriadis once referred sardonically to Trotskyists as the Stalinist bureaucracy in exile. Trotskyists have long dominated the revolutionary tradition on the Western left, yet their proposals for socialist transition have been largely rhetorical. Trotskyist politics, in default, have effectively become apologetics for Eastern European regimes or else enthusiasms for Central American struggles. Socialism has come, in this tradition, to be identified with 'victories' elsewhere, while the authoritarian 'excesses' of such new regimes are excused as historically 'necessary'. At the same time, it has now become commonplace on the Western left to insist that socialism will be democratic or it will not be at all. There is a growing realisation that the revolutionary tradition is not only mistaken, or misleading: it is also dangerous, and this is evident not only in the arguments of emigrés like the Budapest School, but also in the pleas of belated heretics like Poulantzas. Bolshevism ought now to be seen as a problem.

Trotskyism is important because it is part of this problem. Its democratic impulse is weak, and is structured by the Jacobin legacy; this is why Trotskyism is an obstacle to the cause of socialism. The problem with Jacobinism, stated plainly, is that it is a form of politics which seeks human elevation but kills people: it seeks to improve humanity from above, whether they like it or not. It kills people, or justifies murders by others, and then blames History. Bolshevism is an extension of this tradition, and Trotskyism is its most developed theoretical expression. This book examines Trotsky and Trotskyism by analysing the work of Trotsky himself and several major subsequent Trotskyists — James, Dunayevskaya, Mandel and

1

Deutscher. Its focus is the question of the transition to socialism, the philosophy of history in Trotskyism, and the hegemony of the Soviet and Jacobin experience within its thinking.

The argument proceeds as follows. Examination of Trotsky, the source, commences with a location of his later, Jacobin, arguments, within his earlier, radical democratic phase, showing that the French Revolution becomes a masterplan for Trotsky only after October. Trotsky's philosophical and political economic views are then examined and related to the Second International milieu within which he worked; significantly, Trotsky took on certain positions, and wrote relatively little of a searching nature in either of these major domains. Trotsky was, of course, far more prolific in writing history; his historiography is examined next, and finally his views on transition in East and West are discussed. This sequence — philosophy, political economy, historiography, and the generalised interest in transition is then followed into the second part, where the views of his intellectual heirs in philosophy — James and Dunayevskaya, in economy — Mandel, in historiography — Deutscher, are examined and criticised. James and Dunayevskaya are shown to remain more faithful to the democratic but evolutionist aspirations of the younger Trotsky, while Mandel and Deutscher develop in different ways the Jacobin legacy.

There are, then, several themes or purposes in the study. Transition is a theme which runs its whole length. History is also a major theme: the reader more interested in history might begin at Chapter 1, shift to Chapter 3 and proceed to Chapter 7. Readers interested in other particular themes like political economy or philosophy could follow a similar procedure, though these chapters, in the first and second parts alike, have a less unitary nature, as they draw together different arguments sometimes from disparate or meagre sources. The justification for this procedure is that more than other works available on Trotskyism, I seek here to engage the tradition as a tradition or field of discourse, and to do this theoretically and politically. Theory underpins historiography, and politics is borne along by it, but neither are often challenged.

This study seeks to better explain Trotskyism as a way of thinking or a form of argument. The object of the study is to show how Trotskyism functions as a political discourse which

2

can be read through its language and metaphor, which are symptomatic of its Jacobinism and the automatic marxism of the Second International. Trotsky's work rests on a series of generative and evolutionary metaphors which guarantee socialism and, after 1917, predispose him to Jacobin outcomes. The language of automatic marxism then permeates subsequent Trotskyist argument, emerging in different ways in necessitarian philosophies of history, making the transition to socialism a non-problem. The proposals of Trotskyism for a transition to socialism in the West dissolve when its telos is removed. Even some Trotskyists have now realised the vacuity of their tradition, politically; but they still work within it, by now openly supporting Stalinism as the world-historic revolutionary trend.

Trotskyism, then, is far from exhausted. Its criticism and rejection is one condition upon which socialists must face the future. Socialists must henceforth learn from history, no longer to idolise it.

Acknowledgements

This book has been a long time coming. Consequently I have accumulated many debts, intellectual, political and personal, which must be acknowledged. Alastair Davidson, Martin Jay and Baruch Knei-Paz played a vital role in the development of these arguments. Zawar Hanfi, Johann Arnason, Ferenc Fehér, Agnes Heller, George Markus and Cornelius Castoriadis helped to educate me: without their patience and inspiration this book would not have been possible. Over the years I have discussed the problems involved with many, among them Julian Triado, Rob Watts, John Murphy, Boris Frankel, Alan Roberts, Steve Wright, Michael Eldred, Michael Löwy, James O'Connor and Lewis Siegelbaum. I am grateful to all. Peter Sowden at Croom Helm was helpful and supportive, as was Croom Helm's anonymous reader. The thesis on which this book is based would not have been possible without the help of the librarians of the Houghton Library at Harvard and at Wayne State in Detroit. I am also indebted to the staff of the British Library and the Marx Memorial Library in London, and to the staff at Monash Library and Victoria's State Library. The manuscript was typed by Sandra Zurbo and Livia Helou. Authors suffer for the writing of books, but they choose to; families do not. My own parents and the Korbels supported me in ways which cannot be described. Dor did even more, which can even less be explained (I embrace you, full of thanks!). This book is for her, my dearest friend, and for Nikolai, whose generation deserves a better world, and needs the honesty to admit the difficulty of making it.

Peter Beilharz

Note

An earlier version of Chapter 3 appeared as 'Trotsky as Historian', in *History Workshop*, 20 (1985); my thanks to Routledge and Kegan Paul and Gareth Stedman Jones. References to Trotsky's Archives are by permission of the Houghton Library.

Part One
Trotsky: the Source

1
Introduction:
Trotsky and the Jacobin Legacy

'Good and bad citizens'

Leon Trotsky has passed into popular imagination as the Man of October, the hyperbolshevik, and later as the romantic in exile, spurned equally by the regime which he had helped to create and by the capitalist societies which he vilified. But there is another, forgotten Trotsky, who began his political life differently. Before October Trotsky shared in the political culture of the Second International; he imbibed its cosmopolitanism, its enthusiasm for education and enlightenment. This was a world in which socialism was seen to be inevitable, in which marxism was a science no less than Darwinism, a world where progress was believed to forge onward unabated, where the mass was seen as being the party, where a whole growing socialist community would exist within the bowels of bourgeois society, debating in *Die Neue Zeit*, reading anthropology, awaiting the carcass of capitalist civilisation to rot, arguing about the necessity or irrelevance of the general strike to finishing the process. Trotsky's politics, in this milieu, were spontaneist; his self-conception was that of the revolutionary intellectual rather than the professional revolutionary. Like Rosa Luxemburg he stood apart from others, not least of all because of his concern with prefigurative politics.[1] Most significantly, the young Trotsky was a democrat, a vehement opponent of Jacobinism, that very tradition which he was later so brilliantly to extend.

Ironically, then, given the accepted images of Trotsky, his political career began with the vilification of Bolshevism. The central vehicle of his polemic against Lenin, the 1904 missal

9

Introduction

Our Political Tasks, still awaits an English translation; one can understand why. *Our Political Tasks* is as vitriolic and penetrating as any polemic to come from the pen of the later Trotsky; only its object is the very politics which he later came to make canon. Trotsky here severed Lenin's claim that Jacobinism and Social Democracy could be amalgamated; Jacobinism was a specific historical product, he claimed, which had no substantial compatibility with the socialist project as he then identified it.[2] Trotsky repeated earlier allegations that Lenin was Robespierre, caricatured. Jacobinism represented the acme of bourgeois radicalism: in theory, the rights of man and citizen, in practice, the guillotine.[3] Bolshevism had a decapitationist logic; according to Trotsky, Robespierre's maxim – 'I know only of two parties, good and bad citizens' — was inscribed on Lenin's heart.[4] The Bolsheviks consequently represented disaster for Russian Social Democracy: presenting themselves as agents of proletarian liberation, they would produce rather dictatorship over the proletariat.[5]

Who, after October, would recognise Trotsky in these words? Certainly not the Trotskyist tradition, which reduced *Our Political Tasks* to its much celebrated qualms about 'substitutionism', which Trotsky intended against Lenin but could now be directed, retrospectively, against the demonic Stalin. For Trotsky's own trajectory into Bolshevism saw him elevate just this maxim of Robespierre — 'good and bad citizens' — into a marxist cosmology, adding the signifiers 'proletarian' to good and 'bourgeois' to bad credentials respectively. This lapse into Jacobinism can be witnessed in Trotsky, however, not only in the perilous period of war communism but also through the thirties. It becomes a permanent motif in the Trotskyist tradition because it is a lasting feature of Trotsky's Bolshevism; even the later Trotsky's few doubts about this tradition never became substantial.[6]

Trotsky's Jacobin credentials are evident not only in *Terrorism and Communism* but also, later, in *Their Morals and Ours* and *In Defense of Marxism*. *Terrorism and Communism* remains a fascinating work, as H. N. Brailsford put it, 'by far the most typical expression of the Bolshevik temperament which the revolution has produced'.[7] Max Shachtman concurs: it is a High Bolshevik text, but importantly *not* an aberrant one compared to Trotsky's later thought.[8] In it Trotsky rebuts Kautsky's work of the same name. He denounces the idea he

10

had earlier advocated, that Bolshevism viewed itself as the sole repository of the Truth.[9] He lambasts the idea of democracy, itself so central to *Our Political Tasks*; he denies the substitutionism thesis.[10] Trotsky's defence of revolutionary terror in the Russian Revolution introduces the notion of. . .good and bad citizens, or at least good and bad classes; terrorism directed toward the latter is historically and politically necessary, therefore proper.[11] Similarly Trotsky decrees that there are good and bad newspapers, good and bad Taylorism, good and bad armies.[12] Here the dualisms of the Enlightenment are refracted into public life, via state power.[13] The language used by Trotsky to put his case is that of Jacobinism, though it also has other connotations for denizens of the twentieth century: 'To make the individual sacred we must destroy the social order which crucifies him. And this problem can only be solved by blood and iron.'[14] The language decisively expelled from argument by the early Trotsky has returned with a vengeance, as the Bolshevism which the young Trotsky declared degenerate is now alleged to be amalgamated with the Russian proletariat.[15]

Trotsky's Jacobinism may be especially vociferous in the period of war communism, but it is by no means limited to it. In *Their Morals and Ours* (1938) the same dualisms are introduced — morality has a class character, there are only bad and good citizens; them, and us. . .[16] Morality is a closed matter — it lies with the proletariat, and, by historic delegation, with the Party. *In Defense of Marxism* reveals a similar logic — Trotsky's dualistic approach to morals is here taken to its logical conclusion. The opposition within the Party must have a class basis for its mistaken views; it is found to be that of the petty-bourgeoisie, the declining class which must now choose whether to affiliate with the good or bad citizens. Uncertainty and disagreement: here are petty-bourgeoisie traits; for the disappearing class must surely have vacillating positions, such as:

> . . . a disdainful attitude toward theory [!] and an inclination toward eclecticism; disrespect for the tradition of their own organisation; anxiety for personal 'independence' at the expense of anxiety for objective truth; nervousness instead of consistency; readiness to jump from one position to another; lack of understanding of revolutionary centralism and hostility toward it. . .[17]

11

all in contrast to proletarian dialectics. Dialectics had by now come to mean the apologetic hat tricks for which Trotsky already had some weakness; in *Terrorism and Communism*, for example, he had put the later notorious case that the proletarian state withered and intensified at the same time.[18]

Yet within the space of years Trotsky's Jacobin image of man as a lazy animal needing coercion is supplanted by the idyll of Olympian self-perfection in *Literature and Revolution*.[19] Here Trotsky posits the developmental face of Jacobinism, his image of perfection from above, introduced by the cultural superman of socialism, the Faustian technologist carving up nature, rationalising and planning everything which moves as well as nature's inert being.[20] Trotsky's is a vision of ultramodernism very much contiguous with that analysed by Berman in his book, *All That Is Solid Melts Into Air*; Trotsky shares with Faust even the commitment to militarisation of labour, so that the Will to Reason might finally come to temporal fruition.[21] Trotsky's messianism, ironically, grows inversely as the Soviet situation deteriorates. When Trotsky had been completely routed, among his last words to the Central Committee were these: 'Expel me, but you will not prevent the victory of the opposition!'[22] Trotsky could not conceive that history was not on his side, and so in a period of decay and defeat could nevertheless let his imagination soar to utopian heights. Supermen socialists were therefore concocted by Trotsky in an environment where even a decade later, 'you can't find decent buttons' and where 'on our most important highway. . .automobiles can make only ten kilometres an hour'.[23] Yet Trotsky assures the reader that these supermen will be 'stronger, wiser and subtler', more musical in style and voice, excelling even Aristotle, Goethe and Marx.[24] Heroic individuals populate his mind, while the masses toiled on for their bread: the conception of history here in Trotsky was aristocratic.

Trotsky and the French Revolution

Trotsky's post-October arguments have a direct relation to the French Revolution, or at least to the Bolshevik conception of it. As we have seen, the young Trotsky had nothing but contempt for Jacobin Social Democracy, and made this judgement on

Introduction

moral and historiographical grounds alike. In a contemporaneous text, *Results and Prospects* (1905), Trotsky elaborated his historiographical principles and detailed his reservations about unversalising the French Revolution as though it were a general typology. He argued, rather, for the unique specificity of experiences like those which occurred in 1789, 1848 and 1905.[25] After his conversion to Bolshevism, and in response to the attack on his own Bolshevik credentials, Trotsky however openly embraced this notion of the universality of the great French experience. As is well known, he came to parallel the entire process of Soviet 'degeneration' with the alleged masterplan of the French Revolution, popularising notions like Thermidor to explain his own political defeat. This language had awkward resonances, for Trotsky himself had of course earlier been cast as an aspiring Bonaparte.[26]

By 1926 Trotsky was prepared to justify his own record before the Central Control Commission in precisely Jacobin terms. Trotsky now finally recognised the real affinity between Jacobinism and Bolshevism, though at the historiographical expense of collapsing their two Revolutions. He argued that the history of the French Revolution ought now be mandatory reading for Party members, as the Russian Revolution had followed in its path. The crucial thing, Trotsky argued against Comrade Soltz, was that like the French Revolution the Russian, too, was divided into two chapters, one of ascendancy, followed by another of decline. 'None of us is scared by firing squads. . .But the thing is to know *whom to shoot and in accordance with which chapter.*'[27] Shooting enemies of the Revolution in the chapter of ascent was quite normal and in accordance with history's general plot. Trotsky's defence is intriguing, but its significance may have been lost on an audience which had already identified the Left Opposition as bad citizens, and this despite or even because of the generalised influence of the French Revolution among Russian radicals.[28]

Trotsky's trajectory illustrates the power of metaphorical thinking in socialist historiography, and also its weakness. Furet has explained some of the problems involved in his important study, *Interpreting the French Revolution*. Furet argues that the French and Russian Revolutions have been forcibly made mutually reflexive and constitutive by left historians: 'the historiographical discourses about the two revolutions became fused and infected each other. The Bolsheviks were given

13

Introduction

Jacobin ancestors, and the Jacobins were made to anticipate the communists'.[29] More, Furet argues, the French Revolution, understood in this typological sense, never occurred.[30] To illustrate the problem, Furet conjures up an image of his own: Bolshevism and Jacobinism, he says, have been treated as two successive 'liberations', nested like a set of Russian dolls.[31] More specifically, Furet argues that it is only with the French Revolution that leftist politics develops its own novel language of truth and falsehood, good and evil; good citizens and bad citizens, Bolsheviks and traitors . . .[32]

These problems are not unique to Trotskyism, indeed Furet discusses them rather with reference to the dominant communist tradition of historiography in France. But these problems need to be separated out from the problems in Marx's own historiography. As Fehér has shown, the French Revolutions were decisively influential as models for Marx's politics.[33] Further, it is now widely recognised that Marx's historiography or philosophy of history was deeply metaphorical itself: Hayden White, for example, has shown how fundamental was Marx's reliance on the device of metonymy, while Alvin Gouldner has argued that marxism is definitionally metaphorical.[34] It was Marx, of course, who described French history in tragi-comic form, who spoke of revolution as the 'old mole', who, steeped in classical literature, structured even his most systematic work, *Capital*, through the imagery of Shakespeare, Goethe and Dante. But because Marx eschewed Jacobinism he never spoke of good and bad citizens, nor did he make the fatal mistake of identifying history with Party or State: despite the clearly teleological nature of his historiography, Marx, like the young Trotsky, refused history a terrestrial expression in the form of a vanguard.

The situation in the theory of the Bolshevik Trotsky and in Trotskyism generally is different. This is so not only because of Trotskyism's substitutionist chains of 'representative' logic which bind together History, Class, Party and Leadership, nor even primarily because of the implication of Trotskyism in the Soviet experience. More fundamental here is the Jacobin anthropology, which Marx never entertained. As Fehér explains, the central political feature of Jacobinism is the principle of the anthropological perfectibility of man, understood as a condition to be implemented from above. Though thinking primarily of Lenin and Trotsky, Fehér extends this

14

judgement on Jacobinism: 'All revolutionary leaders have combined radical voluntarism and anthropological pessimism.'[35] On this view, Jacobinism combines a _public_ doctrine — the uncritically held notion of human perfectibility — with a _secret_ doctrine, a desperate pessimism, which can be traced back genealogically to Rousseau.[36] Of conceptual teleology Marx was certainly guilty, and frequently; Marx was convinced that socialist revolution was immanent to capitalist development, and in this he was conspicuously mistaken. Neither the historical _deus ex machina_ of his writings on French history, nor the conceptual dialectics of capital in the _Grundrisse_, nor yet again the historical telos imputed to the proletariat in the _Manifesto_ or in the penultimate chapter of _Capital_ have any substantive basis. Trotskyism shares with Marx this historically deceptive, if politically innocent, metaphorical basis: but it mediates it, necessarily, through two further categories to which Marx was indifferent, if not hostile: Party, and (Soviet) State. Whereas history remains in a sense an abstract universal for Marx, it becomes with Trotsky a concretised process: the old mole surfaces in Petrograd, unwittingly delegates its historic vocation to the Bolsheviks and receives — a hiding.

The Bolsheviks felt compelled to summon the imagery and metaphor of the French Revolution to explain and legitimate their own because they, too, were Jacobins. Trotskyism has then become a language of persuasion, of justification, of legitimation, a rhetoric necessarily bound to so-called actually existing socialism. It is in this sense a language of the past, representing a retrospective politics rather than a radical or democratic socialist politics for the West today. This is why so much of its vocabulary is 'dead' metaphor, banal or even fatal. As Susan Sontag has shown, biological metaphor was a staple of Bolshevik discourse, as fundamental to it as was its prognostic issue in surgical intervention.[37] Live, or vivifying metaphor we can, with Ricoeur, define as that which adds or creates meaning, which allows the intuitive perception of the similar in the dissimilar.[38] Dead, or deceptive metaphor in this context, claims to reveal similarity or identity (for example, between French and Russian history) at the expense of their differences. As Barthes suggests, in its myth-function it naturalises history, here by making it conform to the putatively general contours of revolution.[39]

Introduction

Ricoeur has argued, after Aristotle, that poetics and rhetoric seek out similarities.[40] History, in contrast, ought perhaps to be conceived as a discourse which seeks out difference. While the creative use of metaphor expands discourse, or enlightens an audience, banal or dead metaphor encloses it by appealing to the obvious — the biological, the evolutionary, the Great Revolution as typology. The function of Trotskyism, as a rhetorical historiography, is not enlightenment but persuasion. It is a discourse of closure, a monologue of resplendent elegance, rather than an invitation to dialogue. Trotskyism, I will argue in this study, functions so as to persuade the audience by means undisclosed, by installing necessitarian devices which sweep the audience into Bolshevik conclusions. This process can be seen in Trotsky's own work, in his philosophical and economic premises, in his historiography and in his stand on the Soviet Union, and can be traced through major Trotskyist thinkers like James, Dunayevskaya, Mandel and especially Deutscher. With Trotsky, we begin.

Notes

1. Trotsky, *My Life* (Penguin, Harmondsworth, 1975), Chs 3–5; B. Knei-Paz, 'The Political and Cultural Formation of Leon Trotsky'; *Thesis Eleven, 3* (1981), pp. 89–105; P. Beilharz, 'The Other Trotsky', *Thesis Eleven, 3*, pp. 106–13; A. Brossat, *Aux origines de la révolution permanente — la pensée politique du jeune Trotsky* (Maspéro, Paris, 1974); H. J. Steinberg, 'Trockij und die marxistische Debatte in der Periode der II Internationale' in F. Gori (ed.) *Pensiero e azione politica di Lev Trockij* (2 vols., Olschki, Florence, 1982), vol. 1, pp. 61–9; N. Geras, 'Trockij and Rosa Luxemburg' in Gori, ibid., pp. 165–83; D. K. Rowney, 'The Generation of October', unpublished PhD Thesis, University of Indiana, 1965.
2. Trotsky, *Nos tâches politiques* (Belfond, Paris, 1970), Ch. 4. The 1980 English translation by Brian Pearce, announced by New Left Books, has not yet seen the light of day.
3. Ibid., p. 189.
4. Ibid., pp. 194, 197.
5. Ibid., p. 207.
6. I therefore dispute the view of A. Macintyre in *After Virtue* (Notre Dame, University Press, 1981), p. 243f, and implicit in my earlier essay, 'Trotsky's Marxism — Permanent Involution?', *Telos, 39* (1979), pp. 151–2.
7. H. N. Brailsford, Preface to Trotsky, *In Defence of Terrorism* (Labour Publishing Co., London, 1921) p. ii.
8. M. Shachtman, Foreword to Trotsky, *Terrorism and Communism*

16

Introduction

(Ann Arbor, Michigan, 1972), p. vii; compare Trotsky's 1936 French Preface and 1935 English Introduction.

9. Trotsky, *Nos tâches*, p. 198; compare *Terrorism and Communism*, p. 60.

10. Trotsky, *Terrorism and Communism*, p. 109.

11. Ibid., p. 59.

12. Ibid., pp.61, 149, 172.

13. See C. Taylor, *Hegel* (Cambridge, Cambridge University Press, 1975), Ch. 1; C. Perelman and L. Olbrechts-Tyteca, *The New Rhetoric* (Notre Dame, University Press, 1971), Sec. 91.

14. Trotsky, *Terrorism and Communism*, p. 63.

15. Ibid., p. 98.

16. Trotsky, *Their Morals and Ours* (New Park, London, 1974), p. 12.

17. Trotsky, *In Defense of Marxism* (Pathfinder, New York, 1973), p. 43.

18. Trotsky, *Terrorism and Communism*, p. 170; and see F. Fehér, A. Heller and G. Markus, *Dictatorship Over Needs* (Blackwell, Oxford, 1984), Ch. 7.

19. Trotsky, *Terrorism and Communism*, p. 133; Trotsky, *Literature and Revolution* (Ann Arbor, Michigan, 1971), Ch. 8.

20. Trotsky, *Literature and Revolution*, p. 250ff.

21. M. Berman, *All That Is Solid Melts Into Air* (Simon and Schuster, New York, 1982), Ch. 1.

22. Quoted in R. Day, *Leon Trotsky and the Politics of Economic Isolation* (Cambridge, Cambridge University Press, 1973), p. 176.

23. Trotsky, *The Revolution Betrayed* (Pathfinder, New York, 1972), p. 13f.

24. Trotsky, *Literature and Revolution*, p. 256.

25. Trotsky, 'Results and Prospects' in *The Permanent Revolution* (Pathfinder, New York, 1974), and see generally B. Knei-Paz, *The Social and Political Thought of Leon Trotsky* (Oxford, Oxford University Press, 1978), Ch. 4.

26. See Knei-Paz, Ch. 10.

27. Trotsky, 'First Speech at the Session of the Central Control Commission' in *The Stalin School of Falsification* (New Park, London, 1974), p. 113.

28. See generally A. Mathiez, 'Bolshevism and Jacobinism', *Dissent*, Winter 1955; D. Law, 'Trockij and Thermidor' in Gori, *Pensiero e azione politica di Lev Trockij*, vol. 2, pp. 443–9.

29. F. Furet, *Interpreting the French Revolution* (Cambridge, Cambridge University Press, 1981), p. 6; A. Heller, *A Theory of History* (Routledge and Kegan Paul, London, 1982), p. 179.

30. *Interpreting the French Revolution*, p. 118f; and see F. Furet and D. Richet, *The French Revolution* (Macmillan, New York, 1970); T. Skocpol, *States and Social Revolutions* (Cambridge, Cambridge University Press, 1979), Ch. 5.

31. Furet, *Interpreting the French Revolution*, p. 13.

32. Ibid., p. 26.

33. F. Fehér, 'The French Revolutions as Models for Marx's

Introduction

'Conception of Politics', *Thesis Eleven, 8* (1984).

34. H. White, *Metahistory* (Johns Hopkins, Baltimore, 1973), Ch. 8; A. Gouldner, 'The Metaphoricality of Marxism and the Context-Freeing Grammar of Socialism', *Theory and Society* (1974).

35. F. Fehér, 'The Dictatorship Over Needs', *Telos, 35* (1978), p. 34.

36. F. Fehér, A. Heller and G. Markus, *Dictatorship Over Needs*, p. 225; Markus, 'Practical Social Rationality in Marx', *Dialectical Anthropology, 5* (1980), Part 2, p. 27.

37. S. Sontag, *Illness as Metaphor* (Farrar, Straus and Giroux, New York, 1978), p. 82.

38. P. Ricoeur, *The Rule of Metaphor* (Routledge and Kegan Paul, London, 1978), p. 6.

39. R. Barthes, *Mythologies* (Paladin, London, 1976), p. 142f.

40. Ricoeur, *The Rule of Metaphor*, p. 27.

2
The Theoretical Foundations of Trotsky's Marxism: Philosophy and Political Economy

What was the context of Trotsky's intellectual formation? How did the culture of the Second International frame his later thinking? The broad affinity of the young Trotsky with the milieu of German Social Democracy has already been noted. Like his entire generation, Trotsky was deeply influenced by Kautsky and Plekhanov. As Trotsky reminisces in his 1929 'attempt at an autobiography':

> It was in my cell [at the turn of the century] that I read with delight two well-known essays by an old Hegelian-Marxist, Antonio Labriola. . . .Labriola had mastered the materialist dialectics, if not in politics — in which he was helpless — at least in the philosophy of history. The brilliant dillettantism of his exposition actually concealed a very profound insight. He made short work of the theory of multiple factors which were supposed to dwell on the Olympus of history and rule our fates from there. . .although thirty years have gone by since I read his essays, the general trend of his argument is still firmly entrenched in my memory, together with his continuous refrain of 'Ideas do not drop from the sky'.[1]

Labriola's essays presumed a knowledge which Trotsky lacked, 'for which', he confesses, 'I had to substitute guesswork'. The guesswork was later compounded by combination with the arguments of the more orthodox representatives of the Second International. 'In the writings of Marx, Engels, Plekhanov and Mehring, I later found confirmation for what in prison seemed to me only a guess needing verification and theoretical justification.'[2] Mehring shared the economism and penchant for gynaecological metaphor so characteristic of the Second International; his work rests on the classical view in which History is a process marching onward to inevitable proletarian victory.[3] Labriola is a more interesting case. His philosophical views were rather uniquely sophisticated in the largely dogmatic milieu of classical marxism. More, his views are interesting because they provide not proof for, but rather refutation of, Trotsky's own positions. Labriola was an opponent of the monism dominant in the Second International.[4] His was a novel view, which questioned the orthodox dualisms of material/ideal, base/superstructure,[5] and consequently also questioned the Jacobin dualisms of good and evil, God and Devil, optimism and pessimism.[6] Far from supporting the theoretical edifice which Trotsky was constructing, Labriola criticises the entire problematic which would turn history into a moral play by substituting a teleological philosophy of history for an understanding of history itself.

Trotsky's understanding of Labriola appears in fact to identify positively with positions put by Lafargue. Lafargue was a far less sensitive thinker than Labriola; he was given to eclecticism and often to self-contradiction. It was Lafargue and not Labriola who popularised the slogan of 'the right to be lazy', with which Trotsky seems to associate Labriola.[7] Certainly it was Lafargue rather than Labriola who shared with Trotsky the misanthropology of the 'lazy animal',[8] while the glimpses of utopia in Trotsky's work are also reminiscent of Lafargue's conceptions.[9] What then was Trotsky's relation to the pope and cardinal of classical marxism?

Though Trotsky wrote little by way of direct commentary on their philosophical views, a number of fundamental affinities are evident. Trotsky shared with Kautsky the dominant conception of r/evolution in its peculiarly Darwinistic variant.[10] Kautsky had also done much to popularise the notion that ethics was a subsidiary, and inconsequential matter; marxists, after all, possessed Science.[11] Kautsky had also developed the schema of class bipolarisation, the two-class model bequeathed by Marx which subsequently became stock in trade for orthodox marxists.[12] Needless to say, neither Kautsky nor Plekhanov could stomach Trotsky's heresy in replacing the so-called stagist conception of history with the theory of Permanent Revolution. Yet the influence of Plekhanov in philosophical matters is equally plain. It was Plekhanov, rather than the more sophisticated Kautsky, who popularised 'dialectics' and Dialectical Materialism and, with it, propagated the monist conception of history. It was Plekhanov, rather than Labriola, who had railed against the 'factor' theory of history.[13] Plekhanov also foreshadows central theoretical problems regarding the individual and history, freedom and necessity, which emerge as fundamental in Trotsky's historiography and especially in Deutscher's. Like Trotsky, Plekhanov argues against the 'factor' theory, but necessarily from within it; for monism itself is but an immanent attempt to transcend dualism by cancelling the other factor.[14] To Plekhanov's monism there corresponds his necessitarian philosophy of history. Plekhanov argues that necessity *is* freedom.[15] For Plekhanov, as for Calvin before and Deutscher after him, historical predestination is a track upon which will is set.[16] Humans are free to the extent that they know natural and social laws and submit to them.[17] Should, then, any central actor be struck down by the proverbial falling brick, history's plot would still unfold, more or less unaffected.[18] More than Kautsky, then, Plekhanov develops the language of necessity central to Jacobinism and to the Trotskyist tradition. Morality is made effectively redundant, prostrate before the laws of nature or society: one simply *submits*, if not to the Party then at least to History. Squeezed out by the nomological weight of History, value freedom issues in the end of value.

Beyond the sources:
Trotsky's dialectical materialism

If Trotsky wrote little directly on philosophical matters before October, the subsequent period was to be no more edifying. We can, however, still read Trotsky's positions through his texts. For Trotsky did in the later period engage two major polemics on philosophy: and it is surely significant that he refused to discuss philosophy other than polemically. We have already noted Trotsky's contempt for questions of morality, his presupposition that the Party is the proper arbiter of matters public.[19] The later Trotsky regards morality in general as premarxist and therefore obsolete.[20] It is a straightforward matter: there are their morals, and ours . . .,[21] the Kantian

21

categorical imperative is dismissed as shell without content.[22] Here Trotsky follows Engels, in presuming that, in the dualistic terms of positivism, science replaces philosophy.[23] Morality is then replaced by science, passed on by history to the Party (and in *In Defense of Marxism*, to its leaders).

In what did this science consist? In dialectics. Like morality, Trotsky simply presumes that dialectics exist: they are known, held in trust by the Fourth International. This self-righteous attitude produces arguments which themselves remain remarkably unconvincing. The arguments put in *In Defense of Marxism* are in style and substance little improvement on Stalin's catechism in *Dialectical and Historical Materialism*. The tone of the arguments in *In Defense of Marxism* is itself striking. After manifesting some theoretical uncertainty and democratic enthusiasms in the 1937 work *The Revolution Betrayed*[24] Trotsky reasserts his dogmatism by 1939, refuting even the idea of an inner-party referendum because not all opinions are equal.[25] Doubtless the context of these writings is important: already in a state of siege within and without, the Fourth International was now faced by the prospect of a split and a subsequent decrease in its already sparse numbers. It can be conceded that these were not ideal circumstances for a leisurely reflection on Trotsky's part; but Trotsky was capable of literary profusion in worse circumstances yet. At any rate, the text of *In Defense of Marxism* is less simply urgent than it is plainly vitriolic and dogmatic. Trotsky makes it clear that Trotskyism is the sole heir of marxism; to dispute with Trotsky is to break with marxism. The text is heavy with medical metaphor: the opposition is cast as gangrenous, as an abscess demanding lancing. A schoolmasterly Trotsky dispenses the ABCs of marxist science in a style both aggressive and self-righteous:

1. Quantity changes into quality.[26]
2. Everything is in motion (A is not A).[27]
3. Nature itself is dialectical: Darwin was an unconscious dialectician. A natural dialectic works itself out through agents.[28]

The first and second principles, like their equivalent formulations in alternative variants of Dialectical Materialism, are merely common sense. If 'dialectical thinking is related to vulgar thinking in the same way that a motion picture is related to a still photograph',[29] then almost all historians today are by definition marxists. The third principle, the 'dialectics of nature', tells more of Trotsky's affinity with the common wisdom of the Second International. Dialectics are taken to be a biological fact[30]; dialectical thinking is seen as an outgrowth of the dialectic of nature.[31] Trotsky's reference to Darwinism, to atomic weights and chemical elements, confirm his location in the Engels lineage of marxism. All phenomena are subsumed to the category of evolution: forms of thought allegedly *grow* like everything else.[32] Marx's contribution to social theory is therefore understood as equivalent to Darwin's in natural science.[33] This definition places Marx with Lewis Henry Morgan in accordance with Second International wisdom; Marx's achievement is recast as the discovery of a form of classification, that is, Marx's practice and method are presumed to be identical to those of natural science. Further, the argument enlists Marx as support for a general theory of modes of production, where advancing forces of production (technology) break through successive relations of production, in accordance with the classic scheme of automatic marxism. Far from possessing the 'scientific' status which Trotsky attaches to it, this philosophy of history can solve the problems of humanity only with the device of teleology and guarantee.

In Trotsky a quasi-religious faith in the inevitability of socialism provides the motor force for Dialectics. 'Laws of motion' in Trotsky function as the force of progress. According to Trotsky, this position is both Aristotelian (formal) and Hegelian (dialectical).[34] Both the peasant woman adding salt to soup, and the fox in hunt or flight, 'prove' Aristotelian and Hegelian logic, living these logics out without ever understanding them.[35] Trotsky takes Hegel more seriously than he does Kant, but nowhere engages his thought systematically. Hegel is put to the most sophistic of ends, as when Trotsky justifies terror with reference to the principle of contradiction.[36] Hegel is also fundamental to Trotsky's philosophy of history, as will be seen later. With specific reference to philosophical premises it can be argued that Trotsky vacillates between the dualistic categories form and content, appearance and essence, as circumstance necessitates. It is this vacillation which explains how it is that while, say, the premisses of the theory of Permanent Revolution are essentialist and economistic, Trotsky's method can also be formalistic, as it is in his analysis of the USSR. Whatever the limitations of Shachtman's own position in the inner-party debate, the victim whom Trotsky called 'gangrenous' at least perceived the relation between formalistic logic and its conclusions in Trotsky's characterisation of the USSR, where socialist legal forms allegedly determined the socialist content of society. In Trotsky preordained definitions establish conclusions in advance. Trotsky warns dogmatically that political conclusions cannot be made empirically.[37] His arguments are typically presented in formal style: if A, B, then C. A is asserted and beyond discussion; it usually has its source in evolutionist common sense. This indicates a fundamental limit in Trotsky's politics. The necessity of the syllogism denies the very contingency which is the stuff of politics.

Finally, Trotsky's philosophical self-certainty seems to produce an instrumental attitude to theory, which is seen as a tool-box or surgical kit held in the exclusive possession of those who, whether by birth or by choice, have taken the proletarian road.[38] Here Trotsky reintroduces the junction between class-morality and class-philosophy, the position traditionally associated with Stalinism, which can be traced back to Jacobinism. There are only two classes and therefore only two moralities: as more generally with the revolutionary tradition, any proposed 'third way' must by definition be a petty-bourgeois way.[39] In seeking an attitude of 'revolutionary scepticism' towards theory and towards the basic premises of marxism, Dwight MacDonald revealed himself to Trotsky as no less than a traitor.[40] Trotsky casts his opponents in *Their Morals and Ours* as religious zealots. Peasants as another 'third class' are always presumed to approximate to the petty-bourgeoisie: by nature they are untrustworthy and vacillating.[41] Whatever the differences between Trotsky and Stalin, there is a clear identity in their attitudes to theory as the direct reflection of objective class origin.[42] The good worker, instinctively socialist, is naturally free of petty-bourgeois filth. Clearly there is continuity between the early and later Trotsky in this metaphysical premiss of a morally superior proletariat. Political and moral problems are simply brushed aside by reference to the alleged class origins of the opponent. Ironically, then, while Trotsky lacks an elaborated morality his view of history and humanity is saturated with Jacobin moralism.

This deficit and its overcompensation are the root of Trotsky's inability to move beyond the status of the loyal oppositionist, even when the regime he defends has a price on his head.

Political economy in Trotsky

In 1859 Marx wrote a new Preface, replacing the old 1857 'Introduction' to his *A Contribution to the Critique of Political Economy*. These few pages — perhaps less, few paragraphs — were to determine the physiognomy of subsequent traditions of marxism until the rise of western marxism and the Frankfurt School. The generations of the Second and Third Internationals and those who were influenced by them were to speak of this Preface as a brilliant summary of historical materialism. The real content of the Preface was a schematic notion of history as process and interrelation, where some phenomena found correspondence in others, and a problematical formula suggesting that forces of production (usually understood to mean technology), serving as the motor of history, broke through successive relations of production.

Notwithstanding the revival of enthusiasm for the Preface inspired by G. A. Cohen's *Karl Marx's Theory of History, A Defense*, its theorems are somewhat less than edifying for temporal socialists today.[43] Yet the economism in Marx, established as a central principle by the Second International, remains widely influential, even if it is strategically useless: marxists are more at home with their texts than with politics. Trotskyism again is centrally complicit in this saga, for Trotsky retained and developed the forces-relations theorem in the theory of Permanent Revolution. In common again with the Second International, Trotsky viewed *Capital* as a book about surplus-value, exploitation and capitalist collapse, burdened with the 'mysteries of dialectics' and 'the Hegelian triad'.[44] Bebel would, in Trotsky's judgement, have been a better expositor of these problems than the pedantic Dr Marx.[45]

In political economy as in philosophy, Trotsky wrote little systematic work and imbibed rather the general categories of the Second International. One of the few exceptions came in his Preface to a special edition of *The Living Thoughts of Karl Marx* published in 1939. The text itself was organised by Otto Rühle; the introduction, by Trotsky, has only a passing relation

25

to the text itself. Trotsky introduces Marx as the best exponent of the labour theory of value: Marx is the Red Ricardo, a commonplace in *fin-de-siècle* marxism.[46] Trotsky takes the 1859 schema to be Marx's special message; where Trotsky refers to *Capital* it is to its apocalyptic penultimate chapter. The case is simple, if only the useless intellectuals could understand; socialism is inevitable.[47] Trotsky's arguments here explain what he would have called the 'ABCs' of political economy and their predictive character. He polemicises against Sombart and monopoly capital while avoiding the anomalies and controversies internal to marxist economics. He presents allegedly inevitable laws as the substance of a proletarian science.

It may be the case that Trotsky's views on political economy had other sources beyond the shared heritage of the Second International. Richard Day has argued that Trotsky's views on economic policy were far more reasonable and pragmatic than is often thought;[48] perhaps this accords with his other adminis-trative experience, as in the period of civil war. But if the young Trotsky substituted guesswork for hard labour in philosophy, the later Trotsky sought the advice of others in economy. According to Van Heijenoort, his secretary in exile, the only persons with whom Trotsky ever contemplated a literary collaboration were economists: Field, a Trotskyist and Wall Street economist, in Prinkipo; Sternberg, who despite substantial differences with Trotsky, was intended to write the economic section of the New International's program, in Saint-Palais; Rühle, a sometime council communist, in Mexico. Van Heijenoort reads this as suggesting a lack of confidence on Trotsky's part in his command of economics;[49] the idea is a provocative one, more, given his earlier reliance on Rakovsky and Preobrazhensky. In light of this situation, our analysis here can only be further extended through the examination of specific economic themes in Trotsky's work. The theory of Permanent Revolution, the cyclical nature of economy, the questions of Americanism and class are cases in point. Each indicates in a different way the difficulties produced by Trotsky's acceptance of orthodox wisdom.

Trotsky's practice of political economy

The theory of Permanent Revolution

The theory of Permanent Revolution is the keystone of Trotsky's economic and political theory. As Knei-Paz shows, the theory itself was more or less completely formulated by Trotsky already in 1905;[50] the crucial modification, later, is the addition of the revolutionary party as the midwife, nay, *surgeon* of the revolution. The theory itself has two parts. The first new axiom of Trotskyism is that bourgeois revolutions become, in the twentieth century, impossible: they may be initiated as bourgeois revolutions, but can only result in proletarian revolution. The second new axiom is that, because international capital breaks through the relations of the nation-state, revolution also becomes necessarily international. This dual telescoping process presumed by Trotsky to be everywhere underway is clearly economistic, presuming that economic developments determine the political, and it is also universalistic, presuming that world developments determine the national and cultural. As capitalist civilisation slides into the twenty-first century, it can only be observed that Trotsky's conclusions, if not his premises, were hopelessly wide of the mark.

Trotsky's sensitivity to the problem of the world system was, however, acute, and he has taken on the role of internationalist *par excellence*. But as Trotsky explains, for him:

> internationalism is no abstract principle but a theoretical and political reflection of the character of world economy, of the world development of productive forces and the world scale of class struggle. . .Marxism takes its point of departure from world economy, not as a sum of national parts but as a mighty and independent reality. . .the national state. . .has long ago outlived itself and. . .has turned into a brake upon the development of the productive forces. National capitalism cannot be even understood, let alone reconstructed, except as a part of world economy.[51]

However, Trotsky's understanding of the developing inter-

27

nationalisation of capital is also projected onto socialist struggle: this process has, for Trotsky, prepared world economy as a whole for socialist transformation.[52] The internationalisation of capitalist economy is taken to indicate a correlative internationalisation of national politics, leaving the world as such ripe for socialist revolution. Trotsky's sound analytical basis — 'national capitalism cannot be. . .understood except as a part of world economy' — is translated into political necessity, as though national culture and politics simply wither with the internationalisation of production, distribution and finance. Rather than taking a distance from the forces/ relations formula of the 1859 Preface, the theory of Permanent Revolution universalises it, projecting it onto the world system and reinforcing thereby the fictitious notion of 'automatic' revolution. Trotsky's profound understanding of the importance of the world system is effectively denied by its association with the notion of world revolution.

The cyclical nature of economy

In contemporary scholarship the question of the world system is intimately bound up with that of the cyclical nature of its development. The central early theorist in this connection was N. D. Kondratiev, one of the earliest proponents of the idea that 50-year-long cycles were a fundamental principle of capitalist production. Today Kondratiev is common intellectual property, basic to the work of not only Mandel but also of Rostow. The situation was different in Trotsky's time. Kondratiev wrote in the early twenties, and Trotsky did not hesitate to contest Kondratiev's arguments about capitalist equilibrium. Kondratiev explained the 1920–1 economic crisis as a 'normal' crisis, one functional to capital in liquidating its internal disparities and establishing a new equilibrium. The capitalist crisis therefore signalled a downturn prior to the next protracted upturn.[53] Trotsky distinguished himself both from Kondratiev and from many other Bolsheviks by denying both the restoration of capitalist equilibrium and the contending argument, which anticipated imminent collapse.[54] Instead Trotsky anticipated the restoration of equilibrium at such a depressed level as would incur prolonged and bloody decay.

The central difference between Kondratiev and Trotsky was

that between the former's 'smooth' developmental trends and
the latter's preference for broken, fragmented developments
(epochs or periods) in keeping with the principle of uneven
development.[56] As Day has it, 'Kondratiev treated Trotsky's
"external conditions" as passive manifestations of the long
cycle itself, rather than as shocks to the capitalist system
emanating from without'.[57] Trotsky's protest against
Kondratiev is at base methodological: he seems to be denying
the possibility of definitive explanation in the analysis of
current history.[58] But the analytic void thus created cannot be
filled simply by writing history after the fact: cycles, for
Trotsky, derive from the developing productive forces.[59]
Again, the positive critical perspective is followed by mere
intuition: 'History is explained by the development of
productive forces', which can be separated out as prime mover.
Trotsky must reject Kondratiev's long cycles because they
violate his own philosophy of history: Trotsky's perspective is
that of a socialist telos, while Kondratiev's is implicitly one of
capitalist repetition. Rather than pursue a specific analysis of
history using critical categories, Trotsky pits the principle of
repetition against his own socialist telos. Trotsky exposes
notions of stasis or repetition, but substitutes for them notions
of necessary progress. Desire again overrides Trotsky's earlier
sensitivity to the principle of uneven development. Once more
the spiral staircase of the 1859 Preface guarantees the future of
socialism.

The question of Americanism

The infatuation of Bolshevism with French history is
frequently noted. Less often observed is the infatuation with
American technology or *Amerikanski tempo*.[60] For Trotsky the
refutation of Kondratiev's general theory of cycles was already
apparent in the decline of Europe and the rise of American
capital. Trotsky's enthusiasm for the powers of American
society seems at first to be anomalous; indeed, it complements
the ambiguity in Trotsky's marxism between a technological
determinism on the one hand, and the professed political
voluntarism in the strategy of Permanent Revolution on the
other. Trotsky's enthusiasm is less for American society or

politics than for its technology or productive forces. Thus he argues:

> To have Bolshevism shod in the American way — there is our task! We must get shod technologically with American nails. . .Americanised Bolshevism will crush and conquer imperialist Americanism.[61]

And again:

> Soviet forms of property on a basis of the most modern achievements of American technique transplanted into all branches of economic life — that would indeed be the first stage of socialism.[62]

Taking technology to be effectively neutral, presuming Franklin's toolmaker anthropology, Trotsky's admiration for Americanism culminates in the conclusion that American forces of production plus Soviet relations of production equals socialism. Khrushchev, in this specific sense, was the direct descendant of Trotsky; the utopia outlined in *Literature and Revolution* binds the two images of socialism together, Khrushchev's hare-brained agricultural schemes meet the superindustrialiser Commissar Trotsky's fantasies of carving up Mont Blanc, reviving Atlantis, remaking both nature and society *Amerikanski tempo*, with a Bolshevik twist.

The problem of class

Marxism has long been hamstrung by dual theories of class.[63] Trotsky follows the marxian capital-analysis tradition, working with the definition of class in the *Communist Manifesto* or *Capital* Chapter 32 or with the earlier marxian writings, where classes function as personified Hegelian actors. Classes function predominantly as historic agents in Trotsky: in any particular epoch there is a class of progress and a class of reaction (minor classes like the petty-bourgeoisie being doomed to decline). The vision of history implicit in this view of class is that of a moral play; there are only two classes, good and bad . . .

In certain texts such as the *New Communist Manifesto* and the Introduction to the first Afrikaans translation of the Marx-

Engels *Manifesto*, Trotsky portrays class in the traditional simplistic terms of two opposed camps. Trotsky accepts the wisdom of the Second International as enshrined in the *Erfurt Program* and the *Manifesto*: the middle class lacks historic vocation and is, therefore, doomed.[64] Elsewhere the proletariat is treated as a quasi-mythical character, as in *1905*. This mass-instinctual actor is finally transformed by the post-October substitution of the Party for the proletariat. Thereafter the proletariat is conceivable only as a class whose historic interests are embodied in the workers' Party/State: this remains the premiss until, facing Stalinism, Trotsky tentatively disentangles his earlier integration of party and class.

Trotsky is not alone in giving insufficient consideration to class theory. The point of criticism is therefore only that an intellectual of Trotsky's calibre should have been capable of a more balanced and systematic approach to the treatment of the problem of class. Certainly others, like Gramsci, did better at understanding the permanence of third classes and national cultural configurations. Trotsky in comparison did not approach the problem of class in its specificity from either the theoretical or the historical perspective. He avoids both crucial problems: the analytical question of relation to mode of production or organisation, and the separate problem of the self-constitution of classes. He specifies neither class 'in itself' with reference to production relations, nor class 'for itself' with reference to problems of consciousness and action. Instead Trotsky's class analysis remains prescriptive or instinctive, working at the level of 'good classes' and 'bad classes'. Robespierre would have approved.

Trotsky is far from uniformly insensitive to these problems, but the spectre of the class actor never quite disappears from his writing. A distance from essentialist notions of class is for example apparent in Trotsky's criticism of the 1936 'Stalin Constitution', where the argument is advanced that 'in reality classes are heterogeneous' and 'torn by inner antagonisms'.[65] Trotsky nevertheless maintains that the proletariat is still 'the least heterogeneous class of capitalist society'.[66] By the time of writing *The Transitional Program* of 1938, the proletariat is again perceived to be wracked by a deep disquiet — 'the multimillioned masses again and again enter the road of revolution', a pathway which is blocked only by the bureaucratic machines of the movements that claim to serve them.[67]

31

Classes are presumed to be unitary and poised for action, to function as though they are personified objective class interests. Instead of difference and specificity, the metaphor of guarantee re-enters. In this conceptual constellation humans are reduced to the mere agents of an evolutionary process.[68] How easily they become its victims.

Conclusions

Could it be the case that, in all these criticisms, Trotsky is merely representative of his milieu? The answer to this question is no. If Trotsky's theoretical background was classical Second International, the logic of his political practice during and after October was a clear break with that background. The theory of Permanent Revolution violated the Second International's political wisdom; and Trotsky's early sensitivity to uneven development provided a potential means to transcend the dominant evolutionary scheme of history. It is this very innovation and originality in Trotsky which justifies the high standards of criticism applied here. Trotsky had available to him the theoretical and textual means to produce a reworked understanding of the critical foundations of marxism. His intellectual capacity was by no means inadequate to the task. But the maintenance of residual categories of orthodox marxist common sense was to prevent a systematic rethinking of philosophy or economy, with the result that Trotsky's political analysis was to be secretly structured by positions and values which were beyond consideration. As will be seen in the following chapters, both Trotsky's historical work and his analysis of the question of transition were to be overdetermined and obstructed by the kinds of conceptual trickery latent in the teleological guarantees of Dialectical Materialism and of a political economy subsumed to it.

Notes

1. Trotsky, *My Life* (Penguin, Harmondsworth, 1975), p. 123.
2. Ibid., p. 127
3. F. Mehring, *Philosophische Aufsätze* (Dietz, Berlin, 1961).
4. A. Labriola, *Essays on the Materialist Conception of History* (Kerr, Chicago, 1908), p. 162.

5. Ibid., pp. 104–9, 165.

6. Labriola, *Socialism and Philosophy* (Kerr, Chicago, 1918), p. 106f.

7. Trotsky, *Terrorism and Communism* (Ann Arbor, Michigan, 1972), p. 133.

8. See generally P. Lafargue, *The Right to be Lazy* (Kerr, Chicago, 1907).

9. Ibid., for example, pp. 16, 56, 12, 57ff, 103, 109.

10. See J. Molyneux, *Leon Trotsky's Theory of Revolution* (Harvester, Brighton, 1981), Introduction.

11. See, for example, Kautsky, *Ethics and the Materialist Conception of History* (Kerr, Chicago, 1906), Ch. 5; R. Hilferding, *Finance Capital,* (Routledge and Kegan Paul, London, 1981), Preface.

12. A. Przeworski, *Capitalism and Social Democracy* (Cambridge, Cambridge University Press, 1985), Ch. 2; J. Cohen, *Class and Civil Society* (Martin Robertson, London, 1983).

13. G. Plekhanov, 'On the "Economic Factor"' in *Selected Philosophical Works* (4 vols., Progress, Moscow, 1977), vol. 2, pp. 251–82.

14. See generally Plekhanov, 'On the "Economic Factor"' and 'On the Individual's Role in History', *Selected Philosophical Works*, vol. 2, pp. 285–315.

15. Ibid., pp. 285, 291f.

16. Ibid.

17. Plekhanov, 'For the Sixtieth Anniversary of Hegel's Death', *Selected Philosophical Works*, vol. 1, p. 427.

18. Plekhanov, 'On the Individual's Role', p. 305ff.

19. Trotsky, *Their Morals and Ours* (New Park, London, 1974), p. 9.

20. Trotsky, *In Defense of Marxism* (Pathfinder, New York, 1973), p. 166.

21. Trotsky, *Their Morals*, p. 12.

22. Ibid., p. 13.

23. Engels, 'Ludwig Feuerbach and the End of Classical German Philosophy' in Marx and Engels, *Selected Works* (Progress, Moscow, 1970, one volume edn), p. 595.

24. Trotsky, *The Revolution Betrayed* (Pathfinder, New York, 1972), pp. 107, 267, 276, 290, 270f, 258f.

25. Trotsky, *In Defense of Marxism*, pp. 34–6.

26. Ibid., p. 50f.

27. Ibid.

28. Ibid., p. 51f, and see pp. 104, 108, where Dialectic functions as *Geist.*

29. Ibid., p. 50f.

30. Ibid., p. 51. This proposal is later contradicted (p. 76) and then reasserted (p. 81).

31. Ibid., p. 51.

32. Ibid., p. 52.

33. Ibid., and see Trotsky, 'Philosophical Tendencies of Bureaucratism' in *Challenge of the Left Opposition, 1928–29* (Pathfinder, New York, 1981), pp. 397, 399.

34. Trotsky, *In Defense*, p. 72.
35. Ibid., p. 84.
36. Trotsky, *Terrorism and Communism*, p. 53.
37. Trotsky, *In Defense*, p. 56.
38. Ibid., pp. 45, 181.
39. Ibid., p. 167.
40. Ibid., p. 182f.
41. See, for example, Lenin and Trotsky, *Kronstadt* (Monad, New York, 1979), p. 81; Trotsky, *Permanent Revolution* (Pathfinder, New York, 1974), p. 205.
42. Trotsky, *In Defense*, pp. 59f, 94, 167.
43. G. A. Cohen, *Karl Marx's Theory of History, A Defense* (Oxford, Oxford University Press, 1978). Compare Beilharz, 'Marxism and History', *Thesis Eleven*, 2 (1981), and see P. Corrigan, H. Ramsay, D. Sayer, *Socialist Construction and Marxist Theory* (Macmillan, London, 1978).
44. Trotsky, *The Young Lenin* (Wren, Melbourne, 1972), pp. 127, 181, 183, 187, Trotsky, *Literature and Revolution* (Ann Arbor, Michigan, 1971), pp. 146–7.
45. Trotsky, *Literature and Revolution*, p. 146f.
46. See particularly L. Colletti, 'Bernstein and the Marxism of the Second International', *From Rousseau to Lenin* (Monthly Review, New York, 1972).
47. Trotsky, *The Living Thoughts of Karl Marx* (Longmans, Green and Co., New York, 1939), p. 31.
48. Day, *Leon Trotsky*; and see, for example, Trotsky, 'Toward Capitalism or Socialism?' in *The Challenge of the Left Opposition 1923–25* (Pathfinder, New York, 1975), pp. 319–82.
49. J. Van Heijenoort, *With Trotsky in Exile* (Harvard, Cambridge, 1978), p. 56.
50. Knei-Paz, *Social and Political Thought of Leon Trotsky*, Ch. 4.
51. Trotsky, *Permanent Revolution*, pp. 133, 146, 148.
52. Ibid., p. 279.
53. R. Day, 'The Theory of the Long Cycle: Kondratiev, Trotsky, Mandel', *New Left Review*, 99 (1976), p. 68.
54. Ibid., pp. 68, 70; Trotsky, 'Report on the World Economic Crisis and the Tasks of the Communist International' *The First Five Years of the Communist International* (New Park, London, 1973), vol. 1, pp. 226–78; and 'Flood Tide', *The First Five Years* (Monad, New York, 1972), vol. 2, pp. 74–84.
55. Trotsky, 'Flood Tide', p. 84.
56. Trotsky, 'The Curve of Capitalist Development', *Problems of Everyday Life* (Monad, New York, 1977), pp. 273–80.
57. Day, 'The Theory of the Long Cycle', p. 74.
58. Trotsky, 'The Curve of Capitalist Development', p. 274.
59. Ibid., p. 275.
60. W. H. G. Armytage, *The Rise of the Technocrats* (Routledge and Kegan Paul, London, 1965), interestingly identifies Bolshevism in general but not Trotsky in particular as the exemplary bearer of this banner; the lapse is similar to that in Berman, *All That is Solid Melts Into*

Air.

61. Trotsky, 'Perspectives of World Development', *Europe and America: Two Speeches on Imperialism* (Merit, New York, 1971), p. 33.
62. Trotsky, *The Revolution Betrayed*, p. 61.
63. See Beilharz, 'Theorizing The Middle Class', *Arena, 72* (1985).
64. Trotsky, 'Manifesto of the Communist International to the Workers of the World', *The First Five Years*, vol. 1 pp. 43–54; 'Ninety Years of the Communist Manifesto' *Writings 1937–38* (Pathfinder, New York, 1976), pp. 18–27.
65. Trotsky, *The Revolution Betrayed*, p. 267.
66. Ibid.
67. Trotsky, *The Transitional Program for Socialist Revolution* (Pathfinder, New York, 1977), p. 112.
68. Trotsky, *The Living Thoughts of Karl Marx*, p. 8

3
Trotsky and History

From the *Times Literary Supplement* to the *Sunday Telegraph*, from Kingsley Martin to Isaac Deutscher, the authorities represented in the presentation of the three volume English edition of *The History of the Russian Revolution* all agree that Trotsky's historical work has no parallel save perhaps Churchill's. Scholarly opinion broadly concurs. For the historian and Trotskyist Perry Anderson, Trotsky was the first great marxist historian: 'For a long time *The History of the Russian Revolution* remained unique in the literature of historical materialism.'[1] Others have viewed Trotsky enthusiastically as an historian producing the 'literature of revolution'.[2] Given the dominant tendency to identify Trotsky as 'the man of October', it is not surprising that *The History of the Russian Revolution* tends to eclipse Trotsky's other historical works. Trotsky's historical practice in fact produced works of an extreme variation. There is a marked unevenness between and even within some texts. Such unevenness is best revealed in the analysis not only of the classic *History*, but also of the earlier work, *1905*. That unevenness is further illuminated by the exposure of the historical presuppositions at work in Trotsky's biography of Stalin. The interpretation of these texts together can yield a deeper understanding of the problematic at work in Trotsky, the deep structure of which has been indicated in the previous chapters of this study. The teleological notions of history already evident in his philosophy and economy emerge fully only in the consideration of Trotsky's historical writing itself.

'1905'

Overshadowed by the *History*, *1905* remains an underrated series of studies. In accordance with his earlier rejection of textual fundamentalism,[3] Trotsky's studies in *1905* provide a marxist economic history marked by sensitivity to specificity and a theoretical rigour bringing to mind even contemporary debates like the *Science and Society* dispute between Sweezy, Dobb and others over the question of the transition from feudalism to capitalism and whether its source was in the application of merchant capital to artisan production, or was internal to the new mode of production itself.[4]

Trotsky's explanation of the peculiarities of the Russian situation commence from its 'hothouse' development. Capital is imported, it is not accumulated within Russia's national confines as it was in the British case. Though substantially feudal, Russia is also characterised by the existence of highly intensive capitalist industry prior even to the abolition of serfdom. The emergence of 'free', geographically and socially mobile labour in Russia at the hands of the tsarist state thus contrasts with its organic emergence in the classic British case of capitalist development.[5] In Russia it is only with the abolition of serfdom in 1861 that labourers become formally free to work where they will and to make their way up the ladder of the class hierarchy. Where in Britain modern towns emerge as productive centres, Trotsky explains the emergence of Russian towns primarily as administrative centres or trade markets. The Russian towns are commercial rather than productive centres and are therefore understood as dependent links with the world system of capital rather than as self-sufficient industrial-productive bases.[6] All Russia's characteristics combine to produce the picture of its uneven development. Trotsky's own words provide an apt summary, and indicate something of his literary verve:

Within this vast space every epoch of human culture is to be found: from the primeval barbarism of the northern forests, where people eat raw fish and worship blocks of wood, to the modern social relations of the capitalist city, where socialist workers consciously recognise themselves as participants in world politics and keep a watchful eye on events in the Balkans and on the debates in the German

37

Reichstag. The most concentrated industry in Europe based on the most backward agriculture in Europe. The most colossal state apparatus in the world making use of every achievement of modern technological progress in order to retard the historical progress of its own country.[7]

Yet the importation of capital and its social relations into Russia was to place a time bomb under the tsarist edifice, leaving in question only the nature of the outcome consequent on social explosions.

Trotsky followed Plekhanov in borrowing heavily from the Russian historians, who gave special importance to the social and economic role of the state. Like Plekhanov, Trotsky saw climate and geography as partially explanatory factors for the peculiarities of Russian history.[8] Going beyond Plekhanov, Trotsky came to view the absence of the Occidental city as the crucial factor distinguishing Russian from Western European feudalism. In this regard it was Parvus and not Plekhanov[9] who influenced Trotsky. Parvus had observed in his period of collaboration with Trotsky that Russian towns were closer to the Chinese, administrative centres doubling as bazaars. As Trotsky was to put it in *Results and Prospects*, the Russian towns performed only a consumptive not a productive role,[10] this fact accounting for the relative absence of a politically inspired bourgeoisie or petty-bourgeoisie, and therefore providing the historical basis for the theory of Permanent Revolution. While the urban centres, lacking their own bourgeoisie, served as outposts for world capital, the vast spaces of Russia remained largely untouched by bourgeois culture or politics.

The catalysing influence of Parvus in this period of Trotsky's formation helped Trotsky to transcend the existing wisdom of Menshevism. Going beyond Plekhanov, Trotsky analysed the specifics of the experience that was unique to Russia. The theory of Permanent Revolution at this stage of Trotsky's formation related specifically to Russia; it was not at this stage the universally applicable formula which it was later to become in *The Permanent Revolution*. The Trotsky of *1905* denied the general philosophy of history of the kind which was popularised by Plekhanov. Indeed, for the young Trotsky 'where there are no "special features", there is no history, but only a sort of pseudo-materialistic geometry'.[11] It was only later that Trotsky was to deny such 'special features' and to construct such a 'geometry' of his own.

The high quality of the analyses in *1905* should not be taken
to indicate an internal uniformity in the collection. The seeds
of the philosophy of history later to be modified and made
explicit already exist in its pages. Trotsky's use of theatrical
metaphor is particularly striking. He relates the experience of
the trial of the Soviet of workers' deputies as theatre — perhaps
because it actually resembled theatre more closely than
history.[12] But the choice of the theatrical form of historical
presentation is more significant yet, as is shown elsewhere:
'Classes cannot be seen at a glance — they usually remain
behind the scenes . . . [and later, P.B.] . . . Gapon's priestly robe
was only a prop in the drama; the protagonist was the
proletariat.'[13] The generative metaphor at work here suggests
that history is a moral play in which justice will confirm the
proletarian cause in the long run. Generative metaphors we
take to be those which generate their own conclusions or
solutions. Their use is fundamental to Trotsky; the abscess
needs lancing, the gangrenous limb amputation, a medical
intervention (by Trotsky) restoring health, growth or development. This biological analogy is, of course, symptomatic of the
Second International's conflation of natural and social
sciences. This type of metaphorical appeal is precritical and
areflective, playing on the persuasive power of the 'obvious'
and the 'certain' to the detriment of the uncertain and the
complex, and inserting, in this case, a motor of inherent
development.[14]Thus the imagery of 'titanic struggle',[15] the
resort to the images of growth and decay, the device of
personification and the imagery of clothing. In 'My Speech
Before the Court', Trotsky personifies the insurrection: 'An
insurrection of the masses, gentlemen of the bench, is not
made: *it accomplishes itself.* It is the result of social relations, not
the product of a plan. It cannot be created; it can be
foreseen.'[16] A sharper example is provided by Trotsky's
personification of the 1905 strike:

Where the telegraph refused to serve *it*, *it* cut the wires or
overturned the telegraph poles. *It* halted railway engines
and let off their steam. *It* . . . [etc, P.B.] *It* used every possible
means. *It* appealed, convinced, implored . . . *it* threatened,
terrorised, threw stones, finally fired off *its* Brownings. *It*
wanted to achieve *its* aim at whatever cost.[17]

While the literary device is compelling, it can hardly be accepted as licence in historical analysis. For the strike is hereby given a primordial necessity: 'This strike is not merely itself. . .[but] is obedient to the will of the revolution which has sent it down through the land.'[18]

History here drifts through the realm of literature and into that of theology. In the first instance the implication of such imagery is that the strike authors the strikers; in the second, that the strike itself is authored by the revolution. History becomes the playground of divine but delegated intervention. The image is one of rebirth via superhuman agency.[19] Doubtless Trotsky succeeds in conveying the sense of spontaneity unique to such periods with consummate skill. Spontaneity is precisely the key, for it corresponds with his pre-October understanding of politics. Yet while the young Trotsky is free of the belief in a vanguard which stands in for the mass in politics, it must be observed that the argument for spontaneity was to provide no practical alternative to vanguardism. Though rousing the urban masses, the events of 1905 nevertheless resulted in defeat. The ancillary argument, that the 1905 events in functioning as the 'dress rehearsal' for October were no defeat but merely the preliminary to success, solves the problem only by collapsing the unique nature of the events of 1905 into a preordained view of (delayed) necessity, reasserting the view of history as a moral play, only with altered chronology. If history is to be viewed not as theatre but rather as a realm of structural obstacles and human possibilities, a somewhat more contingent approach to its understanding and writing might be necessary.

Finally, the more significant point in this context is that this kind of argument is more than receptive to Jacobin outcomes, in politics and historiography alike. The argument being put here is *not* that Trotskyism is bad because metaphorical; there is *no* discourse outside metaphor. The problem rather is that this kind of Second International discourse, with its language of generation/degeneration, necessity and *nomos*, itself invites Jacobin intervention, itself begs for the Bolshevik scalpel which lances the abscess that the Plekhanovs and Kautskys merely watched and monitored. Trotsky's Jacobinism can therefore be observed in his historiography as well.

'The History of the Russian Revolution': history as theatre and theatre as history

Trotsky's *History of the Russian Revolution* is a remarkable work from any point of view. At its best the narrative of the *History* runs like a transcribed oration: quickening, resting, quickening again, it has a great power of persuasion on this immediate level. Like John Reed's *Ten Days that Shook the World*, it has a strange power to convey the intensity of events; this urgency, coupled with Trotsky's literary gifts and his firsthand knowledge, combine to produce a text of extraordinary influence and value. Lunacharsky characterised Trotsky's achievements well when he wrote that Trotsky's 'articles and books are, as it were, frozen speech — he was literary in his oratory and an orator in literature'.[20] Trotsky's unique contribution as historian is to convey so effectively the feeling of 1917. His narrative is excellent, his images of the dog-tired proletarian enthusiasms of 1917 are evocative in the extreme.[21] Trotsky fascinates the reader with devices such as the change of tense from past to present correlative with the shift from context to the actual unfolding of events.[22] His is a masterly technique.

The *History* opens in a similar manner to *1905*, beginning with the peculiarities of Russia's development. Like *1905*, if to a lesser extent, the analysis of prerevolutionary Russia in the *History* is marked by a notable sensitivity to uneven development.[23] Trotsky repeats the argument about the insignificance of the Russian towns before explaining the broader effects of the war and of tsardom's decay. Next the reader is taken through the February events to the July days, and finally to October and the conquest of power. Radically diverging critics all affirm that it is a gripping story.

A deeper reading, however, reveals the same generative structure to be at work, constructing in advance a textual frame within which the reader cannot but agree with the author. The field of chosen metaphor is again primarily the organic one of evolution so fundamental to Second International thinking. In one place Trotsky almost seems to acknowledge the generative structure at work in his writing:

Physical analogies with revolution come so naturally [!] that some of them have become worn-out metaphors: 'Volcanic

41

eruption', 'birth of a new society', 'boiling point'. . .Under
the simple literary image there is concealed here an intuitive
grasp of the laws of the dialectic — that is, the logic of evolution.[24]

Trotsky's language is instructive: physical analogies are not
illegitimate, only overused; they emerge naturally, revealing
intuitive understanding of the working out of the laws of an
evolutionist world view. Consequently it should come as no
surprise that 'worn-out metaphors' pervade the *History of the
Russian Revolution*. As has been seen in Chapter Two of this
study, the context for the use of such metaphor is a
metaphysics called 'dialectics', which identifies social life with
natural science, so that both are seen to be subject to the gover-
nance of law and therefore given to predictability. Trotsky
thereby establishes a preordained teleology which ensures
both the defeat of various enemies and the inevitability of the
Bolshevik victory through the use of metaphorical device.
Images of natural necessity including boiling, eruption, tidal
and solar movements occur frequently in the text.[25] 'Molecular
processes' are taken to be at work:[26] Trotsky uses the Hegelian
concepts of essence and appearance in order to assure that
whatever the face of events suggests, history is really on his side
'below the surface', for the Bolsheviks were 'revolutionists of
the deed and not the gesture, of the essence and not the
form'.[27]

Just as humans are powerless before the movement of flood
or molecules or before the necessity of gravity or the seasons,
so are they impotent in the face of death or birth. Trotsky
revels in gynaecological metaphor and in the imagery of death
and disease.[28] The choice of the images of death and birth is
especially significant, for they allow the combination of
teleology of necessity with the fact of the power of the experts
to intervene. The Bolsheviks with Lenin and Trotsky at their
head emerge as the gynaecologists of the Russian Revolution.[29]
As Sontag observes, 'Disease metaphors were a staple of
Bolshevik polemics, and Trotsky, the most gifted of all
communist polemicists, used them with the greatest profusion'.[30] In this Trotsky conforms to a broader social tendency
to characterise any object of disapproval as diseased. Disease
and health are in general presented as a mutually exclusive
couple. However, in Trotsky this broader social trait takes a

particularly extreme form, so that disputation (that is, pluralism) equals 'disease', where 'health' seems to be associated with the image of a monovocal, stable society. The kind of argument which Sontag advances — that illness is not appropriate as metaphor — is dismissed in advance by the Bolsheviks. For Trotsky the process of world revolution is written into the very order of things, but 'those who know' must step in to take control of events. In this regard Trotsky's text is entirely a foregone conclusion, it is 'history read backwards', establishing the 'fruit' already in 'seed' in the beginning. The 'seed' is in fact only a retrospective projection of the author's modified Second International world view.

Beyond this level of metaphor in Trotsky's *History* is another equally provocative, the image of history as theatre. As a preliminary, it is appropriate here to introduce Trotsky's later views on historiography. In a manner quite distinct to that of his self-understanding in *1905*,[31] Trotsky insists that the *History of the Russian Revolution* is a work of history, to be understood as the science of history.[32] The exposure of laws — the primary historical task involved — necessitates for Trotsky the application of the method of historic objectivism.[33] The precise nature of these laws, whether they are properly social or natural, is never made clear. The 'laws' of uneven and combined development are 'applied' only occasionally and elliptically in the *History*.

It is this pursuit of 'objectivism' which makes necessary Trotsky's use of the third person in the text — for the later Trotsky the use of the 'subjective tone' is not permissible in the writing of history.[34] The use of the third person is a peculiar device, though it must be conceded that Trotsky finds himself in a rare predicament as the historian-cum-revolutionary participant. However, the resulting effects are perhaps worse than the problem which the device seeks to solve. In writing himself out of the text as subject, Trotsky ensures that he reappears as agent, as the bearer of an historical process already in motion. Further, Trotsky's self-objectification produces an absence that is strikingly present: as Warth puts it, Trotsky's 'use of the third person and quotation when speaking of himself as a historical figure is all the more conspicuous for its attempt at inconspicuousness.'[35] In allocating himself a role in the plot of *History of the Russian Revolution*, Trotsky conforms to the broader marxist tendency, to think in terms of history as theatre and of actors as bearers. Early on in the analysis of tsarism Trotsky makes it clear that the force of the monarchy operates through its bearers.[36] As he puts it, history writes the scripts, the actors have only the scope of interpretation.[37] Subsequent images of the stage, of theatre or the orchestra are again manifold.[38] Either the actors are allotted specific analogical parts — Kerensky and Kornilov, for example, vie for the part of Bonaparte[39] — or else they are personified, where in a fashion reminiscent of *1905* the Soviet or Mass appear on the stage as collective subjects,[40] where, in Jacobin imagery, thousands lift their hand as one man, come out as one man, and so on.[40] Kamenev, Zinoviev and Miliukov all represent types or roles prevented from achieving the status of celebrity by stereotypical flaws in their clay, flaws of intellect or will or both. The treatment of Martov as bearer, as the 'Hamlet of democratic socialism', stands out. Says Trotsky to Martov and his followers: 'You are pitiful isolated individuals; you are bankrupts; your *rôle* is played out. Go where you belong from now on — into the rubbish can of history!'[41] History is a god for Trotsky; he idolises it, though it is later to sit in harsh judgement on him as well, as the defeats of the twenties and thirties accumulate. Trotsky's presentation resembles Sophoclean tragedy with its catharsis and clear moral lessons. Right wins out; tragedy befalls those whose acts are false; catharsis dissolves the anxiety of the audience. The central blunder in Trotsky's text is precisely this presumption, that right — the proletariat — will out, in history as in theatre. The problem foreshadows another: Trotsky, it can be expected, will be in real difficulty attempting to explain the later success of Stalin, for the victory of the mediocre or of the wicked violates his positive philosophy of history, by changing the character of necessity itself.

Trotsky's treatment of his own part and that of Lenin in the Russian Revolution has generated some interest in the past because of his tendency to present the Bolshevik victory as a *fait accompli*.[42] Writing himself out of the text as subject, Trotsky submerges himself in the process allegedly characterised by the 'historic destiny of classes'.[43] In a famous passage in his *1935 Diary*, Trotsky contemplates his own version of the proverbial falling brick. He offers the following as a general explanation of Lenin's role, and his own, in the events that shook the world:

Had I not been present in 1917 in Petersburg, the October Revolution would still have taken place — *on the condition that Lenin was present and in command.* If neither Lenin nor I had been present in Petersburg, there would have been no October Revolution: the leadership of the Bolshevik Party would have prevented it from occurring — of this I have not the slightest doubt! If Lenin had not been in Petersburg, I doubt whether I could have managed to overcome the resistance of the Bolshevik leaders.[44]

How can Trotsky explain that Lenin was the only 'revolutionary' in the Bolshevik Party (himself aside) after April 1917? How can all the dimensions of the picture of necessity established via his elaborate generative metaphorical structure be reconciled with this picture, where all depends on the will and skill of one man? This is the uncomfortable silence in Trotsky's explanation, one which is resolved only falsely by the characterisation of Lenin as the man of decision, as himself the product of necessity: 'Lenin was not an accidental element in the historic development, but a product of the whole past of Russian history. He was embedded in it with deepest roots.'[45] The argument is essentially Plekhanov's. Just as Stalin was later to be cast as the product or personification of 'backwardness', so is Lenin portrayed as the bearer of progress, whose historic mantle is passed on to Trotsky. But if 'great men' merely personify great historical forces, why did Stalin win and Trotsky lose the struggle for power after Lenin's death? And what becomes of the empirical masses?

Trotsky's subsequent difficulties in explaining Stalin's victory did not, however, imperil his philosophy of history, presumably because the self-willed commitment to such a philosophy of history is, strictly speaking, prerational — and Trotsky did see marxism as a matter of faith. This is not to deny that there are real difficulties for Trotsky, the historian, in trying to find a particular place for himself, as actor, in the unfolding of historical events. Whatever the circumstances, Trotsky lacks the critical distance from the events of October to write a more accurate history, not history *wie es eigentlich gewesen war*, but not history 'as it ought have been' either. Trotsky is too historiosophical a marxist to perform adequately the historian's tasks. As Lunacharsky portrayed him, Trotsky always had one eye in the mirror of history. He was always 'ready to make any personal sacrifice, not excluding the greatest sacrifice of all — that of his life, in order to go down in human memory surrounded with the aureole of a genuine revolutionary leader'.[46] Bernard Shaw offers a similarly enlightening reflection on Trotsky: like Lessing, when Trotsky 'cuts off his opponent's head, he holds it up to show that there are no brains in it'.[47] Certainly Trotsky had a sense of the spectacle, of the performance in political and intellectual life. His tendency to conduct the literary executions of various powerful enemies seems to create a situation of reversal — on paper. Trotsky writing in exile can, for a brief moment, relive better times, when historical justice chose the victors and the defeated with more discernment. In exile, the glory of the apogee of his personal life is therefore made somehow permanent. The rhetor of Petrograd now addresses a distant audience; the world historic executors are executed by literary means, achieving poetic justice for the Trotsky who could achieve vengeance of no other kind against Stalin or against History. True to his early pseudonym, the 'Pen' never fully understood the limits of its power against the sword.

Trotsky's use of metaphor is however by no means completely vacuous. In some cases its application is superbly sarcastic. Trotsky's use of the image of the theatre is on occasion quite sharp, particularly in those instances where it was the circumstances themselves which did the mocking, as in the example of leftist conferences actually taking place in theatres.[48] Trotsky was an able rhetor indeed; even, and perhaps especially in his most vitriolic moments, he was a master of language, whether caricaturing the crepuscular Kerensky, or portraying Kautsky in his slippers, or teasing Hilferding, who enters the revolutionary epoch with his heavy book on his back, a turtle-like porter.[49] Elsewhere mechanistic imagery is put to good use:

The fact that the earth's axis is merely an imaginary line does not of course prevent the earth from rotating on its axis. In like manner the Kornilov operations rotated around an imaginary insurrection of the Bolsheviks as round its own axis.[50]

Other mechanical metaphors — the most famous of them being the image that mass is to party as is steam to piston box —

are less convincing if ingenious in conception.[51] Indeed, some examples are awkward in the extreme. Among them, Trotsky applies in his *History* an image of Bonapartism which resurfaces in his analysis of fascism. 'If you stick two forks into a cork symmetrically, it will, under very great oscillations from side to side, keep its balance even on a pinpoint: that is the mechanical model of the Bonapartist superarbiter.'[52] The symbol invoked, if curious,is not unreasonable: the image summoned is one of a tenuous but adequate self-suspension, momentary and contradictory. More perplexing from the viewpoints of politics and physics alike is the contraption presented as Bonapartism in 'The Workers' State, Thermidor and Bonapartism', which '. . .by its very essence, cannot long maintain itself; a sphere balanced on the point of a pyramid must invariably roll down on one side or the other'.[53] Trotsky proceeds to disavow the historical analogy with Napoleon, but not the physical image — as though the political world were analogous to the contrived vacuums of the laboratory.

Yet Trotsky can simultaneously apply with much effect punning images like that of the theatre, actual and metaphorical, and can produce such movingly tragic parody as his Aesopian tale of Social-fascism in 'What Next?':

A cattle dealer once drove some bulls to the slaughterhouse. And the butcher came nigh with his sharp knife. 'Let us close ranks and jack up this executioner on our horns', suggested one of the bulls.'If you please, in what way is the butcher any worse than the dealer who drove us hither with his cudgel?' replied the bulls, who had received their political education in Manuilsky's Institute. 'But we shall be able to attend to the dealer as well afterwards!' 'Nothing doing', replied the bulls, firm in their principles, to the counsellor. 'You are trying to shield our enemies from the left; you are a social-butcher yourself.' And they refused to close ranks.[54]

The difficulty lies not in Trotsky's use of metaphor but in its misuse. The certainty installed by the use of generative metaphor, whether in natural, mechanical or gynaecological form, establishes a discourse in which Trotsky's teleological philosophy of history presents itself as an indisputable science of history. In historiography Trotsky's marxism is therefore myth presented as science, and it is this which sets Trotsky apart from Sorel. Whatever the apparent similarities between Trotsky and Sorel, Sorel refused both teleology and Darwinism in theory, and self-consciously presents the myth of the general strike as myth, not as theory, for it has a functional rather than scientific character. Trotsky's presentation of marxism, in contrast, is mythical despite itself, and is mythical despite (or through) Trotsky's pretensions to scientific 'objectivism'. In consequence, the *History of the Russian Revolution* cannot warrant the general acclaim given it as a work of history — on the contrary, critical readers must refuse to be part of its captive audience.

For a captive audience is what Trotsky achieves in works like the *History*, through his use of language. The reader receives not only a signifier and a signified, but a teleological association as well, usually drawn from the language of Jacobinism, whether its active or passive mood. Trotskyists in this sense speak a language other than that of theory or common sense: concepts like 'class', 'history', 'strike', 'crisis', 'movement' or 'development', 'action' or 'actor', take on an additional associational meaning within Trotskyist discourse. The Trotskyist discourse exemplified in the *History* is a language of seduction. As Barthes explains, what allows the reader to consume myth innocently is that s/he does not see it as a semiological system but as an inductive one: the language of myth in this specific sense naturalises its object, presents a system of values as a system of facts.[55] In this specific sense Trotsky's historiography functions as what Barthes calls a mythology: it is an inclusive discourse, with a necessitarian plot.

'Stalin'

Trotsky's biography of Stalin provides further material for the interpretation of Trotsky's historical and historiographical premises. The problematical nature of the text should be noted from the beginning. Only the first seven chapters and the appendix, 'Three Concepts of the Russian Revolution', were worked up by Trotsky himself, the remaining five chapters and two supplements being a combination of Trotsky's text in rough, his own citations, and editorial summaries and interpolations by Charles Malamuth. The text is incomplete, uneven, and mediocre when placed alongside the *History of the Russian Revolution.* Unlike the *History,* Trotsky's biography of Stalin uses both personal reminiscences and the first person. Again unlike the *History,* detail extended to the point of trivia overpowers both narrative and analysis. There is a relative absence of metaphor and particularly generative metaphor from the text, apparently because the decay of Soviet socialism is inexplicable for Trotsky, and the likelihood of rectifying intervention at this stage becomes increasingly rhetorical. But it is these very weaknesses which make Trotsky's *Stalin* a revealing text.

Trotsky's attempt to analyse Stalin borders on the psychopathological approach. The work is dominated by the attempt to establish the character of Stalin. Trotsky denies that he hates Stalin[56] but finds him to be mediocre in the extreme, and uniformly so across the years. Neither 'a thinker, a writer, nor an orator', Stalin was incapable of ever initiating anything.[57] He was without linguistic flair,[58] ugly, had no memory and felt compassion for neither man nor beast.[59] Significantly, Trotsky emphasises Stalin's alleged pessimism and irrationalism, attitudes which are held in clear contrast to his own optimistic and rationalistic positions (the latter being positions which are presumed by Trotsky to be essential to marxism). Stalin was ill-spoken, ill-read and provincial.[60] He has a strong will but a weak intellect, is power hungry and conspiring.[61] He is capricious, primitive, morose, slow, vile, banal, dry;[62] inconsiderate, rude, ambitious, choleric, sly, stupid, vulgar, unforgiving, empiricist and opportunist.[63]

Beneath this Trotskyist torrent of abuse exists an undeveloped contextual explanation of Stalin's character. Early on, Trotsky presents Stalin as representative of Russian backwardness, viewing Asiatic patriarchy and Asiatic cruelty as specifically Georgian remnants in Stalin's make-up.[64] Trotsky offers a glimmering reflection of the images of apparent stasis in *1905* and in his *History,* portraying Georgia as a land of bazaars epitomising Russian backwardness.[65] The image recurs later, when Trotsky presents Stalin as the personification of bureaucracy, a shift which is quite in order given Trotsky's conflation of 'bureaucracy' and 'backwardness'. One conclusion can already be advanced: having characterised Stalin as uniformly mediocre, Trotsky can neither explain Stalin's political success nor offer any substantial insights into

his character.[66] This is already particularly evident in his
refusal to allow Stalin any kind of power of initiative. Trotsky's
comments concerning Stalin's alleged lack of imagination
merely indicate that for Trotsky, 'intellect' is identical to
'imagination'. Stalin certainly suffered no shortage of political
'imagination', however brutal. Trotsky, that is to say, equates
intellectual practice and political practice, and this equation
must be seen as the source of his refusal to struggle concretely
against Stalin after Lenin's death.[67] Indeed, there is a strong
sense in which Stalin's victory and Trotsky's defeat were
premissed on Stalin's manipulation of anti-intellectualism. As
Boris Souvarine explains it, Stalin's being other than intellectual was precisely the basis for his victory, for the claim to the
heritage of October was to be based not on eloquence, but on
numbers. In this somewhat more satisfactory explanation, it
must therefore be conceded that Stalin won, victory did not
merely fall like the proverbial ripe fruit into his lap, for Stalin
was the most clever aspirant to power if not the 'best'.[68]

Trotsky fails to credit political skills which do not derive
from the intellect. Trotsky himself rarely had the practical
initiative in the inner-party struggle for leadership. He let pass
the opportunities and responsibilities given him by Lenin to
fight Stalin on the questions of nationality and bureaucracy.
Trotsky denied Max Eastman's exposé of the existing power
struggle and of Lenin's *Testament*. At the Thirteenth Party
Congress in 1924 he put forward arguments which far from
strengthening his own case, actually served to bolster that of
Stalin, morally entrapping himself in his infamous words, 'The
Party is always right', 'My Party, right or wrong'.[69] In his *Lessons
of October* Trotsky chose to attack Stalin's representatives,
Zinoviev and Kamenev, rather than Stalin who himself
shrewdly remained behind the scenes.[70] And in the most
general sense Trotsky accepted the argument about
'Trotskyism' as establishing the parameters of his dispute with
Stalin, fighting on the latter's field of ideology rather than on
the practical field of problems of Soviet construction, further
undermining his reputation with the so-called 'practicals' in
the party. Stalin's defeat of the opposition, the political
victories of the assassination of Kirov, the Shakty plot and
finally, the Purges, all fail to register on Trotsky's scale of initiative: 'Never, in anything or anywhere', was Stalin 'an
initiator'.[71] Trotsky's positive philosophy of history has no

capacity for the measurement of evil in politics: even after Stalinism, politics is seen by Trotsky as the technique through which the progress of humanity unfolds.

This being the case, how is Stalin's victory to be explained? Did Stalin betray the revolution, or did the revolution betray its legitimate heir, Trotsky? Did Stalin author the bureaucracy or was he its product? Trotsky cannot take up these problems directly, for they broach too many fundamental questions. As McNeal puts it, 'In a sense Trotsky struggled to avoid making a Marxist analysis of Stalinism.'[72] Twice Trotsky suggests that Stalin created the machine.[73] Elsewhere the emphasis is on Stalin as progeny of the machine; *The Revolution Betrayed* clearly suggests the latter argument, as does the manuscript, 'What I think of Stalin', where Stalin 'only plucked the ripened fruit of power'.[74] The more 'sociological' analysis implicit here is not reconciled with the more 'pathological' analysis in *Stalin*; Trotsky posits a contradictory schema where the options are necessity or accident, mediated via the introduction of the traditional historiographical form of explanation, the Great Man. Clearly accident cannot be given such a central place in Trotsky's philosophy of history; but nor, after Stalin, can necessity be easily ascribed a primary importance. If Stalin represents the necessary personification of an inevitable bureaucratisation, then Trotsky's rationalist philosophy of history must be modified, allowing 'negative' forces to achieve 'positive' acts. Having endorsed a positive philosophy for so long, Trotsky cannot fully embrace a theory of repetition or decline, let alone countenance a more agnostic position. Though modified on occasions by the harsh realities of world developments in his period of exile, Trotsky's rationalism is far from suppressed. Writing in the period of fascism and Stalinism, Trotsky qualifies the simple unilinear teleology of history only by adding the vacillations of a 'highly complex and paradoxical orbit'.[75] The laws of history still lead to socialism, only the process is complicated by minor turns up and down which serve to delay the inevitable.

This teleological self-certainty resurfaces later in a tragically naïve form: Trotsky still adheres to the belief that 'the vengeance of history is more terrible than the vengeance of the most powerful General Secretary. I venture to think that this is consoling.'[76] But the Muse was little protection against the assassin sent by Stalin to Trotsky's fortress in Coyoacan.

Trotsky's need for consolation manifests itself on the level of faith. The 'ups' and 'downs' of the empirical dimension of politics succumb to the positive philosophy of history for which the only way is up.[77] Logically speaking, the period of decline into the thirties should prompt in Trotsky the rejection of such a philosophy of history and a transference of interest to the empirical problems of consciousness related to decline. Trotsky was rather to reassert his faith. That faith is, as he put it in *The Revolution Betrayed*, 'saturated with the optimism of progress'. Further, for Trotsky, 'It remains of course incomprehensible — at least with a rational approach to history — how and why a faction least of all rich in ideas . . . should have gained the upper hand over all other groups.'[78] But history is not a simple moral play in which Right, however defined, wins out: and Trotsky's explanation of Stalinism and of history remains hopelessly enigmatic, raising problems of reconciliation which were only to be broached later, by Isaac Deutscher.

Viewed from a critical distance, the scenario in Trotsky seems to reduce to an unsatisfactory scheme of personification. Stalin personifies retrogression; Trotsky personifies progress, his immediate defeat to be cancelled out in the advent of a delayed world-historic victory. In this regard Trotsky's understanding of history is indeed reduced to the view of the Great Man of traditional historiography, with the differences that the warring titans represent and personify social classes or social forces. Trotsky self-consciously denies such an interpretation of his historiography: in *Stalinism and Bolshevism* he reprimands Norman Thomas for failing to understand that 'it is not a question of a match between Stalin and Trotsky, but of an antagonism between the bureaucracy and the proletariat'.[79] However, this argument confirms Thomas rather than Trotsky: for 'Stalin' here is bureaucracy personified, while 'Trotsky' is the proletariat personified (if now in a fantastic sense, in exile and via the absent mediation of the new International).

It is this tragic moralism in Trotsky which effectively produces a discourse which prevents a more practical response to the decline of the thirties. Trotsky's response to Stalin's notorious rewriting of history is to reverse the casting of the story, rather than writing the story itself afresh. Trotsky trivialises Stalin in order to idolise Lenin. He informs his readers that Lenin 'wholly inspired' Stalin's only theoretical work, *Marxism and the Nationalities Problem*.[80] He tells that Zinoviev and Kamenev, the good students of Lenin, even came to acquire Lenin's style of handwriting.[81] Trotsky idolises Lenin, identifying with him as a man who could be loved, even worshipped in all his profound humanity.[82] Lenin was infallible: 'Every time that the Bolshevik leaders had to act without Lenin they fell into error.'[83] When it comes to the problem of Lenin's role in history in *Stalin*, Trotsky merely repeats the earlier, circuitous and contradictory explanation, arguing within the space of a page that both accident and necessity determined the outcome of the Russian Revolution.[84] Lenin is portrayed as the apotheosis of October, with Stalin filling the role of its antiChrist. Trotsky's intended innuendo is that it is he who inherits the mantle of Lenin, only somehow the casting is out of synchrony with the unfolding of the plot. The mediocre victor, installed by a quirk of fate, can have but a short reign; who *sees* better wins out in the long run. If Right wins out, then history's passing aberrations need no specific explanation. Through the use of the device of personification, history becomes ultimately the history of essences which work themselves out through humans as agents.

Conclusions

The historical works of Trotsky analysed here all possess some telos which indicates the direction of the future already existent in the present. In *1905* a positive anthropology asserts itself in spontaneous revolutionary politics by manifesting itself in a personified mass. The *History of the Russian Revolution* is a more complex and considered work, in which mass spontaneous will stalls and recedes until the Party machine falls into rhythm with it, at the hands of Lenin and Trotsky. *Stalin* in comparison is a perplexing work with no clear outcome, for in its case Trotsky is faced with the difficult problem of explaining a specific retrogression which violates his philosophy of history. As has been seen, his response is to view Stalinism as a downward political fluctuation on an upward economic curve. So the overall situation is that while Trotsky's optimism is moderated by the passing of the years, it is never fundamentally questioned, let alone surpassed. Radically altered by its authoritarian face in power, Trotsky's

53

anthropology nevertheless remains naïvely, if sadly, optimistic into the years of exile.

Trotsky's major historical writings all share some teleological component; they become more difficult, the more complicit is this teleology with the Soviet experience. Trotsky's own words illustrate the problem, and its transfiguration across the Jacobin-Bolshevik divide. In 1907 the young Trotsky had anticipated that history was a process in which:

> . . . our party [understood in the broad preBolshevik sense, P.B.] . . . will become absorbed without trace in a humanity which, for the first time in history, will be master of its own fate. The whole of history is an enormous machine in the service of our ideals. It works with barbarous slowness, with insensitive cruelty, but it works. But when its omnivorous mechanism swallows up our life's blood for fuel, we feel like calling out to it with all the strength we still possess: 'Faster! — Do it faster!'[85]

In what seems to be a later case, Trotsky saw the relationship between history and Party in a more instrumental sense:

> We work with the most correct and powerful ideas in the world, with inadequate numerical forces and material means. But correct ideas, in the long run, always conquer and make available for themselves the necessary material means and forces.[86]

So is the innocent historical telos of *1905* injected with the spirit of necessity and the logic of apology: history now finds *materials* adequate to its ends. The early vacuous faith in the socialist future gives way to the more forbidding sense, that the new dictatorship will be achieved not merely over the proletariat as collective 'actor', but literally, over the bodies of its component parts. It is this element of the legacy of Trotsky which has become preponderant in the Trotskyist tradition. History has 'done it faster' . . . at the expense of the tradition itself.

Notes

1. P. Anderson, *Arguments Within English Marxism* (NLB, London,

1980), p. 154; compare his earlier, *Considerations on Western Marxism* (NLB, London, 1976), p. 97; and see Deutscher, *The Prophet Outcast*, (Oxford, Oxford University Press, 1970),p. 220ff.

2. N. Geras, 'Literature of Revolution', *New Left Review, 113–14* (1979), pp. 3–41; and see C. Slaughter, *Marxism Ideology and Literature* (Macmillan, London, 1980), Ch. 3. A more sober view, given by Knei-Paz, sees the *History* as a work of art (implicitly, theatre), rather than as a work of history in the strict sense. See Ch. 12 of *The Social and Political Thought of Leon Trotsky*.

3. See, for example, Trotsky, *Results and Prospects*, p. 64, where marxism 'is above all a method of analysis — not analysis of texts, but analysis of social relations'; and *1905* (Penguin, Harmondsworth, 1973), p. 67, where the only acceptable analysis is that which forgoes historical clichés for materialist analysis.

4. See R. Hilton (ed.), *The Transition From Feudalism to Capitalism* (NLB, London, 1976).

5. Trotsky, *1905*, Ch. 2.

6. Trotsky, *1905*, Chs. 1–4.

7. Ibid., p. 53.

8. M. Sawer, *Marxism and the Question of the Asiatic Mode of Production* (Nijhoff, The Hague, 1977), p. 179. See also Trotsky's defence of Plekhanov in Ch. 27 of *1905*.

9. Sawer, *Marxism and the Question*, p. 182. See also Trotsky, *Stalin: An Appraisal of the Man and His Influence* (Hollis & Carter, London, 1947), p. 430f.

10. Trotsky, *Results*, p. 47. Sawer, *Marxism and the Question*, p. 179, indicates that Trotsky never referred directly to the Russian formation as an example of the Asiatic mode of production, perhaps because he saw the Russian formation as characteristically developmental rather than static in nature.

11. Trotsky, *1905*, p. 354.

12. Ibid., Ch. 29.

13. Ibid., pp. 53, 92.

14. See D. Schön, 'Generative Metaphor' in A. Ortony (ed.), *Metaphor and Thought* (Cambridge, Cambridge University Press, 1979), pp. 254–83.

15. Trotsky, *1905*, p. 406.

16. Ibid., p. 409. Emphasis added.

17. Ibid., p. 106f. Emphasis added.

18. Ibid., p. 118.

19. Ibid., p. 194f. Compare *My Life*, p. 307: at the political meetings at the Modern Circus, 'infants were peacefully sucking the breasts from which approving or threatening shouts were coming. The whole crowd was like that, like infants clinging with their dry lips to the nipples of the revolution. But this infant matured quickly.'

20. A. V. Lunacharsky, *Revolutionary Silhouettes* (Allen Lane, London, 1967), p. 65.

21. See, for example, Trotsky, *The History of the Russian Revolution* (Sphere, 3 vols., London, 1967), vol. III, Ch. 7, p. 298.

22. *History*, especially vol. I, pp. 110, 114f.

23. In volume I, Appendix I, Trotsky speaks of Siberia as marked by the combination of 'nomad economic primitiveness with alarm clocks from Warsaw' (p. 431) and observes that around the Belgian and American factory plants are villages of wood and straw which still burn up every year (p. 432).

24. *History*, vol. III, p. 257.

25. For examples of the use of natural necessity, see *History*, vol. 1, p. 18; vol. II, p. 311; vol. III, pp. 66, 107, 250, 318f, 335; for boiling, see vol. I, p. 51; vol. II, p. 27; for the setting sun, vol. I, pp. 106, 216; instincts, vol. I, p. 153; tidal movements, vol. I, pp. 249, 404; vol. II, pp. 252, 274, 276; vol. III, pp. 16, 37, 112, 167, 293, 434; eruptions, vol. I, pp. 257, 361; vol. III, pp. 100, 161, 293, 298.

26. *History*, vol. I, pp. 50, 127, 390, 403; vol. II, p. 243; vol. III, pp. 24, 74.

27. *History*, vol. II, p. 304f.

28. For gynaecology, see *History*, vol. I, pp. 48, 106, 117, 139, 199, 376; vol. III, p. 32, and especially p. 164; for ulcers, death and disease, vol. I, pp. 245, 311, 326, 349; vol. II, pp. 18, 220, 265, 319, 333, 334; vol. III, pp. 37, 64, 70, 95, 100, 123, 159, 161, 168, 213, 234, 255, 283.

29. See generally, M. Daly, *Gyn/Ecology* (The Women's Press, London, 1978), Second Passage.

30. S. Sontag, *Illness as Metaphor* (Farrar, Strauss and Giroux, New York, 1978), p. 82.

31. Compare the Preface to the German edition of *1905*, where the 'subjective tone' is endorsed.

32. *History*, vol. I, pp. 15, 17.

33. *History*, vol. I, pp. 19, 423. Trotsky parallels his task with that of the geologist, vol. II, p. 11. Elsewhere he comments with specific reference to his *History* that 'History is a science no less objective than physiology'. See 'What is Historical Objectivity?', *Writings 1932–33* (Pathfinder, New York, 1972), p. 184.

34. *History*, vol. I, p. 18.

35. R. Warth, 'Leon Trotsky: Writer and Historian', *Journal of Modern History 20(1)* (1948), p. 35.

36. *History*, vol. I, p. 65.

37. Ibid., p. 103.

38. Ibid., pp. 222, 312, 334, 381; vol. II, p. 60; vol. III, pp. 9, 98, 321. A notable example occurs at vol. III, p. 218: 'The social ground shifted noiselessly like a revolving stage, bringing forward the popular masses, carrying away to limbo the rulers of yesterday.' A number of subsidiary questions arise: is it the masses on the stage or their representatives? If not on the stage, is the mass only the audience? To what extent is the action constituted by the director, and to what extent does the director function as censor?

39. *History*, vol. II, Chs 6–7.

40. See, for example, *History* vol. I, p. 160; vol. III, pp. 112f, 154.

41. *History*, vol. III, p. 289. Emphasis added.

42. An early criticism which has dated little is that of L. Gottschalk, 'Leon Trotsky and the Natural History of Revolutions', *American Journal of Sociology XLIV(3)* (1938); see also Warth, *passim*, and B. D.

Trotsky and History

Wolfe, 'Leon Trotsky as Historian', *Slavic Review*, October 1961.
43. *History*, vol. III, p. 68.
44. *Trotsky's Diary in Exile 1935* (Atheneum, New York, 1974), p. 46.
This tension in Trotsky between individual and historic forces resurfaces later in the same entry, where Trotsky laments that he alone must now arm a new generation for world revolution in the Fourth International (p. 47).
45. *History*, vol. I, pp. 271, 310; Ch. 15.
46. Lunacharsky, *Revolutionary Silhouettes*, p. 68.
47. G. B. Shaw, 'Trotsky, the Prince of Pamphleteers', 1922, quoted in G. Breitman and G. Saunders, *Introduction to Portraits Personal and Political by Leon Trotsky* (Pathfinder, New York, 1977), p. 8.
48. *History*, vol. II, Ch. 7 and p. 316.
49. Ibid., p. 333; Trotsky, *Terrorism and Communism*, pp. 28, 180.
50. *History*, vol. II, p. 204.
51. *History*, vol. I, pp. 17, 394, 422; vol. II, p. 205; vol. III, pp. 112f, 262, 264, 271. In addition, there are strangely subconscious mechanical metaphors at work in the *History*. The first, ironical given Trotsky's later reputation as 'the man with the train' in the Civil War, is that of revolution as the locomotive of history, vol. III, pp. 60, 169, 317. The second is the ironical reference to the 'forging of the steel', which conjures up the image of Stalin in the mind of the reader but apparently not in that of the author, vol. I, pp. 257, 325, 403; vol. III, p. 160.
52. *History*, vol. II, p. 155; compare 'The Only Road' in Trotsky, *The Struggle Against Fascism in Germany* (Pathfinder, New York, 1972), p. 276.
53. 'The Workers' State, Thermidor and Bonapartism', *Writings, 1934–35* (Pathfinder, New York, 1971), p. 181f.
54. Trotsky, *The Struggle Against Fascism in Germany*, p. 254.
55. Barthes, *Mythologies*, p. 131; Preface and Conclusion.
56. Trotsky, *Stalin*, p. 372.
57. Ibid., pp. 67, 118, 182, 213, 393, 119.
58. Ibid., pp. 119, 259.
59. Ibid., pp. 3, 10, 11, 414.
60. Ibid., pp. 22, 34, 40, 75, 194. Interestingly, Trotsky fails to take up the relationship of Stalin's provincialism to his nationalism.
61. Ibid., pp. 51, 52, 54, 120f.
62. Ibid., pp. 66, 179.
63. Ibid., pp. 75, 171, 173, 177, 202, 203, 207, 237.
64. Ibid., p. 2.
65. Ibid., p. 13.
66. Trotsky notes that Stalin is possessed by 'extreme Oriental laziness' and by trivialities, ibid., pp. 65, 140, 206, 393, 420. This latter is one of many *tu quoques* in Trotsky's text. The biographer's trivia, in addition to the abovementioned, also take in Stalin's rheumatism, the questions of his marriage to a believer and his skill as huntsman (mediocre again) as well as his truancy from meetings (pp. 6, 86, 172, 224). Trotsky is obsessed by questions of when Stalin did what (for

example, p. 50), and with Stalin's place in the hierarchy of Old Bolsheviks (Stalin is always last on the list, pp. 261, 334). More explicit *tu quoques* include his own version of the Doctors' Plot (against Lenin, p. 372ff), the charge that the young Stalin was neither party builder nor centralist (neither was Trotsky!) and the gleeful discovery of Stalin's potentially Menshevik background (pp. 41, 50).

67. Ibid., p. 83f.
68. B. Souvarine, *Stalin. A Critical Survey of Bolshevism* (Longmans, Green and Co., New York, 1939), pp. 348, 411.
69. See, *The Challenge of the Left Opposition 1923–25*, p. 161.
70. Trotsky even portrays Stalin as stage-manager, as director-in-the-wings, in *Stalin* pp. 232, 237, 378, 413, but this image has no effect on his conscious assessment of Stalin's organisational capacity. As has been seen, for Trotsky history writes the scripts, so the director can have no part larger than that of the actors in the play.
71. Ibid., p. 119.
72. R. McNeal, 'Trotskyist Interpretations of Stalinism' in R. Tucker (ed.), *Stalinism: Essays In Historical Interpretation* (Norton, New York, 1977), p. 51.
73. Trotsky, *Stalin*, pp. 368, 393.
74. *Exile Papers of Lev Trotskii*, 15734, p. 1; Trotsky, *The Revolution Betrayed* (Pathfinder, New York, 1972), Ch. 5.
75. Trotsky, *Stalin*, p. xiii.
76. Ibid., p. 383.
77. Ibid., p. 403.
78. Trotsky, *The Revolution Betrayed*, pp. 45, 44, and compare p. 86.
79. 'Stalinism and Bolshevism', *Writings 1936–37* (Pathfinder, New York, 1978), p. 429.
80. Trotsky, *Stalin*, p. 157.
81. Ibid., p. 158.
82. Ibid., p. 195.
83. Ibid., p. 204.
84. Ibid., p. 205.
85. 'Instead of a Preface to the Second Part', *1905*, p.365; 'Against Pessimism', *Writings 1936–37* (Pathfinder, New York, 1978), p. 193.
86. Trotsky to Cannon, quoted in J. G. Wright, 'Trotsky's Struggle for the Fourth International', *Towards A History of the Fourth International* (SWP Education for Socialists Series, New York, 1973), Part 2, p. 7.

4
Trotsky's Politics:
the Question of Transition

Trotsky's marxism is built on the premisses of automaticity and historical guarantee. Certainty about the outcome of inevitable socialism is written into Trotsky's ambiguous anthropology and his philosophical and economic premisses, and is applied within his historical work and historiographical considerations through Jacobin metaphor. Arriving now at the question of transition in Trotsky, it will become evident that his analysis of this question is already circumscribed and foreclosed by these positions. Here a new theme is introduced: the question of the nature of the Soviet regime. The question of the nature of the Soviet Union remains at the centre of Trotsky's thought ever after 1917. For the purpose of this analysis, the question of transition needs to be divided into two parts: the question of the nature of the USSR and its transition, and the question raised by the *Transitional Program*, that of the transition to socialism in the West. This distinction is then followed through in the criticism of James, Dunayevskaya, Mandel and Deutscher.

Trotsky's analysis of the USSR

Trotsky's understanding of the USSR is spread across many writings, particularly those of the thirties, in which he attempted to come to grips with the phenomenon of Stalinism. Many of his specific works, such as his study of German fascism, include analytic observations about the USSR, and there are miscellaneous considerations on the problem spread throughout the 14-volume *Writings*. In addition there is a range of related archival material, mostly relating to the inner-party dispute over the nature of the USSR. Criticism of Trotsky here will focus on his major relevant work, *The Revolution Betrayed*. Written in 1936, published in 1937, *The Revolution Betrayed* has taken on the status of a classic. It is equalled only by the *History of the Russian Revolution* both in terms of impact and novelty. In its own time the importance of *The Revolution Betrayed* was even greater than that of the *History*. In the thirties alternative explanations of the nature of the USSR included the liberal apologetics of the Webbs, the obscure convergence theory of Bruno Rizzi popularised by James Burnham, and the 'state capitalist' analysis of the half-submerged tradition of council communism. Trotsky's analysis was in this context both a political and an analytical achieve-ment. Where the Friends of the Soviet Union accepted and applauded its image as though it were its reality, the intrans-igent leftist critics saw only the similarities between East and West and few of their differences. This is not to say that *The Revolution Betrayed* was an adequate book, but rather that it was an important one. *The Revolution Betrayed* is a crucial political development, continuing the critical legacy of the Left Oppos-ition; as Bolshevik criticism, it is entirely immanent, measuring Stalinism only against the image of October without beginning to criticise Bolshevism itself.

The Revolution Betrayed — this criticism of Stalinism — actually begins with a defence of Soviet economic achieve-ments. Yet even before it commences a tragic postscript undercuts the argument: 'POSTSCRIPT: This book was completed and sent to the publishers before the "terrorist" conspiracy trial at Moscow was announced. . .September 1936.'[1] It is not clear what value can be ascribed to 'economic growth' at the cost of forced collectivisation and industriali-sation followed by the Great Purges. What is clear is that there is much at stake here for Trotsky: for already in the first pages of *The Revolution Betrayed* the USSR appears despite all as essentially socialist, that is, as possessing the basic elements of socialist economy. Whether the real problem of the 'betrayal' of the revolution is to be located in developments in the state or in the economy is never quite clear: certainly the emphasis is on the former.

How does Trotsky define the nature of the USSR? In his fourth chapter, 'The Struggle for the Productivity of Labor',

Trotsky establishes that Stakhanovism, the forced-compulsory labour which intensifies the production and labour process, resembles the extraction of absolute surplus value characteristic of the process of primitive capitalist accumulation.[2] Production relations in Soviet industry, that is to say, mirror those in the earliest stages of capitalist development. On this understanding the object under analysis is a socialist economy in the early phases of generalised capitalist development, an economy marked by the most primitive and extreme exploitation of labour.

In Chapter Six of *The Revolution Betrayed*, entitled 'The Growth of Inequality and Social Antagonisms', Trotsky reveals that feudal relations are dominant in the countryside, where small, private plots are coupled with compulsory labour for the state.[3] In conjunction with the previous notion, the cumulative definition of the USSR must therefore be that it is a socialist economy with capitalistic relations dominating in industry and with feudal or petty-bourgeois relations dominant in agriculture. But the analysis becomes more complex yet. For Trotsky the new society is a combination of socialist production and bourgeois distribution:

Two opposite tendencies are growing up out of the depth of the Soviet regime. To the extent that, in contrast to decaying capitalism, it develops the productive forces, it is preparing the economic basis for socialism. To the extent that, for the benefit of an upper stratum it carries to more and more extreme expression bourgeois norms of distribution, it is preparing a capitalist restoration. This contrast between forms of property and norms of distribution cannot grow indefinitely. Either the bourgeois norm must in one form or another spread to the means of production, or the norms of distribution must be brought into correspondence with the socialist property system.[4]

Trotsky is unable to perceive the USSR as a new society whose present form is permanent. He applies instead a universal sociological typology. Modern societies can only be capitalist *or* socialist: this is the duality which establishes the metaphorical constellation within which marxist orthodoxy operates. In this fixed scheme the social reality of the USSR can only fit somewhere 'in between' these two essential notions. For

61

Trotsky the USSR is therefore in transition between capitalism and socialism. Which way will it go? Trotsky replies that to betray the revolution is not sufficient to defeat it:

As a conscious political force the bureaucracy has betrayed the revolution. But a victorious revolution is fortunately not only a program and a banner, not only political institutions but also a system of social relations. To betray it is not enough. You need to overthrow it. The October revolution has been betrayed by the ruling stratum, but not yet overthrown. It has a great power of resistance, coinciding with the established property relations, with the living force of the proletariat, the consciousness of its best elements, the impasse of world capitalism and the inevitability of world revolution.[5]

But Trotsky continues: 'The Question of the character of the Soviet Union [is] not yet decided by history.' Here Trotsky's sensitivity for specificity reappears briefly; he hesitates for a moment to characterise the new society as other than contradictory. A more elaborated definition follows:

The Soviet Union is a contradictory society halfway between capitalism and socialism, in which: (a) the productive forces are still far from adequate to give the state property a socialist character; (b) the tendency toward primitive accumulation created by want breaks out through innumerable pores of the planned economy; (c) norms of distribution preserving a bourgeois character lie at the basis of a new differentiation of society; (d) the economic growth, while slowly bettering the situation of the toilers, promotes a swift formation of privileged strata; (e) exploiting the social antagonisms, a bureaucracy has converted itself into an uncontrolled caste alien to socialism; (f) the social revolution, betrayed by the ruling party, still exists in the property relations and in the consciousness of the toiling masses; (g) a further development of the accumulating contradictions can lead as well to socialism as back to capitalism; (h) on the road to capitalism the counterrevolution would have to break the resistance of the workers; (i) on the road to socialism the workers would have to overthrow the bureaucracy. In the last analysis, the question will be decided by a struggle of living social forces, both on the national and the world arena.[6]

While Trotsky's *either* capitalist restoration *or* socialist revival avoids the hard and fast categorisations of others like the 'state capitalists', it also avoids the prospects of the regime's permanence. This is a condition entirely in accord with Trotsky's philosophy of history: while categorised as 'contradictory' the USSR is not *simply* contradictory, for contradiction is of course seen as a motor force. The particular Soviet contradiction must therefore drive the economy forward to socialism in accordance with the broader scenario of world revolution. The teleology involved has a significant theoretical effect: Trotsky blames the ills of Soviet society on its incomplete transition, avoiding thereby the problem of the modern state. For Trotsky Soviet bureaucracy is the product of backwardness, not modernity. The state defends privilege and inequality. More emphatically:

. . .the basis of bureaucratic rule is the poverty of society in objects of consumption, with the resulting struggle of each against all. When there is enough goods in a store, the purchasers can come when they want to. When there is little goods, the purchasers are compelled to stand in line. When the lines are very long, it is necessary to appoint a policeman to keep order. Such is the starting point of the power of the Soviet bureaucracy. It knows who is to get something and who has to wait.[7]

Trotsky collapses the coercive into the administrative dimension of the state. If for Trotsky scarcity is the root of the problem, then abundance — high labour productivity organised along American lines — is its solution. For Trotsky 'it is exactly because of its poverty that the Soviet society has hung around its neck the very costly bureaucracy'.[8] Trotsky fails altogether to register the relationship between modernisation and bureaucratisation, to the extent that he suggests the *incompatibility* of bureaucracy with accounting.[9] For this reason Trotsky fails to envisage that abundance itself might generate bureaucracy, for who is to administer the abundance, and who is to produce it, under what conditions?

Since Weber it has been recognised that bureaucracy is a

necessary condition for the reproduction of modern social organisation, rather than merely a precondition necessary for its development. After Weber, the symbiotic relationship between modernity and bureaucracy is generally recognised: against Trotsky, it is held that rational-legal forms of bureaucracy are definitionally incompatible with traditional or charismatic forms of social organisation. In other words, the scale and complexity of capitalist organisation necessitates a coincidental dynamic of rationalisation which is not merely derived from capitalism, but has some measure of independent existence.[10] Like Lenin, Trotsky presumes an inverse relationship between the dynamic of industrialisation and the dynamic of bureaucracy, when in fact the two are intimately bound up together. Neither Trotsky nor Lenin seems aware that from the administrative perspective, industrialisation is a dynamic of increasing complexity rather than of increasing simplicity: labour processes may themselves become simplified, but administration (be it in welfare or any other sphere) becomes ever more complex. The Bolsheviks seem never to have considered the relationship between knowledge and power, nor the broader question of the non-economic sources of power in general: bureaucratic power is subsumed to the problem of class power, its independent dimension is ignored.[11]

Trotsky understands bureaucracy in its pejorative sense alone. He views bureaucracy as the bad habits of his political enemies rather than viewing bureaucrats as functionaries.[12] Trotsky's analytical error underlines his political inability to combat or control Soviet 'bureaucracy' — which in his understanding is characterised precisely by the absence of bureaucratic principles of organisation. It is really something of an irony that Trotsky, characterised by Lenin as stylistically 'administrative', understood bureaucracy neither when he was a bureaucrat, nor when others were, in the Stalinist regime. Trotsky seems to identify the modern state and the feudal state. He denies the positive and necessary role of the state in the capitalist accumulation process, arguing on the contrary that state intervention indicates not progress but reaction. Stalinism for Trotsky can only mean the restriction of the naturally teleological forces of production; the reality of state intervention in the capitalist economy is seen as an obstacle to the unfolding of his philosophy of history.[13] In this regard, his theoretical resistance to the importance of the modern capitalist state is quite in order, resting on his philosophy of history rather than on any theoretical or empirical investigation.

Trotsky cannot adequately register these developments; the acceptance of the Soviet regime as permanent would jeopardise his view of history and call into question the exclusive categories of capitalism and socialism. For similar reasons he must refuse the bureaucracy the nomenclature 'class'. The conceptual basis of this decision is equally ill-considered: it is entirely formalistic. Trotsky explains that the Soviet bureaucracy cannot be a ruling class because it 'has neither stocks nor bonds'.[14] It nevertheless has at its disposition control of the production processes; in the standard marxist definition of class relationships, bureaucracy can be visualised as the 'non-labourer'. But in this understanding it ought be the question of possession or disposition rather than that of legal ownership which is decisive. In the strict sense, the question of the existence of a Soviet ruling class is irrelevant; but Trotsky avoids it for the wrong reason. In his eyes to talk of 'ruling class' is to talk of capitalism, and the USSR is not capitalist: his thought cannot breach this conceptual option. Property, however, should be defined less as a legal than an actual relation. The important question for the classification of the Soviet regime is not 'who owns/who does not own', but 'who makes the decisions/who works without any decision-making power'. The conclusion should not be that the regime is state capitalist, but rather that is is a stable regime of domination with some similarities to capitalism as well as some striking differences.

Such a conclusion is not possible for Trotsky, who refuses to part with his legalistic fiction about Soviet socialism existing still as the lasting legacy of the property forms established by the October Revolution. Yet the caution and the contradiction manifest in the pages of *The Revolution Betrayed* seem to indicate that Trotsky was momentarily uncertain. At one moment, state property is viewed as socialist; at another, state property becomes socialist property to the degree that it ceases to be state property.[15] On one page of *The Revolution Betrayed* nationalisation guarantees the existence of the proletarian state and socialist production relations; while later on the same page, a different image is summoned: the Soviet bureaucracy closely resembles fascism.[16] In one passage revolutionary mass consciousness still exists in the population; in another it does not.[17] Metaphor is summoned again: in one place the 'lava' of

Trotsky's Politics

revolution has not yet cooled; elsewhere it has frozen.[18] Although the bureaucracy cannot be called a ruling class, it is nevertheless in one place referred to as 'like all ruling classes'.[19] Here socialism exists, while there the Soviet state is closer to backward capitalism.[20] Despite the predictable rationalisation, such contradictions do not merely mirror those existing in Soviet reality. On the contrary, the real anomalies of Soviet reality potentially explode the traditional conceptual structure which cannot contain them. The contradictions in Trotsky's argument are symptomatic of a failure to think through the question of the nature of the Soviet state or economy. Sometimes it is merely state property which guarantees the existence of Soviet socialism; at other times higher productivity alone indicates the possibility of socialist victory. Trotsky's response tells us less of the nature of the USSR than it does of his own conceptual framework.

Here again Trotsky operates within categories which originate in the thinking of the Second International, no less than that of Marx. Trotsky elevates to a new height the popular opposition: capitalism or socialism, market or plan. Like Preobrazhensky, Trotsky saw the struggle for Soviet socialism as the struggle between the New Economic Policy and the principle of planning. NEP, Trotsky tells, contained the possibility of dual power between contending classes — thus its threat to socialism.[21] For Trotsky, backyard gardens are morally repugnant: they deny human power and install medieval labour in its place.[22] Collectivisation in comparison implies the dominance of a collective ethic; but smallholdings indicate for Trotsky the growth of individualism.[23] Market relations are taken inevitably to strengthen individualistic tendencies.[24]

Trotsky's fetish of planning should come as no surprise when his rationalism, his enthusiasm for efficiency and technocracy are remembered. Capitalism's crime is for Trotsky its 'anarchy', its inability to control systematically and to breed its unprecedented productive forces.[25] Trotsky's distance from Stalinist 'planomania' did not affect his acceptance of the basic dichotomy of plan and market.[26] Indeed, in one place Trotsky goes so far as to equate 'market' with 'chaos' and 'plan' with 'reason', elsewhere proposing the images of the plan and the unconscious as polar opposites.[27] Planning in Trotsky's lexicon means state planning, introducing one kind of explanation for his identification of 'state' or 'state-owned' with 'socialism'. But as Markus points out, while the dichotomy of market and plan indeed exists in Marx's work, it contains no such statist logic. On the contrary, planning in Marx was understood as the democratic realm of the associated producers.[28] It is something less than a surprise, then, that Trotsky's work lacks a theory of economic democracy. Although his earlier work contains an enthusiasm for political democracy, which is revived in *The Revolution Betrayed*, Trotsky gives only passing attention to the question of democracy in the workplace, or 'workers' control'.[29] He fails to discuss the mechanisms by which 'Soviet democracy' exerts its corrective influence over the central organs of planning. His argument is not strengthened by the historical fact that by this stage of Soviet development neither soviets nor unions were functioning any longer.

Suggestions that Trotsky may have seen market and plan as symbiotically related in the twenties are weakened by difficulties in periodisation.[30] Writing in 1924, Preobrazhensky envisaged the coexistence of market and plan as lasting 'ten, twenty, and we must expect, thirty years'.[31] Trotsky gave no indication of his own sense of the anticipated duration of the Soviet transitional period, which should by rights have been protracted somewhat by the misadventures of Stalinism. Industrialisation itself could indeed have proceeded only at a 'snail's pace' without coercion. Whatever their differences, Trotsky's dilemma resembled Preobrazhensky's, for industrialisation could not proceed apace without civil war or state coercion. The emphasis of the Left Opposition on industrialisation brought with it by logical necessity the principle of central planning. Trotsky was a 'Department I' marxist, his political sympathies were with the forces of technology in Department I which drive the economy, and hence history, forward to socialism. Consequently, Trotsky could never resolve the tension between central planning and 'Soviet democracy'. As he put it in *Terrorism and Communism*, 'our first item is not articles of consumption, but the implements of transport and production'.[32] He urged the producer's view over the consumer's, for the former corresponded with the general indicators of the central plan. This is not to say that Trotsky was insensitive to the question of consumer goods or Department II, but rather that his sensitivity was overridden by the logic of his argument for industrialisation. If planning is to be centralised, then it can only be the prerogative of the state power. Political participation belongs in the first place to the ruling party, even if it is formally extended to others in Trotsky's later writings. Whatever the differences in Trotsky's positions over the years and across changing circumstances, the elements of continuity are clear. The defence of the October Revolution is a constant for Trotsky: but the principle of defence itself presumes what needs to be established. Few with real critical insight could still find positive concrete remnants of the legacy of October in Stalin's Russia.

Beyond 'The Revolution Betrayed'

Three years elapsed between the appearance of *The Revolution Betrayed* and Trotsky's murder in Mexico. Trotsky did not substantially modify his views on the USSR in this period. The *Transitional Program* was however to popularise another definition, that of the USSR as a 'degenerated workers' state':

> The Soviet Union emerged from the October Revolution as a workers' state. State ownership of the means of production, a necessary prerequisite to socialist development, opened up the possibility of rapid growth of the productive forces. But the apparatus of the workers' state underwent a complete degeneration at the same time. . . The USSR thus embodies terrific contradictions. But it still remains a *degenerated workers' state*.[33]

The prognosis following is identical to that in *The Revolution Betrayed*: there are only two possibilities, either capitalist restoration or the revival of soviet democracy.

The notion of Soviet 'degeneration' is not at all incompatible with the classification of the USSR as a society transitional between capitalism and socialism. The notion of degeneration merely extends the metaphorical legacy of the Second International. Trotsky again applies a whole series of metaphors here, organic, institutional and mechanical. He also delves further into the imagery of the French Revolution, but these investigations are less than enlightening because they are typological rather than specific.

As he had long entertained the idea of French precedents, so had Trotsky long refused the idea of Soviet state capitalism. Trotsky's alternative proposal, that of 'degeneration', is of course consitituted with reference to the metaphorical norm, generation. 'Generation' in this context indicates the presence of Trotsky's socialist telos: it is by no means self-evident that a factor of 'progress' or 'generation' is active in the workers' state. Trotsky parallels the workers' state with a diseased liver, which does not cease to be a liver for being diseased.[34] In another place the chosen metaphor is that of a badly damaged automobile — while the mechanic's reaction, 'This is no automobile!' is readily understandable, the fact of its damage does not alter the automobile's objective status; it is still an automobile.[35] But the metaphor most belaboured by Trotsky is that of the corrupt trade union. The corrupt trade union despite its corruption still serves the workers.[36] The analogy here is complete: 'In the last [!] analysis a workers' state is a trade union which has conquered power.' Trotsky makes no distinction between a first approximation and a final analysis. As Trotskyists defend unions even though they be corrupt, so should they defend the degenerated workers' state.[37]

Trotsky's best considered metaphor is hopelessly inadequate. To use the appropriate language, Trotsky's problem is that he avoids the 'dialectics of quantity and quality'. How far can this process of degeneration proceed? At what stage can it be determined that the workers' interests are still being catered for? Trade unions, even corrupt ones, are after all bound by bourgeois law; they do not administer social regimes but contest one part of their terrain, taking up primarily questions of wages and conditions for those who labour. Trade unions are functional to bourgeois society, as the right of the organisation of interests is an accepted norm of its legality; trade unions are an identifiable part of the operation of bourgeois society. The existence of the workers' state, in comparison, rests on mere assurance. While in itself quite convincing, Trotsky's refusal of the category 'state capitalism' was possible only at the cost of a slide into the presupposition that the Soviet Union must be socialist, only 'degenerated'. The introduction of various forms of generative or degenerative metaphor suggests a strategic resort to a range of rationalisations sufficient to foreclose the discussion of the question of the nature of the USSR. The formalistic analysis introduced by

Trotsky avoids the primary definitional question: in what senses was the Soviet regime recognisably 'socialist' in the first place? The automobile, the liver and the trade union are determinate objects or facts, the existence or condition of which can be verified on the level of common sense or science. Trotsky's subterfuge avoids both the conceptual challenge and the historical factors involved, backing around both questions: what was the nature of the regime in the beginning? And, what has it come to be after two decades of chaos and coercion?

Only once did Trotsky seemingly ponder the possibility of the complete degeneration of the USSR. In 'The USSR in War' Trotsky gave an either/or prognosis: the Second World War would seal the fate of the Soviet Union, either provoking proletarian revolution or else witnessing further decay, the latter 'signalizing the eclipse of civilisation'.[38] In the latter event, the USSR would then have to be seen as the precursor of a new exploiting regime on an international scale.[39] The status of this speculation is problematical. In a later contribution to the inner-party debate Trotsky confirms the rhetorical nature of his negative proposal. He reveals that he could not give credibility to the scenario of decay into complete degeneration; the perspective of the proletariat must be 'invincible revolutionary optimism'.[40] The pessimistic scenario of decline therefore functions as a strawman and a mere inversion of generative imagery: it is not for Trotsky an option that warrants serious consideration. Certainty is still conceived to be written into the order of history, and the Soviet proletariat must redeem itself: for the Soviet degeneration, after all, was only due to the 'belatedness of the world revolution'.[41] The problem of the national explanation of the new society is eclipsed by reference to the metaphysics of world revolution: had only the world proletariat adhered to the task given it by history. . .[42]

Trotsky's analysis of the USSR divides into a minimum and a maximum program: defence of the existing Soviet reality is justified by reference to the metaphysics of world revolution. When the latter overcomes the momentary obstacles imposed on it the former will cease to be a problem. The 'revolution betrayed' will be absolved by a telos that is merely delayed. In the meantime, in Knei-Paz's words, for Trotsky 'a Stalinist Soviet Union was better than no Soviet Union at all'.[43] Since he constituted his personal and political identity with singular

70

reference to the Soviet Union, Trotsky was in no position to analyse it adequately. The course of the Russian Revolution had 'betrayed' Trotsky, but he could not betray it.

But the association was more than merely personal or psychological. The necessitarian component of Trotsky's philosophy of history predisposed him to the Hegelian 'cunning of history'; history had to 'do it faster', but 'the dialectic of the historic process has more than once cruelly punished those who tried to jeer at it.'[44] True enough, Trotsky never jeered at dialectics, but knelt before them, and before History itself. Given that socialism was understood by Trotsky *essentially* to be a matter of nationalisation, the extension of Soviet power into the Second World War could only be understood as History's own cunning at work. The invasion of Poland by the Red Army was therefore greeted by Trotsky as a step forward; and though he remained ambivalent about the consequences of the extension of Soviet power, his positive appraisal in this instance did lay the way for the later hegemony of the necessitarian view within the Fourth International.[45] Ironically enough, Trotsky's Bolshevism was in this sense self-destructive: for his followers were, in the long run, to scramble after the old mole the world about, effectively eschewing their own vocation as the new vanguard and liquidating the Fourth International itself.

Transition in the West: 'The Transitional Program'

Trotsky's fundamental optimism remained unaltered by the developments of the thirties. In some senses Trotsky's optimism might be said to have become even more accentuated, for he saw those developments and the impending war as providing even better opportunities for world socialist revolution. Having revealed its own political bankruptcy, the decline of the Third International now necessitated establishment of the Fourth. As always, the masses were held to be yearning for revolution, but retarded by their own labour leaders. Trotsky's overall position suggests that transition was under way everywhere except on the level of party leadership. Here again we see the tension between necessity and voluntarism in Trotsky.

The programatic document of the new International

71

embodying these principles was *The Death Agony of Capitalism and the Tasks of the Fourth International*, which subsequently came to be known as *The Transitional Program*. Trotsky here begins with the problem of leadership and its relation to the present crisis:

> The world political situation as a whole is chiefly charac-
> terised by a historical crisis of the leadership of the
> proletariat. The economic prerequisite for the proletarian
> revolution has already in general achieved the highest point
> of fruition that can be reached under capitalism. Mankind's
> productive forces stagnate . . . all talk to the effect that
> historical conditions have not yet 'ripened' for socialism is
> the product of ignorance or conscious deception [!]. The
> objective prerequisites for the proletarian revolution have
> not only 'ripened', they have begun to get somewhat rotten
> . . . The historical crisis of mankind is reduced to the crisis of
> the revolutionary leadership . . . the chief obstacle in the
> path of transforming the [existing, P.B.] pre-revolutionary
> condition into a revolutionary one is the opportunist
> character of proletarian leadership.[46]

Trotsky's analysis is characterised by a level of generality completely inappropriate to the discussion of the subject at hand. Its underpinning is the familiar language of Jacobinism, indicating the necessity of correct intervention against the renegade leaders in order to forestall decay and return the biological process of evolution to its natural course.[47] Trotsky's focus on the question of leadership to the detriment of all else is to be expected, for this is the very *raison d'être* of the Fourth International as the 'alternative' proletarian leadership. Already in its opening words, *The Transitional Program* is presented as a solution on the level of leadership rather than that of mass activity.

Trotsky proceeds to define the nature of the *Program* and its demands in the following terms:

> It is necessary to help the masses in the process of the daily
> struggle to find the bridge between present demands and
> the socialist program of the revolution. This bridge should
> include a system of *transitional demands*, stemming from
> today's conditions and from today's consciousness of wide

layers of the working class and unalterably leading to one final conclusion: the conquest of power by the proletariat.[48]

Trotsky is concerned to contrast this program with that of the 'Classical Social Democracy', with its distinction between 'minimum' and 'maximum' programs. In the self-understanding of Social Democracy, it was the case that 'between the minimum and maximum program, no bridge existed':

> Insofar as the old partial, 'minimal' demands of the masses clash with the destructive and degrading tendencies of decadent capitalism — and this occurs at each step — the Fourth International advances a system of *transitional demands*, the essence of which is contained in the fact that ever more openly and decisively they will be directed against the very foundations of the bourgeois regime. The old 'minimal program' is superseded by the *transitional program*, the task of which lies in systematic mobilisation of the masses for the proletarian revolution.[49]

What is the nature of these transitional demands? The demands themselves include a sliding scale of wages and hours (wage indexation and work sharing), the disclosure of business secrets, the extension of public works, workers' control and selective nationalisation and the defence of the existing democratic rights and conditions of life.[50] None of these demands seem to be revolutionary in character, least of all judged by Trotsky's own criteria, nor are the means by which they might engender the transition to socialism at all evident.

This raises the question: how transitional in fact is the *Transitional Program*? One group of intransigent American Trotskyists has put forward the argument that it is not transitional at all, nor was it intended to be. Commenting on the passage of the *Program* just quoted, their verdict is that Trotsky clearly meant the transitional program to be a substitute for the 'minimal' program and not for the 'maximal' program of socialist revolution.[51] As evidence to support their argument, the anonymous authors cite the words of Trotsky in a discussion of the Draft Program, where he argues that 'the strategy brings the reader only to the doorstep. It is a program for action from today until the beginning of the socialist revolution.'[52] In their polemic against the Socialist Workers'

Party, the dominant American Trotskyist party which takes the *Transitional Program* to be a revolutionary program, the authors wish to set the transitional demands apart from the socialist revolution proper. They seem ultimately to be suggesting that transitional measures merely serve to discredit the non-revolutionary left by exposing their inadequacy to the task of fundamental social change. Their argument is of course based on the highest authority, Trotsky himself. But is Trotsky's textual position so clear cut?

A more thorough textual examination of the arguments involved reveals yet again contradiction in Trotsky's position. In one place, Trotsky seems to concede that the transitional demands are substantially reformist in nature.[53] The logic involved here is similar to that at work in the quotation at the foot of p.73: the demands are seen not as identical with, but as preparatory to, the socialist revolution.[54] Yet elsewhere Trotsky suggests that the immediate demands will themselves have a revolutionary effect: 'Not one of our demands will be realised under capitalism. That is why we are calling them transitional demands. It creates a bridge to the mentality of the workers and then a material bridge to the socialist revolution.'[55] The logic at work in this passage corresponds with the widely received understanding of the *Transitional Program* as itself a part of the revolutionary process rather than belonging to the period preliminary to that process. As Trotsky put it in a passage quoted earlier, in expeditionary image, the program bridges minimum and maximum programs, rather than simply providing a modified version of the former. No final conclusion can be drawn on the question of the self-conscious understanding of the place of the *Transitional Program* in Trotsky's marxism: like so much else in his work, its condition is contradictory, the contradictions providing the ground which sustains the array of interpretations characteristic of modern Trotskyism.

Is the *Transitional Program* transitional measured by criteria other than those of internal criticism? As has been noted, the real *motif* of the program is the question of leadership. Transition to socialism on a world scale is presumed to be a process already under way, but blocked by the bad leadership of the Stalinist and reformist parties. This political analysis rests on the accepted wisdom of economic determinism, and invokes the language of Jacobinism. The objective situation of world

Trotsky's Politics

capitalism is understood to be 'ripe', even 'overripe'. Bourgeois
civilisation rots: revolution is summoned. Trotsky is at a loss to
explain the political 'backwardness' of the (American) working
class in the face of this objective 'ripeness'; the factor of bad
leadership is introduced as *de facto* explanation for the situation.[56] The echoes of the Jacobin anthropology are clear:
socialism is written into the order of things, but its expression is
prevented by a particular form of political domination.
Instinctively socialist strivings are manifested only to be
repressed by leaderships which consider themselves to have a
concrete interest in the maintenance of the status quo. Trotsky
introduces such precritical views in order to explain the dislo-
cation between 'subjective' and 'objective' factors, bypassing
the problem of mass consciousness and its role in the process of
social change.

Trotsky's understanding of consciousness harks back to
Marx. There is an implicit assumption in Trotsky that since
'being determines consciousness', the nature of proletarian
existence in a situation of crisis can only induce a mass break
into socialist politics. Trotsky conceives proletarian
consciousness as mere superstructure, as the effect of an
economy credited with exclusive causal powers. Trotsky's
dependence on Marx's 1859 Preface is evident: for the Preface
explains only how consciousness is reproduced, not how it is
changed.[57] Also implicit in Trotsky's writing is the class univer-
salism of Marx's early works, that position which later came to
be associated with the Lukácsian notion of 'class imputation'.
As the alleged bearer of the historic interests of mankind, the
proletariat has a particular duty which it is obliged to fulfil. It is
a class which can be jolted from its momentary slumbers by the
emergence of a really revolutionary leadership — that of the
Fourth International.

Trotsky's response to the problem of mass consciousness
consists, therefore, in the presentation of a *Program*. For
Trotsky a correct program — one corresponding to the
objective situation — must override the immediate empirical
consciousness of the proletariat.[58] Those who know — the
vanguard of the Fourth International — determine the real
nature of the objective situation in order to bring the
consciousness of the masses into conformity with it. Trotsky's
dual error consists in an ideological misreading of objective
'ripeness' coupled with the denial of the legitimacy of the

75

masses' empirical consciousness. The response which calls for the 'Correct Program' avoids the real problems of everyday consciousness, instead turning the notion of transition into sloganising and propaganda: as though when the masses hear the word, they will know to act.[59]

In Trotsky's scenario the workers are apathetic not because their empirical realities and needs remain unaddressed, but because they lack a *Program*.[60] This is the source of the modern Trotskyist tragi-comedy, where the would-be generals seek out an army, offering the utopia of barracks-communism in exchange for a *Program*. This spectacle is deeply rooted in the logic of the *Transitional Program*, in its assumption that the correct leadership armed with correct knowledge need only bring mass consciousness into conformity with objective reality in order to formalise the already existing transition to socialism latent in the 'crisis'. Beyond the dimension of Trotsky's self-understanding or immanent criticism, it is clear that rather than confronting the real human problems involved in the quest for social change, the *Transitional Program* simply reasserts Trotsky's mythical philosophy of history, this time in the form of a proletarian eschatology.

Specific problems of transition in the West

Trotsky transforms the Heracleitan intellectual common sense about understanding the world as motion into a mythical maxim of permanent transition. The *Transitional Program* itself begs the question of the transitional epoch.[61] Trotsky simply presumes that the transitional epoch exists. His analyses of the British General Strike and the Spanish Revolution confirm this picture.[62] More striking yet are his portrayals of imminent transition in the United States and France. The least positive indication in these cases is read as a signpost on the road to socialism. Trotsky's understanding of transition in the United States rests on the base of the classical crisis principle. In the Preconference Discussions for the founding of the Fourth International, he comments:

> There cannot be any reason to believe that American capitalism can of itself become a sound, healthy capitalism, that it can absorb the 13 million unemployed. . .Every

76

unemployed person sees that the employed have work. He will look for work and, not finding any, will enter into the unemployed movement.[63]

Trotsky sees the immediate condition of economic crisis as irreversible and insoluble, suggesting that of necessity the impoverished will turn to the workers' movement, subsequently to be revolutionised. His catastrophic view of capital's impending doom is nowhere better witnessed than in his myopic view of the New Deal. Trotsky argues that New Deal politics, like Popular Front politics in France, open no new exit from the economic blind alley.[64] Elsewhere he suggests that the New Deal is directed into the same channels as the policy of Fascism.[65] Here Trotsky applies the first principles of the theory of collapse: the collapse of capitalist economy means not only the collapse of the political superstructure, but also heralds the victory of socialism.[66] That Trotsky's scenario bears little relation to the specifics of American society is particularly evident in his comments on unionism and the labour movement. In accordance with the automatic connotations of the theory of collapse, Trotsky blurs the different developments in unionism, portraying the rapid growth of industrial unionism as 'the most indisputable expression of the instinctive striving of the American workers to raise themselves to the level of the tasks imposed [!] on them by history'.[67] In keeping with his focus on leadership, Trotsky blames reactionary organisation and leadership for the failure of the masses to act.

Trotsky typifies the American unions with reference to their equivalents in Britain. According to Trotsky, 'Now that genuine trade unions exist, they must make the same evolution as the English trade unions. . .on the basis of declining capitalism, they are forced to turn to political action',[68] and implicitly to political action of no ordinary type. Trotsky's failure to negotiate the specific American situation is functional to his revolutionary philosophy of history: the details are filled out in accordance with the latter. Perhaps this much on Trotsky's part is understandable, but beyond this there is his tendency to prophesy about the impending arrival of the non-existent American labour party. In a discussion entitled 'The Problem of the Labor Party', Trotsky fails to register the most tangible, relevant problem: that of its non-existence.[69] The development of the labour party is presumed as part of an overarching set of unstated but classical prerequisites necessary for the 'transition' to socialism: the existence of a labour party is one precondition for socialist revolution, therefore it will come into existence of itself. 'When and how the labor party will be formed, and through what stages and splits it will pass, the future will disclose.' Further, Trotsky continues:

> In its very essence the Labor Party can preserve progressive significance only during a comparatively short transitional period. The further sharpening of the revolutionary situation will inevitably break the shell of the labor party and permit the Socialist Workers' Party [US representatives of the Fourth International] to rally around the banner of the Fourth International the revolutionary vanguard of the American proletariat.[70]

The non-existent labour party, a mere 'shell' of superficiality representing a more fundamental and dynamic essence, withers before it has even grown. In Trotsky's messianic outlook, the non-existent labour party is shattered, to be replaced by a new International whose existence is only marginally more concrete.

Trotsky's insensitivity to the problems involved, given the relative absence of a tradition of political organisation in the American labour movement, is symptomatic of a deeper *parti pris* at work. The underlying notion is that parties, as part of the political realm, are the function of properly 'objective' developments: the 'labor party' is therefore called into existence, as it were, by the latent transition in economy. As regards the American case, it functions here only as a delayed version of the British: the unilinear theory of universal history indicates that where a particular case is 'behind' temporally, it will in time duplicate and perhaps even outstrip earlier precedents. The development of American industrial unionism and its 'logical' concomitant, the labour party, have been delayed, but will out. Transition here is taken to be the norm: it cannot adequately be stated as a problem, let alone solved, within this framework.

The language of Trotsky's analysis of transition in France is equally associational: the title of the final chapter of *Whither France?* indicates the outcome already in advance: 'The French

Revolution has Begun'.[71] Coupled with the signifier 'crisis' is the Trotskyist signified: socialist revolution. Trotsky's general scenario consists of a mechanical juxtaposition of alternatives: given that transition is an actual fact, the only question is, which transition? the transition to socialism or barbarism? the Soviet path or that of Italian Fascism?[72] As in Trotsky's argument about America, history here is taken to be in motion, only there are two alternative roads, to use a favoured image. The problem is to get the masses over the bridge and onto the right road. Trotsky views the French situation as being as revolutionary as it possibly could be, given the non-revolutionary policies followed by the working–class parties.[73] There is no suggestion that leaderships might reflect mass opinion rather than deny it.

This presumption in Trotsky links in with the earlier discussion of Jacobinism. To span concepts, 'transition', as 'progress' or 'necessity', is already latent in the Jacobin anthropology; it serves as a first principle in Trotsky's politics. This problem in Trotsky has some echoes in the work of Michels. Like Michels the early Trotsky feels disdain for the organisational dead weight of the Social Democratic Party. The later Trotsky expands this disdain to the Communist Parties as well. However, the Bolshevik Trotsky excludes his own organisation, the Fourth International, from the operation of the 'iron law of oligarchy', an exclusion which the more sober Michels would hardly allow. In Michels' seemingly prophetic words, while accepting the existence of the iron law, 'the Marxists hasten to add that the socialist party is quite free from these dangers'.[74] For Trotsky, in comparison, there are two kinds of parties, ours and theirs. For the Bolshevik Party became another first principle for the later Trotsky. But there is no substance in the 'military analogy' with the politics of social change, regardless of how radical the new vanguard claims to be. The impotence of Trotskyist politics is bound up with its focus on the cultivation of the vanguard and its contempt for the empirically existing masses. If it is at all meaningful to talk about a possible transition to socialism, then it need be acknowledged that those masses must be taken into consideration as they are, and not as they 'ought to be'. If the discussion of transition is divorced from mass popular politics, it remains, as with Trotsky, on the level of eschatological guarantee: and this holds true for East and West. The 'theory of transition' in Trotsky's thought asserts in both spheres what it must prove. Even within his own metaphorical framework, Trotsky fails to realise that political faith does not move mountains which must be climbed.

Conclusions

Trotsky's orthodoxy in philosophy and economy has resounding effects throughout his analytical work. As his historical work is strewn with conclusions established in advance, so is Trotsky's analysis of transition a foregone conclusion. Trotsky is incapable of assessing critically the changing nature of the Soviet regime, turning instead to the faith of necessity in order to solve on paper the problems of socialism in East and West alike. Inasmuch as socialism is held to be deeply inscribed both in the nature of man and on the historic agenda of the twentieth century, critical doubts as to the real achievements of mankind or of the century are foreclosed. The practical outcome, which will be felt throughout the remainder of this book, is the contradictory conclusion which suggests that modern society is already transitional to socialism, while the discussion about transition is nevertheless overdetermined by the question of the nature of the USSR. Trotskyist theories of the transition to socialism developed after Trotsky are still irredeemably bound into associations with the Soviet experience. Trotskyists after Trotsky may alter their periodisation of Soviet 'degeneration', but they all associate with the achievements of October in one period or another.

While there can be no suggestion that the question of socialism could be discussed today without reference to the Soviet experience, it is another thing altogether to reduce the discussion to that experience, as though in some early stage of its development the 'secret' of transition might be gleaned from its record. Even Trotsky had a partial insight into the limited relevance of the Russian Revolution to the broader question of transition, though this also was to be suppressed. In the text of *The Revolution Betrayed* itself Trotsky quotes a document of the Left Opposition from 1927, where the following rhetorical conjecture is made:

If you admit the possibility of its [the capitalist world's, P.B.] flourishing anew for a period of decades then the talk of socialism in our backward country is pitiable tripe. Then it will be necessary to say that we were mistaken in our appraisal of the whole epoch as an epoch of capitalist decay. Then the Soviet Republic will prove to have been the second experiment in proletarian dictatorship since the Paris Commune, broader and more fruitful, but only an experiment. . .[75]

Some commentators have suggested that the best criticism of certain critics of Trotsky is to be found in Trotsky himself. It seems here to be the case that on the contrary, the potential refutation of Trotsky's arguments may be found in the occasional insights of the momentarily critical Trotsky. The Trotskyist tradition, in comparison, has a historical existence and political continuity in which self-refutation is in general structurally precluded, where conceptual structures have only hardened and become hackneyed, long having lost the degree and kind of self-contradiction characteristic of Trotsky's own thought.

Notes

1. Trotsky, *The Revolution Betrayed* (Pathfinder, New York, 1972), p. 4.
2. Ibid., pp. 78–85.
3. Ibid., pp. 126, 132.
4. Ibid., p. 244.
5. Ibid., p. 251f.
6. Ibid., p. 255.
7. Ibid., pp. 58, 112.
8. Ibid., p. 217.
9. Ibid., p. 274.
10. Weber, *Economy and Society* (two vols., California University Press, 1978), vol. I, p. 220f.
11. See B. Knei-Paz, *Leon Trotsky* (Oxford University Press, Oxford, 1978), Ch. 3, especially pp. 100ff; and see A. Polan, *Lenin and the End of Politics* (Methuen, London, 1984).
12. But see 'The New Course' in *Challenge of the Left Opposition 1923–25* (Pathfinder, New York) p. 91f.
13. Trotsky, *The Revolution Betrayed*, p. 246.
14. Ibid., p. 249.
15. Ibid., pp. 236, 237.

81

Trotsky's Politics

16. Ibid., p. 248.
17. Ibid., pp. 255, 257.
18. Ibid., pp. 270, 271, cf. p. 272.
19. Ibid., Ch. 9, p. 274.
20. Ibid., pp. 252, 258.
21. 'Preface to *La Revolution Defigurée*' in *Writings 1929*, p. 119; 'Toward Capitalism or Socialism?' in *Challenge of the Left Opposition 1923–25*, p. 327.
22. Trotsky, *The Revolution Betrayed*, p. 126.
23. Ibid., p. 130.
24. Ibid., pp. 132, 176.
25. Ibid., p. 19.
26. See for example, Day, *Leon Trotsky*, p. 183.
27. *The Living Thoughts of Karl Marx*. p. 43; *History of the Russian Revolution*, vol. III, p. 322.
28. Fehér/Heller/Markus, *Dictatorship Over Needs*, p. 11.
29. Trotsky, *The Revolution Betrayed*, pp. 160, 263, 267; compare p. 94f; 'The Soviet Economy in Danger', *Writings 1932* (Pathfinder, New York, 1973), p. 273ff.
30. Day, *Leon Trotsky*, p. 185.
31. Preobrazhensky, *The New Economics* (Oxford, University Press, 1965), p. 59.
32. Trotsky, *Terrorism and Communism* (Ann Arbor, Michigan, 1972), p. 160.
33. Trotsky *The Transitional Program for Socialist Revolution*, p. 142.
34. 'Not a Workers' and Not a Bourgeois State?', *Writings 1937–38*, p. 64f.
35. 'Again and Once More Again on the Nature of the USSR', *In Defense of Marxism*, p. 25.
36. 'Not a Workers' and Not a Bourgeois State?', p. 64f.
37. 'Again and Once More Again', p. 25.
38. 'The USSR in War', *In Defense of Marxism*, p. 8f.
39. Ibid.
40. 'Again and Once More Again', p. 31f.
41. Trotsky, *The Revolution Betrayed*, p. 278.
42. Ibid., and see p. 23.
43. Knei-Paz, *Leon Trotsky*, p. 411.
44. *In Defense*, p. 104.
45. Ibid., p. 18ff.
46. Trotsky, *The Transitional Program for Socialist Revolution*, p. 111f.
47. Ibid., pp. 112–13. Elsewhere, the imagery is of tidal forces: 'The approaching historical wave will raise it [the Fourth International] on its crest', p. 148.
48. Ibid., p. 114.
49. Ibid., pp. 114, 115.
50. Ibid., p. 115ff.
51. (Anonymous) 'Myth and Reality of the Transitional Program'. *Socialist Voice*, 8 (1979), publication of the League for the Revolutionary Party, New York, p.18.

Trotsky's Politics

52. Ibid., p. 18; Trotsky, *Transitional Program for Socialist Revolution*, p. 173.

53. Trotsky, *Transitional Program*, p. 122.

54. Interestingly, the drafts for the *Transitional Program* contain a subtitle which is absent from the published version: 'Mobilisation of the Masses Around Transitional Demands in Preparation for the Conquest of Power', *Trotsky Archives*, 4341.2, 4341.3.

55. Preconference Discussions, in *Transitional Program for Socialist Revolution*, p. 159. Emphasis added.

56. Preconference Discussions, p. 155.

57. Draft Discussions, in *Transitional Program* p. 99.

58. Preconference Discussions, pp. 157, 176.

59. Draft Discussions, p. 85.

60. Preconference Discussions, pp. 166. 172.

61. See, for example, *Transitional Program*, p. 118.

62. See Trotsky, *Where is Britain Going?* (New Park, London, 1970), and *The Spanish Revolution 1931–39* (Pathfinder, New York, 1973).

63. Preconference Discussions, *The Transitional Program for Socialist Revolution*, p. 187f.

64. *Transitional Program*, p. 111.

65. *The Living Thoughts of Karl Marx*, pp. 25, 38.

66. See ibid., p. 22.

67. *Transitional Program*, p. 113.

68. Preconference Discussions, p. 163.

69. Draft Discussions, p. 107.

70. Draft Discussions, p. 108.

71. Trotsky, *Whither France?* (Merit, New York, 1968).

72. *Whither France?*, for example, pp. 6, 46, 49, 51ff, 60.

73. Ibid., p. 50.

74. R. Michels, *Political Parties* (Jarrold, London, 1915), p. 44.

75. See Trotsky, *The Revolution Betrayed*, p. 297.

Part Two
Trotskyism: the Intellectual Heirs

5
Philosophy and Transition: C.L.R. James and Raya Dunayevskaya

Trotsky's arguments about transition are constructed in the shadow of the Soviet experience. The same is true of the arguments of his followers, even if some of them reverse his understanding of the significance of the Russian experience or shade their interpretations with more nuance. The thinkers examined in this second part all emerged directly from the political milieu of organised Trotskyism. Mandel and Deutscher, who remained closer to orthodox Trotskyism, will be discussed in subsequent chapters. C.L.R. James ('J.R. Johnson') and Raya Dunayevskaya ('Freddie Forest') were in comparison the central heretics of the Johnson-Forest 'state capitalist' tendency, which worked within American Trotskyism between 1941 and 1951. James and Dunayevskaya left organised Trotskyism in 1951 and collaborated on the 'Correspondence Committees' from 1953 to 1955, when they split. Dunayevskaya then established 'News and Letters' which, with its newspaper of the same name, still functions today. While remaining politically active, James did not have a formal organisational following, though there were enthusiasts for his thought grouped around journals like *Radical America* and *Cultural Correspondence*. Both James and Dunayevskaya had collaborated with Trotsky in the earlier period. James partici-pated in the Founding Conference of the Fourth International as British delegate and was responsible for raising discussion of the Negro problem in the Fourth International. Dunayevskaya assisted the operations of the *Bulletin of the Opposition* and worked as secretary to Trotsky in Mexico between 1937 and 1938, breaking with him over the Stalin-Hitler pact, as she refused any longer to follow Trotsky's defence of the USSR.

The Johnson-Forest Tendency arose within and against the Workers' Party, which was associated with Max Shachtman and his analysis of the USSR as 'bureaucratic collectivism'. Dunayevskaya and James developed an alternative explanation of the USSR: they developed the other half of the socialism/capitalism dyad, arguing that the Russian regime was state capitalist in nature. Both Dunayevskaya and James were philosophers with a special interest in Hegel; Dunayevskaya translated the first English versions of both Marx's *Paris Manuscripts* and Lenin's *Philosophical Notebooks*. Both thinkers made detailed analyses of the Russian economy; both were to take on the characteristically Trotskyist enthusiasm for Lenin and Lenin's regime. While Dunayevskaya's interests are wide-ranging, her works — notably *Marxism and Freedom* and *Philosophy and Revolution* — are characterised by thematic unity and clarity of style. James, in contrast, has interests even more diverse than Trotsky: his writings include a book on cricket (*Beyond A Boundary*), historical analysis (*The Black Jacobins*), novels and literary criticism (particularly on Melville). In contrast to Dunayevskaya, whose political interests still have a distinctly North American orientation, James became a publicist for the Pan African movement.

As intellectuals and activists James and Dunayevskaya are therefore both complementary and contrasting. Their criticisms of Trotsky, their philosophical interests and their own analyses of transition provide reflections of some of Trotsky's positions as well as revealing the novelties of their own developments. Their major contribution, the argument about state capitalism, remains one of the most influential of radical interpretations of the Soviet state. As one of the most innovative variants of Trotskyism, this argument affords a clear view of the libertarian limits to which Trotskyist thinking can be pushed. James will be dealt with first, then Dunayevskaya.

James's assessment of Trotsky and Lenin

James's position on Trotsky commences with the problem of Trotsky's conceptual rigidity. According to James, Trotsky's equation of 'nationalised property' with 'the workers' state' in *The Revolution Betrayed*, indicates that Trotsky would rather let marxism perish than change its obsolete categories. Trotsky's limit is that he attempts to think through new problems, such as the question of the nature of the USSR, within old forms. James applies Hegelian categories to the criticism of Trotsky: Trotsky remains on the level of persistent Understanding, and it is this which explains his fixation. Trotskyism remains fixed within categories which no longer exist. Unlike Lenin, Trotsky failed to consider the Hegelian legacy of marxism.[1] James's criticism is both general and specific: 'Trotskyism. . .completely failed to study p. 244 of the *Logic*'[2] and therefore avoided coming to grips with the philosophical foundation of its mistaken ways. Instead Trotsky remains imprisoned within Understanding, unable to grasp the fact that Understanding is merely the preparatory step to Reason. Trotsky's scorn for the concrete drives him into the arms of Menshevism, where he can develop only 'thin abstractions. . .without content'.[3] Quoting Hegel, James proceeds to demonstrate his case:

Understanding takes the concrete and makes that into a Universal. It therefore sees the Universal only as determinate Universality: and therefore the concrete, the Individual, which it has elevated into this position has taken upon itself the tremendous task of determining itself (self-relation). For this the concrete thus pushed up into the situation of Universal is quite unfitted.

'Does this sound abstract?' James interpolates — 'Not to me. We have seen nationalised property, the concrete in Russia, taken and pushed into the position of Universal.'[4] Trotsky's method, according to James, then, is to take the being of the finite and make it into an Absolute: he takes a moment of the Universal and transforms it into the Universal itself — 'Whence these tears', so speaks James in evangelical despair of Trotsky's philosophical misadventures.[5]

For James *Lenin* becomes critical Reason incarnate.[6] Trotsky, in comparison, was wrong 'on every serious point'.[7] Yet James's criticisms of Trotsky are single minded: he always concentrates on the category of nationalised property.[8] Trotsky's failure is then restated as the false universalisation of the moment of nationalised property and the Plan. Property for James is mere appearance: what are essential are the real production relations operative in the USSR.[9] James explains

89

his argument in a review of *The Revolution Betrayed*, 'After Ten Years'. Trotsky's central focus is on planning, his interest is in consumption rather than production, in equality rather than in the nature of the prevailing social relations. James turns the early Marx against Trotsky: as Marx had it, alienated labour precedes private property, rather than vice versa.[10] Trotsky's argument is held to be deficient in that it concentrates on the formal or legal dimensions of the USSR to the exclusion of its active labour process.[11] This is an argument common to James and Dunayevskaya: the view is one of society from below, through the prism of labour, which is seen as the vital determinant of social classification.

Though highly critical of Trotsky, James nevertheless concedes that Trotsky's theory is the source of his own understanding. Like Stalinism, Trotskyism for James is essential and rational, though both theories are now obsolete.[12] James recognises that Trotsky is essential to the progress of marxist thought because error is the dynamic of truth. In what, then, does James's own Trotskyism consist? His specific endorsements of Trotsky are few. In his orthodox Trotskyist phase, he accepts the principle of uneven development, but retitles it the law of historical compensation, transforming backwardness into a dynamic of social transition.[13] He judges Trotsky a 'great executive, an organiser and administrator of the first rank' and follows Trotskyist tradition in praising Trotsky's analysis of fascism.[14] Beyond these tacit endorsements, there exists a series of affinities with Trotsky: a love of Lenin; a belief in Dialectical Materialism's capacity to function as an epistemological master-key; and its teleological outcome manifested in an extreme optimism, anticipating inevitable evolution.

James deems Lenin superior to Trotsky because Lenin speaks of Hegel in his *Philosophical Notebooks* of 1914–16. A fundamental import is ascribed to Lenin's philosophical 'turn': his political shifts, for example, the taking up of the slogan 'Turn the Imperialist War into Civil War', are seen by James as philosophical 'leaps'.[15] This judgement corresponds with the argument that Trotsky remains on the level of Understanding, never reaching the Leninist/Hegelian apogee of Reason. Lenin, in comparison, can in James's view make rapid political transitions which are philosophical in source and nature. Lenin also has precisely what Trotsky lacks — a real universal.

Socialism, 'the Universal', is 'looking for somewhere to place itself'.[16] Trotsky is of no help here, as he is obsessed with a false universalisation, state property. Lenin's *State and Revolution* fills the void as philosophical prophecy, as new universal. James regards Lenin's political practice as an attempt to implement practically *State and Revolution*.[17] James does not seem to have contemplated the category 'bad abstraction'; for there could be nothing more fantastic than the project of attempting to realise *State and Revolution* with its maxim — every cook to govern — in the Russia of 1917. Lenin had more sense and less dialectics than this: 'Peace, bread and land' was the terminological currency of a politician, not a philosopher. James, however, interprets Leninism as a utopian theory of universal significance. Himself universalising the particular, he deems Lenin's articles and methods in Russia between 1917 and 1923 to be 'the greatest possible source of theoretical understanding and insight into the world of today'.[18] Like Dunayevskaya, James presents Lenin as a philosophical-political radical who had solutions for all problems. Avoiding problems of complexity and scale, and in this sense reflecting Lenin's own naivety in *State and Revolution*, James argues as though the classical image of Athens could be materialised in the Russia of 1917.[19]

Hegel and the dialectics of certainty in James

James's admittedly sophisticated reading of Hegel in *Notes on Dialectics* is qualified and compromised by his acceptance of the laws of Dialectical Materialism.[20] James applies the historicist Hegel to the history of the working-class movement: the presupposition is that Hegelian logic can reveal where the labour movement is going and how its turns, splits, victories and losses fit into the picture.[21] History for James is teleological by definition: because Reason negates, it must create.[22] Each object has a universal logic which expresses itself with peculiar manifestations in particular examples. Even a house, says James, has dialectical movements of its own.[23] Politics is understood as the movement towards the True and Good. The real is rational, therefore, in the sense that it provides the precondition for the rational.[24] Dialectics is seen as future-oriented and speculative: contradiction is conceived internally as a principle of self-development. All development, not only philosophical, but also directly political, takes place by internal self-movement.[25] A notion of contradiction as immanent self-development is thus inscribed in history: the future of the proletariat, for example, is conceived as coming from within itself.[26] Socialism for James is inevitable 'as a necessity of logical thinking in dialectical terms'.[27] Reason is held to inhere in things, and socialism is seen as political Reason. Thus: 'Under the stress of this violent pressure back and forth, for neither can give way, *the organism boils over* into the Notion. It knows itself for what it is. That stage is not far off for the proletariat'.[28]

Socialism for James is simply inevitable: its inevitability is a 'consciously constructed necessity of thought'.[29] More: socialist thinking is impossible without the presumption of inevitability. 'The inevitability of socialism is the inevitability of the negation of the negation, the third and most important law of the dialectic.'[30] Trotsky would probably dispute little of this, yet he did not explicitly Hegelianise his own understanding of Dialectical Materialism. James's assessment of Trotsky as inadequately Hegelian notwithstanding, there seems to be little substantial difference between Trotsky's more primitive and James's more sophisticated philosophy. Yet even with his additional sophistication James is still capable of crudities far more reminiscent of Trotsky than of Hegel. Like Trotsky, he engages generative metaphor and implicitly divides knowledge into 'proletarian science' and 'bourgeois science'.[31] On occasions James's writing style is even more oratorical than Trotsky's; indeed, in some places it is evangelical in style. James's reaction to the criticism of orthodox marxism is as hostile as Trotsky's own. Sidney Hook, for example, is accused (with special reference to *The Hero in History*) of nothing less than philosophical *crimes* for disputing the possibility of empirically verifying the doctrine that stages develop inevitably from one another.[32] James's argument against Hook proceeds by means of theoretical guilt by ascribed association: James presents Hook's argument as a re-invention of *Dühring*, to be automatically disqualified in advance because Dühring has already been dealt with by Engels. Rather more is learned here about Dühring's limitations than Hook's. As an exercise in obfuscation, James's procedure indicates something about James, whose wilful association with the father of the dialectics of nature is no accident.

The question of James's relation to Engels raises another question, that of his relation to Hegel (and to Marx, for he seems to identify the two). James attempts to rethink Hegel's *Logic* through the prism of the history of the working-class movement, though in such a metaphorical juxtaposition it never becomes clear whether Hegel or that history has priority. James's attitude to Hegel, as to Marx, is reverential. The question of the difference between Marx and Hegel, for example on the question of world-spirit, is consistently avoided. By substituting society (Marx) for religion (Hegel), James achieves the long-sought quest of 'putting Hegel back on his feet'. The self-realisation of spirit in Hegel is recast as the marxian project of the self-realisation of mankind. In this kind of eschatology the result produced is simply Hegel inverted: the philosophy of history proposed for Marx is not substantially different from Hegel's. Further, James falls into the common error of universalising Hegel's dialectic of master and slave.[33] As Gadamer has pointed out, Marx himself illegitimately transfers Hegel's metaphor of master and slave from its original feudal setting into bourgeois society.[34] The conclusion to be drawn is that neither the act of labour nor the dialectic of master and slave has any promethean telos.

James has less to say about Marx. Predictably he is drawn to the apocalyptic in Marx, speaking of the penultimate chapter of *Capital 1* as 'one of the greatest triumphs of the human mind', as it represents what James calls, after Engels, 'The Invading Socialist Society'.[35] Marx is portrayed figuratively as the most idealistic of materialists, while Hegel is presented as the most materialistic of idealists.[36] Hegel and Marx are presented analogically, even interchangeably; Marx appears as Hegel materialised. James therefore conforms to the broader tendency characteristic of marxism to conflate Hegel and Marx, but in a peculiarly metaphorical way. James collapses all intellectual practices into the practice of philosophy, or rather perhaps sees them as emanating from philosophy. Even literature and cricket are subsumed to philosophical judgement in this panlogistic purview. James uses, for example, Heidegger's concept *Dasein* to explain West Indian literature. The parallel is forced, and, as James admits, results from the coincidental in his reading habits.[37] As in the treatment of Hegel and Marx, a series of parallel images is thrown up, which explains very little of the objects being compared. Despite these idiosyncrasies, what is clear is that James views philosophy as a substratum in all discourse. Like other, quite separate strands of Trotskyism such as the Healyites in Britain, James sees philosophy as the essence or fundament of politics.[38]

Hegel is then indented by James as the arbiter of all argument; James indeed presumes that all thinking can be subsumed to Hegel's threefold, ascending differentiation between common sense, understanding and dialectic.[39] Dialectical Materialism here becomes the Master Language: Hegel's *Logic* becomes the bible of socialism ascendant.[40] In historiography, James also follows the argument put by Hegel and especially by Plekhanov: freedom is the materialisation of necessity.[41] Great men, from Wilson Harris to Melville and Garfield Sobers, are represented as bearers of the *Zeitgeist*;[42] politics and history alike are emissions of spirit, and spirit itself is socialism.

The question of transition:
James on state capitalism as the alternative
to Trotsky's explanation of the USSR

For James, unlike Trotsky, the mole has yet to surface (or resurface) in the USSR. Production relations on the factory floor are for James the telling feature of the nature of Soviet society, not its legally 'socialist' property forms. Production relations in the USSR mirror those in the United States: 'an assembly line in Moscow is an assembly line in Detroit'.[43] Both the US and the USSR are seen as materialisations of a broader, world-wide tendency to capitalisation. 'Ford's regime before unionisation is the prototype of production relations in fascist Germany and Stalinist Russia': in Fordism can be seen the embryo of totalitarianism.[44] Elsewhere, James simply calls the USSR a fascist state, or argues like Bruno Rizzi that totalitarianism and fascism are species of one-party state capitalism, the distinguishing feature of the age.[45] The Stalinist bureaucracy is understood as the American bureaucracy taken to its ultimate conclusion. The development of the Russian labour process is viewed as the 'telescopic reenactment of the development of US production'; Stakhanovism is presented as the universal model of the form of leadership appropriate to such systems of domination.[46] The law of value is taken to be operative in the USSR, concretising its definition as state capitalist, a capitalist regime with control centralised in the hands of a single state owner.[47] The introduction of the conveyor belt system in 1943, James argues, corresponds with the admission by the Soviet economist Leontiev that the law of value was operative in the USSR.[48] 'State property and total planning are nothing else but the complete subordination of the proletariat to capital':[49] Soviet planning itself is but a form of capitalist rationality. Trotsky's capitalism/socialism couplet is reduced into one: existing 'socialism' is capitalism. Against Trotsky, James regards the concept of labour as prior to that of property. For James the mere fact of a labour force compelled to sell its labour power 'automatically' indicates the existence of the capitalist system of accumulation.[50] Soviet bureaucrats are therefore seen as bearers of a structure which makes them the functional equivalents of Western capitalists. The proviso is added that the USSR is not the same as the USA, only similar; but whatever the differences, 'the fundamental laws of capitalism operate' in the USSR.[51] Those laws remain undetailed: it can be deduced that they spring from the existence of wage labour, and therefore mirror those alleged to be at work in the US.

How did state capitalism emerge in Russia? James argues that the degeneration of the Russian Revolution evidenced by the 1921–2 trade union debates 'announced the birth of modern state capital' in totalitarian form.[52] The relationship of Stalinism to Leninism is to be explained by the dialectical principle of the unity of opposites: democracy calls forth totalitarianism.[53] Stalinism is seen as a logically necessary response to the Russian Revolution: 'Precisely because the Russian Revolution assumed a new quality in attempting to establish a universal democracy, the Russian counter-revolution assumes a new quality of universal barbarism.'[54] The philosophy of history implicit here is an ironical theorem of progress through retrogression. Tracing the genesis of Stalinism back in European history, James argues that state capitalism is the saving grace of the French Revolution.[55] Menshevism is considered by James to grow into Stalinism as germ grows into plant.[56] This growth is taken to represent the evolution of the petty-bourgeoisie, whose power in James's view lies at the root of the French Revolution, Menshevism and Stalinism. The Communist Party is explained as the form for which the petty-bourgeoisie provides the content.[57] James's peculiar philosophical rhetoric prevents him from engaging a specific theory of the genesis of Stalinism: what is suggested instead is a perverse odyssey in which the petty-bourgeoisie materialises itself in all the known evils of modern history, constructing its road to class power on the bones of humanity.

James in this applies an interesting twist to Trotsky's own perspective, in which the directionless petty-bourgeoisie is merely buffeted between the two major classes. Despite itself, the only class lacking in historic vocation manages now to determine the character of modern history. The relation of this theorem to that of inevitable socialism in James's work is not resolved: the broader possibilities of the historical horizon are obscured. The status of the 'inevitable socialism' to which James has such a basic commitment seems to be cast in doubt. James's assurances that Chapter 32 of *Capital* will still be lived out are no more convincing than the original, perhaps even less so given his inverse theodicy philosophy of history. James makes no differentiation between the way essence works itself out in Russia, Germany or the world at large: 'The proletariat must be revolutionary', says James, 'it must keep on being revolutionary, or it is reduced to nothing and a substitute takes its place.'[58] As in Trotsky's theory, History here both sets the tasks and solves them, punishing the reticent at will. History 'does it faster', at the expense of the proletariat if necessary. James takes his leave, to return to the *Logic* in order to solve the problem of Stalinism.[59]

James's proposals for socialist transition

Despite this dismal scenario for mankind, the certain outcome of socialism is still held by James to be inevitable.[60] Indeed James sees the future already existing in the present in the form of the 'Invading Socialist Society'. It is almost as though socialism already exists, just beneath the social surface, only its arrival has not been declared. James cannot therefore face, let alone answer, the question of transition: as in Trotsky, a residual guarantee of faith always exists to cheer those faced by defeats on all fronts. James's certainty surfaces again and again: in one place, for example, he argues that socialism is inherent in the hearts and minds of American industrial workers. More: the very structure of modern society breeds autonomy in people. [62] Revolutionary activity, says James, is the proletariat's nature; state capitalism itself produces the social and psychological needs which compel the populace to take hold of the state itself.[63] 'Objective necessity compels the proletariat to make permanent the great creative impulses from 1848 to 1917.'[64] The new universal — the abolition of the distinction between party and mass — is already on the agenda in 1948: 'In the advanced countries we are not far from it in actuality.'[65] James anticipates the arrival of socialism before 1958; the passing of the decade is necessary in order to close the gap between Idea and Actuality. Manifestations of these philosophical transitions are taken by James to present themselves throughout the 1940s. In America James follows Trotsky in viewing the CIO as a nascent mass party rather than a union; in Italy and France the prominence of the Communist Parties is taken as a signal of impending revolution.[66] A similar situation exists in Britain for James: in Britain no serious marxist can doubt the revolutionary nature of the working class.[67]

James's prospectus for revolution was not fulfilled by the fifties: as a result his revolutionary attention was turned elsewhere. Reversing the Hegelian view of history as a process with an epicentre shifting from Orient to Occident and reviving his long-established PanAfricanism, James turned to Africa and the third world in search of the revolutionary vanguard. Here, finally, James presents the African anti-colonial movements as potential detonators for other social movements. Nkrumah is seen by James as acting out the ideas of Marx and Lenin. Accra becomes the centre of world revolution.[68] The Ghana revolution is viewed as the first such occurrence since the earliest years of the Russian Revolution. James however does not view Ghana as socialist in the strict sense, nor even as transitional to socialism: rather his verdict is that Ghana experiences the application of a 'socialist pattern of society'.The crucial factor left wanting is the technological basis necessary for socialism.[69] In the US James takes the organised movement of blacks also to function as a detonator for other local social movements. Now James offers enthusiasm for Castro. Like Trotsky, James lapses into the defence of some selected 'approximations' to socialism, coupling this temporal position with an atemporal enthusiasm for abstract utopias. As in Trotsky, there is no explanation in James about how the transition between the concrete cases defended and the utopian end goal is to be achieved. James is clearly hostile towards the vanguard party principle of the later Trotsky, remaining closer to the younger Trotsky's arguments for proletarian self-activity. The major fact of modern politics for James is neither the Party nor Stalinism but the existence of the revolutionary proletariat.[70] But transition for James remains a philosophical proposition projected onto history. In James's panlogistic Trotskyism history becomes the mere servant of a self-evolving Reason.[71] Dunayevskaya's theory is, in comparison, rather less extreme than this.

Dunayevskaya on Trotsky, Lenin and Luxemburg

Dunayevskaya's Hegelian Trotskyism is similar to James's, beginning with a preference for Lenin over Trotsky and ending in the state capitalist argument. Dunayevskaya's admiration for Lenin is even more fulsome than that of James, if somewhat more textually based. Dunayevskaya believes that it was Lenin's consideration of Hegel in 1914–16 which enabled him to produce in *The April Theses* the rationale for the October Revolution. In this understanding, Lenin did not accept Trotsky's theory of Permanent Revolution, Trotskyist claims to the contrary notwithstanding. It was Hegel rather than Trotsky or any other influence who was responsible for Lenin's sensitivity to Russian circumstances, facilitating the Bolsheviks' consequent action upon them.[72] Lenin's encounter with Hegel is given the status of an effective 'epistemological break', allowing Lenin's transportation from the reflectionism of *Materialism and Empirio-Criticism* to the more sophisticated position in the *Philosophical Notebooks*. Dunayevskaya ascribes a central importance to Lenin's Hegelian turn: she argues that Lenin turned to Hegel in order to explain the contradictory developments prompted within the Second International by the Great War. According to Dunayevskaya Lenin came to understand the counterrevolution within the socialist movement as a manifestation of the principle of the unity of opposites.[73]

Dunayevskaya projects the 'philosophical' Lenin of 1914–16 and the politically radical Lenin of 1916–17 backwards and forwards historically, glossing over the authoritarian elements in his theory and practice. Avoiding his espousal of the vanguard party, she ascribes to Lenin her own position of mass self-activity. Such an ascription should not be surprising, for Dunayevskaya implicitly seeks to follow in what she sees as Lenin's footsteps: her task is to provide the philosophical foundation for the new humanism requisite for socialist revolution, through a fresh encounter with Hegel. In her view the theory needed today must be set on a new philosophic foundation with a new concrete universal. Dunayevskaya's choice of universal is that which she ascribes to Lenin: every cook is to govern.[74] Dunayevskaya agrees with James that Trotsky is inferior to Lenin on this score. Lacking an adequate philosophical basis, Trotsky could not make the leap into the realisation that Russia was state capitalist, that the worker's state had been transformed into its opposite.[75] Dunayevskaya seems to understand Trotsky's fetishes of the Party and nationalisation less explicitly than James as the products of poor philosophical schooling. With reference to the problem of nationalisation, Dunayevskaya contends that Trotsky's use of state property, a fixed particular, as a universal, produces a situation in which false universals are disconnected from the self-developing subject (the working class).[76] Trotsky universalises the particular (state property) and avoids the 'labour of the negative', the thinking through of things.[77] Both in theory and in practice Trotsky was thwarted by his failure to follow Lenin and engage Hegel.

Like James, Dunayevskaya has an unconscious empathy with the young Trotsky. Dunayevskaya avoids the arguments of the early Trotsky about the self-developing subject;[78] her criticism of Trotsky rests on a simplification of his actual positions. She reduces the theory of Permanent Revolution to its early, pre-Bolshevik forms: 'Theoretically, his [Trotsky's] whole life can be said to be a series of postscripts to these 1904–06 theses.'[79] Trotsky's concept of the peasantry is not that of the self-developing subject — he fails to redevelop the universals of socialism in accordance with the newly developing objective situation, and therefore cannot place the peasantry in his fixed scheme.[80] Trotsky remains caught, in this view, in his fixed position.

If Dunayevskaya accepts the dominant image of Trotsky as Bolshevik and avoids his early arguments about the self-developing subject, then she has nevertheless over the years come to identify more closely with the spiritual twin of the early Trotsky, Rosa Luxemburg. The object of her most recent work, *Rosa Luxemburg, Women's Liberation and Marx's Philosophy of Revolution*, seems to be to relate the three subjects of her title, or as she would put it, to reveal their immanent connection in the theory and practice of Permanent Revolution. The absence of Trotsky from the title, if not the book, is significant. The implicit judgement is that his revolutionism is spiritually inferior to that of Marx or Luxemburg. Leaving aside here their substantial differences on questions like political economy, their political similarities are evident. Luxemburg and Dunayevskaya alike wish to see bourgeois society overturned by spontaneous social revolution. Their common refusal of vanguard organisation, if not completely unambiguous, nevertheless indicates a shared reliance on the conventional wisdom of orthodoxy about the proletariat as the self-motivating actor who takes centre stage in the next phase of world history. Dunayevskaya nevertheless criticises Luxemburg, as she does the other central revolutionaries of the period, for her refusal to produce a new philosophy of revolution. She relates Luxemburg's 'mistakes' in political economy and over the national question to an insufficient consideration of dialectics, suggesting that Luxemburg saw philosophy, like revolution, as being the result of a spontaneous process of development. Luxemburg's theory and practice are however seen as expressing an intuitive understanding of the principles of Hegelian evolutionism. Luxemburg may not have dealt with Hegel in a theoretical register, but her contribution was nevertheless 'Hegelian'. For her focus was not, like Trotsky's, on some false universal, but rather on the evolutionary principle of 'masses in motion'.

Dunayevskaya on Hegel, Marx and Socialism

Dunayevskaya agrees with James that the road to socialism leads through Hegel. Without a new universal and a new theoretical humanism built upon that new universal, the task cannot even be begun. Dunayevskaya takes dialectics even more seriously than James does. By dialectics is understood not only development through contradiction, but more so, development through absolute negativity. Dialectics is taken as shorthand for development, self-development, development through contradiction, development through transformation into opposites, development through negation and through double negation (negation of the negation).[82] Dialectics is evolutionary by definition: it involves evolution from consciousness to philosophy, from primitive communism to freedom, from class struggle to classless society.[83] Both reality and thought for Dunayevskaya progress through stages in correspondence.[84] Marx's major work is seen as a manifestation of dialectical evolution: 'CAPITAL is the dialectics of bourgeois society, its development and downfall.'[85] Dunayevskaya argues that dialectics is not merely philosophy but life, a fact of life[86] which is to be acted out by the masses: 'Of necessity we are propelled forward, not just to the first, but to the second negation.'[87]

The core of Hegel's method for Dunayevskaya is 'the self-movement which is internally necessary because it is the way of the *organism's* own development'; this was seen by Marx in the self-activity of the proletariat.[88] Politics is understood to have an internal and necessary development. The principle of double negation is given the status of prime mover: it is negation rather than synthesis which is the principle of advance or creation.[89] Dunayevskaya goes so far as to rebuke Adorno's suggestion, in *Negative Dialectics*, that Auschwitz marks the absolute negation. She refuses any proposal that the development initiated by negative dialectics could be retrogressive.[90] Dialectics is inconceivable without teleology; whatever the suffering engendered by passing negations, the historical direction of mankind is inevitably upward — towards socialism. The provider of this political dialectic, the abducted Hegel, emerges again here as something of a revolutionary. The argument is not altogether implausible: Hegel is presented as more revolutionary in effect than in intention, dialectics explain Hegel rather than vice versa, the dialectic which Hegel uncovers overpowers his own intention.[91] The argument seems reminiscent of Marx's 1859 Preface, with the Hegelian dialectic standing in for the dynamic of the productive forces. A sense of necessity or destiny is pervasive in these images. Dunayevskaya links the present revitalisation of the dialectic with the sharp upturn in Hegel studies on the two hundredth anniversary of Hegel's birth (and the one hundredth of Lenin's) and with the political activism of George Jackson.[92] She reads Hegel narcissistically. Hegelian verse is juxtaposed to contemporary political event: thus, for example, Hegel the critic of Rousseau is seen as a latent critic of the modern labour bureaucrat, while other Hegelian fragments are seen as incipient criticisms of Castro, Mao, Djilas and Wright Mills.[93] 'Think of Mao and read the following' — a fragment from the *Phenomenology* follows.[94] True to character, the method of metaphorical juxtaposition here avoids the real meaning of both Hegel and Mao. In similar fashion, Hegel's *Logic* is held to contain anticipatory criticisms of Khrushchev, Bukharin and the Plan; while elsewhere Dunayevskaya has Hegel talking about the Paris Commune and the Soviets.[95] The language of self-development circumscribes all these parallels. Hegel emerges again as the secret theorist of marxism.[96] The same logic which makes Lenin a philosopher now makes Hegel a revolutionary.

Dunayevskaya uses the same formula as James to 'explain' the relation between Hegel and Marx: marxism is the most idealistic of materialisms, while Hegelianism is the most materialistic of idealisms.[97] Great emphasis is placed on the Hegelian dialectic of master and slave and therefore on Marx's comments on the *Phenomenology* in the *Paris Manuscripts*, stressing the centrality of the category labour and the dialectic of negativity. Dunayevskaya is equally vulnerable as is James to the charge of falsely universalising the dialectic of master and slave. James and Dunayevskaya follow Kojève's reading of Hegel, producing a Sisyphean teleology of 'progress' through repetition.

The pivot of Dunayevskaya's marxian Hegelianism is to be found in her ontology of revolutionary labour. Labour is held to be the defining category of humanity;[98] its opposite, capital, urges it into revolutionary activity, prompting a double negation. History as a whole is, for Dunayevskaya, the history of the development of labour. The evolution of man is envisaged as occurring through the stages of the developing labour process. As in James, so in Dunayevskaya does the vocabulary of evolution structure all images of the future. Dunayevskaya views man as a tool-maker striving toward human perfectibility through the revolt against capital: indeed, man's natural mode of being here is revolutionary self-activity. Labour, for Dunayevskaya, is the overarching historical source of human identity, it is the binding constituent of history, it encapsulates the promise of human emancipation. The freedom or servitude of labour therefore becomes the crucial determinant in the classification of different forms of social organisation.

These sentiments are clearly steeped in the humanism of the young Marx. However morally positive her humanism may be, Dunayevskaya's own historiosophy is nevertheless reflected in her acceptance of Marx's insertion of his 1848 politics — the class bipolarisation and inevitable double negation of *The Communist Manifesto* — into his 1867 problematic in the penultimate chapter of *Capital*.[100] Dunayevskaya's revolutionary optimism prevents the registration of the shift in Marx's project from revolutionary politics to structural analysis after the defeat of the 1848 revolutions. Imbued with the spirit of revolutionary inevitability, Dunayevskaya sees only the continuities and not the changes in Marx's trajectory. She does not conceive of the project of *Capital* as an attempt to explain the ability of a resilient bourgeois society to achieve its own self-reproduction, because she does not seem to recognise this key feature of its existence. So optimistic is Dunayevskaya's position that she presents instead a novel argument that Marx's *Capital* is the product of upsurge in class struggles rather than the consequences of their defeat. This elaborate argument is constructed on a parallel reading of Marx's 1859 *Contribution to the Critique of Political Economy* and his 1867 *Capital*. Dunayevskaya takes the *Contribution* to reveal the limits of a theoretical work written when the workers themselves are not in motion. 'CAPITAL, on the other hand, is proof of the creative impact of masses in motion on theory.'[101] Dunayevskaya proceeds to construct the peculiar hypothesis that the American Civil War and the Paris Commune produced in Marx the ability to transcend the intellectual limits of his 1859 work.[102] That Marx's problems in writing *Capital* were those of developing the form of systematic presentation rather than the lull in the class struggle, is beyond Dunayevskaya's ken: here she turns a philosophical (or methodological) problem into a political one. Like James, Dunayevskaya refuses to limit dialectics: she effectively credits politics with the power of directly determining theory. The structure of *Capital* is therefore seen as emerging from the developing class itself.[103] This conclusion results from

Dunayevskaya's labour ontology: marxism is now defined as a *'philosophy* of labour, arrived at naturally out of its own concrete struggles'.[104]

Dunayevskaya's theory of state capitalism and its outcome

Marx's most prescient political prophecy, for Dunayevskaya, was the 'prediction' that capitalism would develop into state capitalism, that the entire social capital would be united in the hands of one single capitalist or corporation.[105] Marx is therefore seen as explaining not only the impending doom of the capitalist mode, but also as anticipating its new totalitarian forms. Totalitarianism is viewed as an effect of the essence of capitalism. The existence of labour power as a commodity is the defining characteristic of capitalism for Dunayevskaya.[106] As in James's theory, so here the argument for Soviet state capitalism departs from the point of labour as it is experienced in the immediate production process.[107] The state capitalist argument has its moral foundations in Dunayevskaya's interpretation of Marx's humanism, most notably in the priority given by young Marx to the labouring activity over its material result or product.

Dunayevskaya's argument about the social character of the USSR is the obverse of Trotsky's: property forms are taken to reflect production relations rather than determine them. Whereas for Trotsky the existence of state property indicates the existence of socialism, for Dunayevskaya the continued existence of production relations of domination indicates the existence of capitalism, with the difference that the function of the capitalist is performed collectively by the state. Trotsky's acknowledgement of the existence of 'bourgeois norms of distribution' in Russia actually indicates for Dunayevskaya the presence of that which he cannot accept: the existence of bourgeois methods of production.[108] The USSR, for Dunayevskaya, is the site of the full 'statification' of production, followed on later by historical repetitions in Eastern Europe and China. State power is defined here reductively as the power to dispose of the labour power of others; state power, that is to say, is defined as economic power. Russian state capitalism is viewed as the ultimate extension of Western capitalism.

An extended definition and characterisation of Russian state capitalism is offered in Dunayevskaya's major work, *Marxism and Freedom*. Dunayevskaya rejects the bipolarised scheme of 'market' and 'plan'. Market and plan are rather part of the same problem. The Plan is a specifically capitalist form of organisation, the planner functions as effective capitalist. The resulting class struggle between planner and planned does not differ in substance to the struggle between capital and labour. The dominance of Department I over Department II of the Soviet economy is symptomatic of state capitalism, Khrushchev's consumerist gestures notwithstanding.[109] The increase in production of luxury consumption goods at the expense of mass consumption goods indicates that the existence of the Soviet ruling class can be established by its role in consumption as well as in production. The single outstanding peculiarity of Russian state capitalism is the existence of forced labour in labour camps:[110] though it could be added that labour in general is neither geographically nor socially 'free'. Further characteristics include the existence of piecework, Stakhanovism, and later, the application of the conveyor belt system. Piecework was finally legitimised by the Stalin Constitution, with its maxim, 'From each according to his abilities, to each according to his work'; while the Moscow Show Trials are taken to signal the consolidation of the new ruling class by clearing a place for it in the production process itself. The existence of Soviet state capitalism is given its final confirmation during the Second War, in the Stalinist expropriation of the vital early parts of the first volume of *Capital* and the corresponding official acknowledgement of the operation of the law of value in the USSR.[111]

For Dunayevskaya the state capitalist counterrevolution is thus fulfilled within the revolution itself. As in James's writing, the schema involved suggests a paradoxically repetitionist philosophy of history. Stalin should, in Dunayevskaya's view, be seen as the perfect representative of counterrevolution because he was, prior to the Russian Revolution, a real revolutionary. Stalin therefore personifies the counter-revolutionary forces existing within the revolutionary movement from its earliest days; his power materialises only when the dialectic of forces within the revolution summons

105

him. The Hitlers, the Mussolinis and Stalins alike represent objective forces in history.[112] It is as though the forces of evil must be exhausted before Right can out: socialism becomes conditional on defeat. History, as in James's theory, is seen as a field where the dialectical principle of unity of opposites works itself out, where no surprises occur to violate its preordained pattern. Only the order of things becomes more convoluted.

If the USSR is the logical extension of the American experience, how then is American capitalism to be explained? Dunayevskaya argues that state capitalism is not a process of continuous development without breaks, but is rather a process of development through transformation into opposites. Though by no means identical twins, 'America is headed in the same direction as Russia'.[113] This case is put the more emphatically because the view 'from below' is similar in Russia and America. Dunayevskaya cites the case of an American worker expected to operate two machines at the same time — a hallmark of the Eastern European labour process. In the US wildcat strikes and black struggles are taken as major indicators of continuing class struggle. Proletarian revolution is, in general, held to be a 'historic necessity' as is crisis prompting capitalist collapse. The means by which the victims of Russian state capitalism are to overthrow the totalitarian regime are not specified; whether the law of motion of capitalism, indicating the growing reserve army of unemployed and falling profit rate, applies also to Russian capitalism is unclear. On all previous indications, it can be deduced that the double negation of *Capital*, the allegedly inevitable 'expropriation of the expropriators', should apply to the USSR just as to the US.

Like James, Dunayevskaya looks further afield in the search for the self-developing subject. She does not, however, settle on charismatic leaders as did James with Nkrumah. The West African and Cuban Revolutions are portrayed as part of the humanist wave, but they must eventually opt for one of the two poles of world capitalism, Soviet or American. Dunayevskaya takes a critical distance from Castro and Debray, enthusing instead for Fanon and Kosik who together are viewed as applying Hegel coincidentally with the radicalisation of the sixties.[114] China, which like the USSR is neither socialist nor an oriental despotism, but a state capitalist regime, is seen to be at risk because revolution and Reason are energies inherent in the Chinese masses.[115] Dunayevskaya is by no means lacking in international perspectives, but she does not turn away from the American situation. In contrast to James, her search for the revolutionary subject leads to a pragmatic identification of the forces of labour rather than a single shifting epicentre: as a result, rank and file workers, blacks, women and youth are understood as the major socialist forces in the US today.

Here the problems of the transition to socialism are at least faced, even if they cannot be resolved because of the residual presence of Hegelianised notions of class. Inasmuch as classes are still conceived as self-developing subjects rather than as empirical groups composed of people with different interests, sometimes contradictory, Dunayevskaya's theory still rests on the teleological foundations common to all variants of 'automatic marxism'. As one reviewer of *Philosophy and Revolution* put it, Dunayevskaya 'seems to expect some orthogenesis in the development of social dialectics in human history'.[116] For all her devotion to the philosophical 'labour of the negative', the logic of Dunayevskaya's position leads her finally toward Trotsky after all, endorsing his fantastic claim that even the 'empiricism of a machine gun' cannot win against dialectics.[117]

Assessment of the state capitalist argument and its explanatory adequacy

Despite their divergence and the differences in their ultimate conclusions, C.L.R. James and Raya Dunayevskaya follow the same path — through a specific reading of Hegel to the argument about state capitalism and mass self-activity as the motive force alone capable of overthrowing it. Both textual and contextual evidence in Dunayevskaya's Archive suggest that of the two, Dunayevskaya performed the more detailed analysis of Hegel, Marx and the USSR. James and Dunayevskaya alike construct their view of state capitalism 'from below', from the view of the labour process as it is experienced on the shop floor itself. That the view 'from below' in the US and the USSR is the same, is indeed a penetrating common sense, and a real advance on Trotsky's own view. However, the view 'from below' understood in this way is purely phenomenological — the experience of work 'feels' the same, yet even on the level of the shop floor there are differences between East and West. An adequate analytical view of the nature of social regimes cannot be constructed 'from below' alone, as though East and West were simply identical. The point about structural differences between East and West brings us into direct confrontation with the state capitalist argument. The state capitalist argument identifies capitalism with modernity. The arguments of James and Dunayevskaya for 'state capitalism' are metaphorical or, in language closer to theirs, fetishistic, inasmuch as they make compulsory equivalence of the different. Where Trotsky applies the concepts capitalism/socialism to the two major world powers, James and Dunayevskaya collapse the US and USSR into the concept capitalism, maintaining socialism as a conceptual or immanent possibility. Neither Dunayevskaya nor James, nor other state capitalists like Tony Cliff, can explain Soviet-type societies in language other than analogical. What is peculiar and specific to these societies is therefore lost from the beginning, bathed in the ether of capital alone. The ultimate extension of this obliteration of difference can be seen in Dunayevskaya's simple dismissal of the market as epiphenomenal and even more blatantly in her claim that 'purges' are a universal phenomenon produced by the capitalist mode of production — as though the dismissal of workers in the US were of the same order as physical liquidation in the Moscow Show Trials.[118] Extraordinary as Dunayevskaya's claim may seem, it is indicative of the conceptual expansion of capitalism: the dimensions of domination unique to the Soviet bloc are thereby reduced to manifestations of its allegedly capitalist mode of production.

Fundamental to the state capitalist argument in James and Dunayevskaya is the use of their most privileged category, labour. The ontology of labour which both read into Hegel and Marx, as has been seen, is a positive ontology: history, despite and through throwbacks, progresses to socialism through the unfolding of the dialectic of labour. Sisyphus is really Prometheus. The unfolding of the dialectic of labour as a general philosophical proposition is held to have, as an accompanying immediate effect,the radicalisation of the bearer or practitioner, the factory labourer, in East and West alike. The labour ontology so basic to the state capitalist argument is never worked up as such; it remains a first principle. Consequently neither theorist explains the difference between work and labour, let alone the relation of labour to the separate sphere of social interaction. Indeed, the clarification of such differentiations must be avoided by the state capitalists, for their argument rests precisely on the association of 'labour' with 'praxis'. To apply Alvin Gouldner's differentiation, the notion of 'praxis' latent in a positive dialectic of labour has two different meanings — what Gouldner calls 'Praxis I' being the unreflective labour on which the reproduction of capitalism depends, while 'Praxis II' indicates rather free labour directed toward the emancipation of workers from 'Praxis I'.[119] The linguistic association of these two meanings is fundamental to the state capitalists' presumption that manual labour has a redeeming revolutionary effect. Without this magical power, ordinary labour re-emerges as what it is, and the socialist telos dissolves.

The priority given to the category labour helps to explain the focus on the labour process or the view 'from below' in Dunayevskaya and James. Both separate the category labour out from the conceptual constellation of *Capital*, avoiding Marx's extended definition of capitalist production as the generalised production of commodities with labour itself functioning as a commodity, the extraction of relative surplus value and the real subsumption of labour to separate capitals, whose share of total social capital is realised through the market. A social formation cannot be characterised by its labour process alone. Nor, in a broader sense, can social analysis ignore the defining character of the political processes which arise with different modes of production: the crucial instance in this case being the forms of liberal democracy corresponding to the development of the capitalist market and mode of production which are totally absent in the Soviet bloc. Because of its single-minded focus on the labour process, the state capitalist argument reveals only the similarities, and occludes the process of the clarification of the problems of the differences between the major industrial social formations and their overall historical direction.

Conclusions: James, Dunayevskaya and Trotsky: and beyond

The privileging of the category labour and of the labour process overdetermines the political perspectives of the state capitalists. In James's case, the defence of contemporary African achievements is coupled to the notion of a syndicalist utopia where cooks might govern, the basic dynamics of which he sees as already enacted in the early days of the Soviet workers' state. James's deeper political affinities may lie with Lenin rather than Trotsky; he associates the early Soviet achievements with Lenin, and seems more often to envisage Trotsky as the 'prophet outcast' than as the 'prophet armed'. Dunayevskaya in contrast seems closer to Trotsky's abstract utopianism, where freedom is understood as a new form of existence beyond the world of production. Dunayevskaya even anticipates the abolition of labour, a mystical turn for her labour ontology.[120] The notion, reminiscent of Trotsky's *Literature and Revolution*, that men and women might suspend the source of their very being contradicts the entire labour ontology, unless art is to be understood as the form of ontological labour appropriate to socialism. Perhaps the logic implied is that the redemptive double negation results in the transcendence of labour as such. But socialism would then entail the end of dialectics.

Despite the absence of Trotsky's defence of the USSR and the addition of considerable philosophical sophistication, Dunayevskaya's and James's theory nevertheless fails to break through the limits of automatic marxism. As in Trotsky, so in James and Dunayevskaya the answer to the question of transition remains assurance, with the difference that where in the language of the Bolshevik Trotsky it is History which drives men forward through the mechanisms of the Party, in the state capitalist argument, it is Man who must drive history. Rhetoric there is, here, but of a different style: man functions as an historical telos which progresses through its own unfolding. The anthropology of the 'state capitalists' thus culminates in a humanist determinism extending that of the young Trotsky. The problem here is that rather than being too much like the Bolshevik Trotsky, they are too much like Marx, or the early Trotsky: not Jacobins, they are nevertheless automatic marxists.

110

The 'state capitalists' can therefore be seen both as filling out Trotsky's marxism and as innovating on the basis of its limited achievements. The process of filling out the philosophical lacunae in Trotsky produces a situation more problematical than the original. James and Dunayevskaya alike associate politics with philosophy (or vice versa) rather than elaborating each separately. In comparison to Trotsky's hesitant and partial engagement of Labriola, Lafargue, Kautsky and Plekhanov, their detailed forays into philosophy and the philosophical in marxism serve only to lead them further astray. They develop Trotsky's theory into a syncretic revolutionary totality, interpreting practice as theory and theory as practice.

It is however their relative philosophical sophistication and their profound humanism which allows the 'state capitalists' to transcend the limits of Trotsky's own characterisation of the USSR. Substituting the image of state capitalism for that of degenerated workers' state, Dunayevskaya and James do not explain the structure of the Soviet regime beyond the analytical level of labour process. Their argument, which might in fact be seen as the materialisation of Trotsky's rhetorical premonition of state capitalism or bureaucratic collectivism in 'The USSR in War', produces a position no less hopelessly metaphorical than Trotsky's own. Where Trotsky remains bound to the historic fact of the existence of the USSR and to the politics of leadership, Dunayevskaya and James find themselves working within a non-fulfilling humanist philosophy of history. The moral superiority and complexity of their arguments cannot serve to make the social explanation of the 'Hegelian Trotskyists' more adequate to the understanding of socialist politics.

The practical superiority of their politics over Trotskyism's warrants emphasis, however. James's return to the concerns of his youth and his origins, while fascinating in themselves, take him outside the scope of this study, into the specific problems of transition in the third world. Such developments notwithstanding, it is doubtless James's refusal of the vanguard principle which is the binding thread of his politics, European and PanAfrican. It is Dunayevskaya who emerges as both more stimulating and more problematical for our purposes. Dunayevskaya's insistence on the autonomy of struggles seems to allow a practical and strategic relativism which is compromised only on the theoretical level, by the syncretism of her labour ontology. Dunayevskaya recognises the real diversity of social struggles, yet nevertheless subsumes them to the premiss of a common striving of labour for autonomy. The array of contemporary struggles is therefore seen as an ultimate expression of *Geistige* 'class struggle' anticipated by Marx rather than as a series of issue-movements which are by nature incommensurate and interest-bound. Dunayevskaya therefore subsumes other struggles to those of labour: black struggles become those of black labour, women's struggles those of female labour.[121] In Dunayevskaya's case, the political results break out of the conceptual premises within which they are constructed. Radical Trotskyism here again shares the grounding of the early Lukács in a labour ontology, a presumed automaticity and the practical endorsement of Lenin. Unlike Lukács, however, both James and Dunayevskaya achieve a more worldly gaze on modern politics. This ambivalence remains the hallmark of their work: a radical, yet ultimately ineffective politics emerges from orthodox philosophical premises. The views of the young Trotsky are thereby preserved; only the permanence of capitalist civilisation vitiates them.

Notes

1. C.L.R. James, *Notes on Dialectics: Hegel, Marx, Lenin* (Allison and Busby, London, 1980), pp. 89, 105, 101.
2. Ibid., p. 124.
3. Ibid., p. 127f.
4. Ibid., p. 129.
5. Ibid., p. 134.
6. Ibid., pp. 138f, 150.
7. Ibid., p. 137.
8. Ibid., p. 162.
9. Ibid., p. 152.
10. James, 'After Ten Years' in *Spheres of Existence* (Allison and Busby, London, 1980), p. 59f.
11. James, 'After Ten Years', p. 61.
12. James, *Notes on Dialectics*, p. 151.
13. Ibid., p. 136.
14. *World Revolution 1917–36. The Rise and Fall of the Communist International* (Secker and Warburg, London, 1937), p. 339f.
15. James, *Notes on Dialectics*, p. 100.
16. Ibid., pp. 100, 127.

17. Ibid., p. 138f.
18. Ibid., p. 147.
19. See, for example, 'Every Cook Can Govern: A Study of Democracy in Ancient Greece' in C. L. R. James, *The Future in the Present* (Allison and Busby, London, 1977), pp. 160–74; and 'What We Owe to Ancient Greece' in *Modern Politics* (Bewick (ed.), Detroit, 1973), p. 3ff. Hegel's devotee obviously gave insufficient attention to the *Philosophy of Right*, where Hegel remarks that only in the modern state is universality bound into particularity. The absence of the concept of subjectivity in Athens undercuts James' attempt to identify the concepts of classical and modern state. See Hegel, *Philosophy of Right* (T. M. Knox ed, Oxford, 1976). Addition to paragraph 260.
20. 'Dialectical 41Materialism and the Fate of Humanity' in James, *Spheres of Existence*, pp. 70–105.
21. James, *Notes on Dialectics*, p. 65.
22. Ibid., p. 23.
23. Ibid., pp. 26, 28.
24. Ibid., p. 93. The political application of this argument is as follows: 'The overcoming of Stalinism is the next stage of infinity' (ibid., p. 103): Stalinism must be seen as a terrible reality which because real is rational (ibid., p. 30). Implicit here is a philosophy of history indicating that progress is achieved through barbarism. 'Dialectical Materialism and the Fate of Humanity', p. 76.
25. 'Modern Politics', in *Radical America*, C. L. R. James Special Issue, *4(4)* (1970), p. 6.
26. James, *Notes on Dialectics*, p. 91f.
27. Ibid., p. 94.
28. Ibid., pp. 94, 111. Emphasis added.
29. 'Dialectical Materialism and the Fate of Humanity', p. 79.
30. 'Dialectical Materialism and the Fate of Humanity', p. 79f.
31. Representative examples include chrysalis and butterfly, ibid., p. 81, and images of ulceration and gangrene, ibid., pp. 78, 100. In 'The Philosophy of History and Necessity', *Spheres of Existence*, 49, Sidney Hook's philosophical carbuncles invite the marxist scalpel.
32. 'The Philosophy of History and Necessity', pp. 50, 54.
33. See, for example, 'Peasants and Workers', *Radical America*, *5(6)* (1971), p. 24ff.
34. H.-G. Gadamer, *Hegel's Dialectic* (Yale, New Haven, 1976), p. 73 and p. 67ff, *passim*.
35. See *Modern Politics*, p. 143, and see generally C. L. R. James, F. Forest and R. Stone, *The Invading Socialist Society* (Bewick (ed.), Detroit, 1972).
36. James, *Notes on Dialectics*, p. 171.
37. James, *Spheres of Existence*, p. 168f.
38. See, for example, C. Slaughter, *Lenin on Dialectics* (Labour Press, Sydney, n.d.).
39. James, *Notes on Dialectics*, p. 18.
40. Ibid., for example, p. 112.
41. James, *The Black Jacobins* (Allison and Busby, London, 1980), p. x.
42. James, *Spheres of Existence*, p. 168f; 'Mariners, Renegades and

Castaways', *Radical America*, 4(4), p. 76; James, *The Future in the Present*, pp. 213, 225.
43. James, *Spheres of Existence*, p. 121.
44. 'State Capitalism and World Revolution' in *Radical America* 4(4), p. 22; 'Peasants and Workers', p. 42f.
45. James, *Notes on Dialectics*, pp. 144, 176; 'Russia — a Fascist State', *New International*, April 1941, p. 54ff; 'Resolution on the Russian Question', *Workers' Party Internal Bulletin*, 19 September 1941.
46. 'State Capitalism and World Revolution', p. 25f.
47. James, *Notes on Dialectics*, p. 13.
48. 'Peasants and Workers', p. 45f.
49. 'The Class Struggle', in James, *The Future in the Present*, p. 139.
50. 'State Capitalism and World Revolution', p. 29.
51. Ibid., p. 29.
52. 'Peasants and Workers', p. 18.
53. 'Dialectical Materialism', p. 74.
54. Ibid., p. 75f.
55. James, *Notes on Dialectics*, p. 188f.
56. Ibid., p. 205.
57. Ibid., p. 210f.
58. Ibid., p. 209.
59. Ibid., p. 210.
60. See generally, for example, James, Forest and Stone, *The Invading Socialist Society*.
61. 'State Capitalism and World Revolution', p. 22.
62. 'The Way Out — World Revolution' in *Radical America*, 5(6), p. 59.
63. James, *Notes on Dialectics*, p. 177.
64. Ibid., p. 179.
65. Ibid., p. 180.
66. Ibid., pp. 61, 179, 181.
67. James, *The Future in the Present*, p. 118.
68. James, *Nkrumah and the Ghana Revolution* (Allison and Busby, London, 1977), pp. 24, 64, 162f, 164.
69. Ibid., p. 171.
70. 'The Revolutionary Answer to the Negro Problem in the United States' in *Radical America*, 4(4), p. 12f.
71. James, *Notes on Dialectics*, pp. 90, 93.
72. Dunayevskaya, 'The Two Russian Revolutions and Once Again, on the Theory of Permanent Revolution' (News and Letters, Political-Philosophic Letter, Detroit, 1979), p. 8.
73. Dunayevskaya, 'Dialectics of Liberation in Thought and in Activity: Absolute Negativity as New Beginning' in *New Essays* (News and Letters, Detroit, 1977), p. 19.
74. *State Capitalism and Marx's Humanism* (News and Letters, Detroit, 1967), pp. 8f, 14.
75. Dunayevskaya, *New Essays*, p.32.
76. Ibid., p. 32f.
77. *Philosophy and Revolution* (Delta, New York, 1973), p. 129.
78. Ibid., p. 127.

79. Ibid., p. 131.
80. *Philosophy and Revolution*, pp. 132, 137.
81. *Rosa Luxemburg, Women's Liberation and Marx's Philosophy of Revolution* (Humanities, New Jersey, 1982), pp. 118, 63, 60.
82. *State Capitalism and Marx's Humanism*, p. 38.
83. Dunayevskaya, *25 Years of Marxist Humanism in the US* (News and Letters, Detroit, 1980), p. 26.
84. *Marxism and Freedom* (Pluto, London, 1975), p. 36.
85. Ibid., p. 91.
86. *Philosophy and Revolution*, p. 13.
87. Ibid., pp. 80, 30, and see p 54.
88. *Marxism and Freedom*, p. 55. Emphasis added.
89. Dunayevskaya, 'Dialectics of Liberation in Thought and Activity', p. 19.
90. Ibid., p. 23.
91. *Philosophy and Revolution*, pp. xv, 6, 32, 38.
92. Ibid.
93. Dunayevskaya, *Dialectics of Liberation* (News and Letters, Detroit, n.d.), pp. 3, 4, 7.
94. Ibid., p.6.
95. Ibid., pp. 16ff, 9.
96. Ibid., p.2.
97. *Marxism and Freedom*, p. 42.
98. Ibid., pp. 55, 66.
99. Ibid., pp., 177, 181.
100. *Marxism and Freedom*, p. 122; *Rosa Luxemburg*, p. 150f.
101. *Marxism and Freedom*, p. 81.
102. Ibid., Ch. 5.
103. Ibid., p. 87.
104. Ibid., p. 90.
105. *Outline of Marx's Capital* (News and Letters, Detroit, 1979), p. 43.
106. *Marx's Capital and Today's Global Crisis*, p. 20.
107. *State Capitalism and Marx's Humanism*, p. 38.
108. *Marxism and Freedom*, p. 223.
109. Ibid., p. 220.
110. Ibid., p. 220f.
111. Ibid., p. 222ff.
112. Ibid., p. 259.
113. Ibid., p. 258f.
114. *Philosophy and Revolution*, p. 278; *New Essays*, p. 23f.
115. *Marxism and Freedom*, p. 310; *New Essays*, p. 15.
116. H. Parsons, review of *Philosophy and Revolution* in *Philosophy and Phenomenological Research, 35* (June 1975), p. 586.
117. *Marxism and Freedom*, p. 63.
118. Ibid., p. 234ff.
119. A. Gouldner, *The Two Marxisms, Contradictions and Anomalies in the Development of Theory* (Seabury, New York, 1980), p. 33. Molyneux suggests that the conflation originates in Trotsky: *Leon Trotsky's Theory of Revolution,* p. 79.
120. *New Essays*, p. 39.

121. *Rosa Luxemburg*, pp. 125, 161, 163. This marxology continually discovers new secrets in old archives, whether they be Marx's ethnological scribblings or mathematical musings. See ibid., Ch. 12; *News and Letters*, January 1985, p. 4.

6
Political Economy and Transition:
Ernest Mandel

Ernest Mandel is probably the best known of all contemporary Trotskyists, and one of the most influential of modern marxist economists. Few figures on the left today create such controversy, attract such adoration and vilification. Mandel is the theoretical and political leader of the United Secretariat of the Fourth International. His arguments remain among the most hegemonic in the revolutionary left today. Born in 1923, Mandel became a revolutionary in 1939, joining the Trotskyist movement in his native Belgium in 1940. He was active in the resistance throughout the occupation. In 1946, under the pseudonym 'Ernest Germain', he was elected to the leadership of the Fourth International, where he was affiliated with Michel Pablo. Throughout the fifties and sixties he was active in the Belgian trade union movement and in the Belgian Socialist Party, within which the Trotskyists then operated. He edited *La Gauche*, organ of the Socialist Party left, before the Trotskyists were expelled from the Party in 1965. An astute dialectician within the Fourth International, Mandel became known as one who changed his positions with ease, rarely pausing to reconcile such shifts with his earlier positions. Mandel is also the author of works of considerable scholarly achievement, most notably *Marxist Economic Theory* and *Late Capitalism*. His works have been published in 30 languages, and range from journalism and programmatic materials to economic treatises and criticism, from sophisticated scholarly interventions to crude Trotskyist polemics. It is this combination of scholarly and political practices which sets Mandel apart from his peers, and which often produces strange effects in 'revolutionary journalism' and 'revolutionary scholarship'.

117

For there is a strong tendency in Mandel to append rhetorical conclusions to substantially empirical and non-revolutionary works. Similarly, earnest theoretical writings like *Late Capitalism* traverse all manner of economic terrains only to issue, unexpectedly, in scenarios of socialist revolution which have no recognisable relationship to the preceding analysis. The tension between science and revolution is by no means evident to Mandel, whose Trotskyist traits include a fundamentalism in which science is held to 'prove' the positions of orthodox marxism, whether basic or modified. For Mandel science itself is a revolutionary weapon, and nowhere is this more clear than in his attempts to apply Marx's 1859 Preface — a scheme which, on historical judgement, explains social stability rather than change — in order to prove the 'inevitability' of socialist revolution. Integrated into his theory of long waves of capitalist development, Mandel's particular variation of the forces-relations formula provides an illustrative case of innovation within the parameters of orthodox marxism.

Mandel's relation to Trotsky

Mandel idolises Trotsky. His *Trotsky — A Study in the Dynamic of His Thought* is little more than hagiography. Trotsky is viewed as the source of the basic truths of modern revolutionary marxism. He is credited with a power of prophesy; he takes on an aura of infallibility.[1] Such problems as are acknowledged in Trotsky's marxism are reduced to questions of mistaken timing or miscalculated prediction.[2] Mandel's admiration is more fulsome for the Bolshevik Trotsky: his attitude towards the young Trotsky is a compromised, vehement yet ambivalent rejection, as Mandel is attracted to the early Trotsky's spontaneism yet repulsed by his anti-Leninism.[3] On balance, Mandel prefers the image of the Bolshevik Trotsky, where spontaneous working-class energy is viewed in Trotskyist manner as a steam which is dissipated in the absence of a Party-piston.[4] Mandel's substantive affinities with Trotsky are many and varied, but are nowhere more apparent than in basic principles. Mandel's anthropological perspectives shift variously with the nature of the subject matter at hand and with the scope of projection. When speaking specifically of people as they are and might be, Mandel espouses a labour ontology, viewing the capacity to perform creative work as a basic characteristic of human nature. This labour ontology produces a basic humanism, manifested in the naïve argument that what people make they can also unmake.[5] Such sentiments are combined with many others. In one place Mandel suggests a dualistic anthropology based on class — the bourgeoisie are by nature competitive, while proletarians are naturally co-operative.[6] In another place Mandel reduces the argument for socialism to a statement of 'faith' in the positive anthropology.[7] In discussing problems of transition, however, Mandel introduces the negative anthropology, arguing that people will strive for better things only under a regime which offers material rewards.[8]

These contradictory positions find their explanation in the Trotskyist determinism which understands egoism as the product of scarcity, and altruism as the result of abundance.[9] Mandel thus views history as the history of the struggle for surplus, as surplus is the condition of existence for class society and, subsequently, for socialism. Mandel's choice of the revolutionary subject capable of achieving such a society is strongly influenced by the Jacobin dimension of Trotskyism. As Mandel himself puts it in one place, the proletariat must emancipate itself; yet only the Party can achieve liberation.[10] This additional level of association is characteristically Trotskyist. Mandel's general debt to Trotsky is evident in his basic working categories, which are those of Dialectical and historical Materialism. Under the pressure of the renewed criticism of the marxist renaissance, Mandel has been obliged to articulate these positions with more clarity than Trotsky ever did. Significantly, however, the result is little improvement on Trotsky's own positions. For Mandel, Dialectical Materialism's basic premiss is that everything changes and is in perpetual motion; this premiss is taken to be a universal truth. 'Motion, universal motion, governs all existence.' This universal motion involves the dialectics of nature as well as those of history and, in addition, the dialectics of knowledge.[11] Dialectical Materialism is the only exception to this rule. It never changes. Mandel outlines the categories of Dialectical logic: the unity and contradiction of opposites, quantitative and qualitative change, negation and surpassing.[12] Contradiction is explained as internal in character, as is content to form; here Mandel

119

offers the significant illustration of the contradiction between forces and relations of production. As will be seen below, the principle of internal contradiction is a binding thread of Mandel's marxism, one which concludes in his theory of endogenous technological revolutions. For it follows from Mandel's first principle, concerning motion, that all 'motion is a function of the internal contradictions of the phenomenon or set of phenomena under consideration'.[13] The epistemological basis of 'automatic marxism' and the theory of Permanent Revolution is here already set in motion.

Dialectical Materialism functions in Mandel's work as the basis of a science which aspires ultimately to an empirical status. The status of marxism itself is viewed as ultimately empirical, though Mandel's own marxism shifts steadily between fact and fancy. Mandel views social science as the empiricist practice of fact-gathering. Social science is understood here as a parallel practice to natural science. Arguing against Korsch, Mandel claims to accept Hilferding's division of marxism into science and revolution. He argues that marxism is meaningless if understood as anything other than science (and science of a most particular kind).[14] Symptomatically, he echoes Engels' claim that empirical proof is the final tribune of epistemology.[15] Mandel makes clear his belief in marxism as a predictive science, implying a literal image of crisis where, in accordance with traditional medical meaning, the specialist diagnoses and awaits the further decline of the patient, world capital.[16] The sequence of Mandel's logic is clear; science can only be revolutionary if it tells the truth; revolution is written into the order of things, therefore an accurate science cannot but be revolutionary.

Mandel's first principles are further clarified in his explanation of the canons of historical materialism. Marxism is explained as a socio-economic determinism 'in the last instance'. 'Historical Materialism is a determinist doctrine', Mandel explains. 'Its fundamental thesis affirms that it is social existence which determines social consciousness.'[17] History for Mandel unfolds through a dialectic of forces and relations of production: each mode of production grows like a human being through phases of vigour and sterility.[18] The scope of Mandel's work indicates that marxism is viewed as a universal theory, and as a theory of universal history, within which the analysis of bourgeois society is merely an application of the 'general' methodology. Nowhere is this universalistic pretension so apparent as in the scope of *Marxist Economic Theory*, where (to name a few), Mandel indiscriminately strings together examples across centuries, from New Guinea to Siberia, from Mesopotamia to Morocco, Cyprus to Ceylon, Samoa to Byzantium — all in order to discover the nature of something called the marxist theory of society.[19]

Leaving aside till later sections Mandel's central affinities with Trotsky in the theory of organisation and transition, two striking similarities should be observed before proceeding to the analysis of Mandel's relation to Marx. First, Mandel's writing is structured by contrived metaphor. As will be seen, his theory depends on metaphor, particularly in his arguments for long waves of capitalist development and for the hybrid, neither capitalist nor socialist, nature of the USSR. More generally speaking, the entire range of Trotskyist metaphor burdens Mandel's texts: instinct, eruption, molecular movement, images of disease and gynaecology introducing the medical experts of the Fourth International and so on.[20] Rarely is Mandel's use of metaphor convincing, and seldom is it conducive to literary persuasion. Mandel is an able rhetor, yet his general style of argument is never so persuasive as Trotsky's. A debater rather than an orator, Mandel is particularly heavy-handed with opponents in argument, and this is a second striking similarity with Trotsky, even though with Mandel it is lifted to new heights. That Mandel should espouse the orthodox bifurcation of knowledge into categories of 'proletarian' and 'bourgeois' science, is perhaps little cause for surprise.[21] But Mandel's criteria for discourse are more stringent yet. In one place, for example, Mandel disallows as 'eclectic', the form of argument which proceeds 'on the one hand [class] — on the other'.[22] Following Trotsky, such uncertainty must, for Mandel, be understood as petty-bourgeois vacillation or outright betrayal. In another significant case, the discursive morals of Stalinism are summoned by Mandel in order to dismiss the arguments of the class traitors, Djilas and Burnham. 'These people have in effect crossed the class lines and joined the bourgeoisie. . .Nothing more needs to be said about this [new class] thesis.'[23] Dubious though he was of Bruno Rizzi's analogous argument, Trotsky at least took it sufficiently seriously to warrant reply, however inadequate that reply may have been. Indeed, it could be said that Trotsky

was obliged to take such arguments seriously, as they
represented legitimate extrapolations of tendencies in his own
thought. With Mandel, in comparison, the polemical sabre has
lost whatever critical edge it had in Trotsky's hand. Relieved of
the contradiction appropriate to a differentiated world and
hardened through constant repetition through changing
times, Mandel's 'discursive' style marks the further consolidation of Trotskyism as an orthodoxy in its own right. This
said, certain absences and presences might be expected in
Mandel's relation to Marx's work.

Mandel's relation to Marx's work

Mandel takes Marx and marxism to be intact, uncorrupted by
internal contradiction and untouched by the twentieth
century's tragedy of errors. For Mandel, the present procla-
mation on the Western left of the 'crisis of marxism' lacks
substantial roots and should be seen as a bourgeois conspiracy
rather than as a practical representation of radical malaise.[24]
Mandel sees himself alone as the true interpreter of Marx, to
the extent that he denies that his own work constitutes one
interpretation of Marx among others. He refuses outright the
hermeneutic principle that the task of constructing truth or
adequacy in understanding lies with the interpreter rather
than the text.[25] Mandel himself clearly constructs his own
Marx.

There are three texts which allow the critical examination of
the relationship between Mandel and Marx: his study of
Marx's own theoretical genesis, and his two major economic
treatises, *Marxist Economic Theory* and *Late Capitalism*. Mandel's
registration of the importance of recent debates is witnessed in
the first work in his intervention in one of the earlier disputes
over the question of the relationship between the work of the
young and the later Marx. In *The Formation of the Economic
Thought of Karl Marx. 1843 to 'Capital'*, Mandel argues a middle
road. According to Mandel, the young Marx sheds his
philosophical chrysalis in order to emerge an *economist*.[26] In
this understanding there could be no other course for Marx
than fully to embrace the *data* which Mandel takes to be the
stuff of real marxist science. Mandel reduces Marx's
contribution to the discovery of the real meaning of the theory

of surplus value.[27] Worse yet, Mandel never comes to his subject matter — the formation of Marx's thought from '1843 to *Capital*'. His analysis halts ten years short of *Capital*, as though the contribution and theoretical system of *Capital* were somehow established in its 'research' (for Mandel, 'data'). *Capital*, for Mandel, existed in Marx's brain already with the (early) solution of the problem of the Ricardian-Malthusian population laws: 'Once this [preparatory] work was accomplished, *Capital* was ready: all that remained was to write it.'[28] Its writing nevertheless took another ten years, a fact which Mandel cannot grasp, as he presumes *Capital* to step fully grown from the earlier drafts in the *Grundrisse*. Theory, too, is telescoped by Permanent Revolution.

Mandel's own major economic works can be seen as attempts at rewriting *Capital* with the 'dialectical scaffolding' removed, substituting his own empirical understanding of science for Marx's Hegelian project. In *Marxist Economic Theory* Mandel fails to constitute the object of his analysis, instead discussing everything under the sun. In the absence of a clearly defined theoretical object Mandel is obliged to discuss universal history. He traces the historical development of universal equivalence and the emergence of commodity production rather than unfolding their modern conceptual dimensions or determinants. Having arrived historically at capitalist production, Mandel offers the classical orthodox arguments in order to characterise it. For Mandel capitalism distinguishes itself by: the existence of the tendency of the profit rate to fall (realised in a cyclical manner); by the contradiction between the effective socialisation of production and the private form of appropriation (the play on words — the implicit elision of the difference between 'socialisation' and 'socialism' — goes undeclared); by the anarchic planlessness of capitalist production; and by the presumed revolutionary proletarian telos which transforms class struggle from the economic level onto the political.[29] This definition provides the framework into which there is accommodated a mass of empirical material which is taken as 'proof' of the validity of the positions of orthodox marxism.

Mandel recognises some of the limits of *Marxist Economic Theory* in the Preface to the German edition of *Late Capitalism*, speaking particularly against its excessively descriptive and insufficiently theoretical nature.[30] Having recognised the problem, however, Mandel does not go far in rectifying it. The structure of *Late Capitalism* resembles in general the structure of the 1857 plan for *Capital* rather than that eventually applied in *Capital* itself, with the exception that, in ending, *Late Capitalism* mirrors the penultimate, apocalyptic chapter of *Capital*. This latter dimension is perhaps *Late Capitalism's* only strong similarity to *Capital* 1 — it mimics the latter's worst thesis, the allegedly inevitable 'double negation' of proletarian revolution. Following carefully executed considerations on analytical problems like the world market, the armaments industry, the service sector and so on, socialist revolution steps unexpectedly from the text: 'The final abolition of capitalist relations of production will be the central objective of the mass revolutionary movement of the international working-class that is now approaching.'[31] Mandel's variation on the marxian double negation can itself be negated on no less than four grounds: the movement of which he speaks is not a mass movement, is not revolutionary, not international, and its impending victory is not imminent; this can be said at least in the absence of a substantial argument to the contrary.

The means by which Mandel claims to construct the argument which supports this structure and its revolutionary issue does not differ radically from the method applied in *Marxist Economic Theory*. In *Marxist Economic Theory*, the structure of *Capital* 1 is viewed as historical-logical in form. In *Late Capitalism*, Mandel reduces method to research, ascribing to Marx his own positivist method of research, 'to-ing' and 'fro-ing' between empirical material (which is taken to be the starting point) and its lawful expression. Mandel proposes a 'six-fold articulation of Marx's dialectical method'. The six stages follow from fact gathering and analysis to the production of laws of motion, the establishment of the relationship between the whole and the parts, with empirical verification of the foregoing stages and, finally, renewed empirical and perhaps theoretical considerations concluding the process.[32]

Much of the controversy surrounding Mandel's work has arisen from this association of the practices of empirical science and marxist theory. Mandel claims, for example, to prove theoretically the argument for the tendency of the profit rate to fall due to the rise in the organic composition of capital (that is, due ultimately to the increase of the proportion of constant capital or technology to that of labour in the production process). As Bob Rowthorn has pointed out, however, in criticism of Mandel, profit rates have fallen in recent years due to 'empirical' rather than 'theoretical' factors — the so-called 'profit squeeze' has limited the share of surplus value going to industrial capital.[33] Mandel, that is to say, attempts to establish an empirical argument by theoretical means; like the state capitalists, he collapses different levels of abstraction appropriate to each form of argument. Another critic of Mandel, Athar Hussain, has argued that Mandel's is a self-verifying and self-congratulatory framework: anything that moves is taken by Mandel to prove his case.[34] Further, the way in which Mandel conducts his empirical analysis undermines his justification for using marxian categories. Mandel simply presumes that statistics 'translate' directly into a marxian discourse, but in the process of, for example, treating price as equivalent to value, he collapses the basic marxian distinction between essence and appearance, thereby jeopardising his own orthodoxy. Mandel makes marxian theory practically obsolete as an analytical device by working on the empirical level, then claiming to prove the dogmas of orthodoxy, his articles of faith beyond discussion, with empirical material which belongs to another discourse altogether. As Mattick explains, however, data is simply not readily convertible into marxian discourse, for Marx's is an abstract theory which, by nature, is ill-disposed purely to empirical verification.[35] Marxists are always right, especially in political economy.

The form of Mandel's argument undermines its *raison d'être* as economics with a marxian intention. It is not enough, for Mandel, to be a competent and original economist: he must also be seen to be a revolutionary economist, on the basis that science is the fount of revolution. Here is the logic of Kautsky and Hilferding: socialism is not only desirable, but necessary. But the projection of modern economic science — with a marxist twist — as revolutionary in effect, and of socialism as necessity, is self-delusion. Science is only what it is: it can 'tell the truth' as best it can, but the most it can possibly achieve is competing representations of the world. The practice of politics, understood as the realm of social change, is another thing altogether. Even prior to a formal consideration of Mandel's treatment of the question of transition a basic misconstruction can be anticipated. Transition cannot be seriously theorised if it is not taken as a political problem in its own right. The economically sophisticated Trotskyism of Ernest Mandel succeeds only in offering more elaborate reasons for its refusal to face this situation.

Transition: Mandel's analysis of Soviet-type societies

Mandel's marxism in general, and his thinking about transition in particular is, like Trotsky's, bound up with the experience of the Russian Revolution. Mandel's treatment of transition in the East will be dealt with first here as a preliminary to the criticism of his proposals for transition to socialism in the West. First, however, some methodological observations are in order. Mandel's writings on the problem of transition are marred by the application of an inappropriate level of generality. Transition in Mandel's usage usually refers to the transition between modes of production in universal history. The proper object of specific transition — in this instance, the transition to a new form of social organisation in the USSR — is deflected from the beginning onto a broader plane via the medium of the general theory of modes of production which Mandel espouses. 'Transition' functions in Mandel's work as an economic category residing 'between' modes of production. 'In transition' comes to function in Mandel's usage as an equivalent to 'in limbo', a fact which militates against the construction of a precise definition of the nature of the USSR.

Mandel constantly avoids analysis of the USSR as a specific case, deflecting discussion onto a quasi-typological plane concerning transitional societies 'in general' in accordance with the transhistorical scheme of 'historical materialism'.[36] Mandel's rhetorical advice that transitions take a long time, or that the USSR is neither here (capitalism) nor there (socialism), can be of little intellectual consolation.[37] For as he himself admits, there can be little parallel in the experiences of the transition from slave, to serf, to free labour and the transition to socialism — in which case, the transhistorical discussion about transition is either obfuscation, or else further proof of Mandel's universalistic pretences. For when pressed to explain the specifics of Soviet transition, Mandel falls back onto common sense — 'transitions take a long time'.[38] But Mandel is not uniformly evasive about the precise nature of the USSR.

His general theory of history, taken from Trotsky, after all indicates that an either/or verdict must be delivered: capitalism *or* socialism, this is the only choice for industrial societies. Mandel is welded, as is Trotsky, to the institutional legacy of the Red October. He is bound to present the course of Soviet history as an artificially prolonged aberration from its original socialist reality and intention. Mandel's earlier diagnosis of the condition of the Soviet state comes directly from the pages of *The Revolution Betrayed*: the Soviet economy is seen as being marked by the contradictory combination of a non-capitalist mode of production and a basically bourgeois mode of distribution, therefore it is transitional between capitalism and socialism, this condition explaining its residual use of capitalist economic categories. For Mandel, as for Trotsky, the contradiction between the Soviet mode of production and its mode of distribution is to be explained by the continued existence of scarcity, that is, by insufficient productivity.[39] Mandel ignores the development of Soviet productivity (or productive forces) which has occurred over 60 years, and this latter without substantially transforming either production relations or distribution. Nothing has changed since the thirties for Mandel: like Trotsky, he follows Preobrazhensky in arguing, still decades later, that the transitional society is marked by the antagonistic coexistence of market and plan.[40]

Mandel's definition therefore suggests that the USSR is a combination of capitalist and socialist elements. When pressed, however, Mandel denies the existence of 'socialist elements' in the USSR.[41] What might its nature then be? In more recent writings, Mandel introduces a new metaphor into the Trotskyist tradition: the argument that the USSR is a hybrid form of society. The modification is as follows:

The production relations specific to the transitional society are thus a hybrid combination of essentially non-capitalist economic planning and the elements of commodity production (with their drive towards private appropriation and private enrichment) which arise from the basically still bourgeois distribution relations.[42]

Elsewhere Mandel compounds metaphors, now adding an astronomical image in order to deal with the problem of how the regime reproduces itself: 'Once launched into orbit, the structure remains in this orbit and can be directed from it only by social revolutions or counterrevolutions, by explosions. . .[or] perturbations.'[43] The continual and increasing contestation of the Trotskyist definition of the USSR since Trotsky's death is evident in Mandel's attempts to discredit alternative theories while attempting to sustain Trotsky's with the 'hybrid' qualification. According to Mandel, the rejection of existing explanations — that the USSR is either capitalist or socialist or else is the regime of a new class — would necessitate the admission that 'we are dealing with the specific, hybrid relations of production of a specific country (or group of countries)'.[44] Yet, again, the fact that Mandel writes in a period of lively marxist debate has had little effect on his basic premises. Nor do his conclusions differ from Trotsky's, notions of the 'hybrid' society notwithstanding. Mandel follows Trotsky's political line — for Mandel, also, the USSR remains a workers' state which, like the corrupt trade union, nevertheless warrants defence — and adheres to Trotsky's strategic response, agreeing that a political revolution will provide the necessary corrective.[45]

In the analysis of other East European societies Mandel follows through the necessitarian logic developed by Trotsky: socialism could now be produced not only from above, but also across national boundaries. He develops a new metaphor to cover the discrepancy between the Soviet state and its progeny — where the USSR has become a degenerated workers' state, the satellites are *deformed*. Though mutant, they maintained real socialist potential because of their paternal pedigree: nationalised forms of property had been endowed upon them by the Soviet Union.[46] Socialism here could not logically be regenerated, nor could the *raison d'être* of the Fourth International any longer easily be defended; the old mole kept breaking through the surface in the wrong places, nowhere near the Trotskyist headquarters. What could Trotskyist leaders like Mandel do, but applaud it?

Like Trotsky, Mandel understands socialism as essentially a matter of planning or nationalisation. Mandel views economic problems as the major problems of the transition to socialism. In *Marxist Economic Theory*, the key problem of the transition period is determining the optimum growth rate; the hardest problems to be solved during the period of transition from capitalism to socialism are those of agriculture and distribu-

128

tion.[47] Since politics follows economics, economics must be given first priority. Mandel's attachment to socialism seems to spring from an interest in efficiency.[48] In keeping with his methodology, his arguments lead logically to priorities which are quantitative rather than qualitative in nature, inclined to the logic of redistribution rather than to that of the restructuring of social relations, and this holds true for East and West alike. Mandel argues as though alienation results from scarcity rather than relations of domination, in Eastern Europe at least, and identifies bureaucratisation with the continued existence of market and money relations rather than with the concentration of power in the Party-state.[49]

What overall judgement can be made of Mandel's position on transition in the East? His earlier formulation, duplicating Trotsky's, is entirely vulnerable to the foregoing criticism of Trotsky's own theory with the qualification that whatever credibility Trotsky's analysis has in 1937, Mandel's repetition lacks decades later. Trotsky's own belief that the USSR was still 'in transition' during his lifetime may be theoretically dubious, but it is not lacking in personal justification or immediate plausibility. That Mandel can simply repeat Trotsky's analysis years later is altogether different. Mandel's justification for this repetition is the combined presupposition that nothing essential has changed, and that the USSR must by definition be transitional in the first place. He refuses the possibility that the USSR might be a permanent social order rather than a society 'in transition'.[50] Mandel does not substantiate his case with adequate empirical or logical evidence. All manner of arguments to the contrary are ignored; only those like state capitalism are engaged, because they can be theoretically pulverised. Mandel insists that the USSR, like all things in a dialectical world, must still be 'going' somewhere. It must be going somewhere, else doubt is cast on the scheme of the general theory of modes of production ending by fiat in capitalism, then socialism. And it must be going towards socialism, as it is a regime allegedly marked by the signs of socialism in the fact of its attachment to the principle of planning.

Mandel's introduction of the notion of the 'hybrid' society must be seen as an ill-chosen revision, intended to close the debate over the question of the nature of the USSR by co-opting elements of the alternative explanations into his own.

The result, the notion of the hybrid society, is a contradictory and potentially explosive one. Mandel's choice of metaphor is particularly inept. That society which is hybrid cannot be heading toward socialism; arbitrary crossbreeding cannot simply be 'undone' by specialists at a later date. The logic of the notion of the hybrid society suggests exactly that which Mandel rejects: that the USSR is a new being, a new society. The derivation of Mandel's metaphor is unclear. If it is vegetable, then the problem arises that the hybrid specimen is not easily propagated. If animal, it may refer to the mule — inelegant but practical, a beast capable of carrying the burden of History. Mandel's hybrid society in any case cannot be undone, so it cannot possess the transitional telos which he ascribes to it. A transitional society is going somewhere; a hybrid society is here to stay, though it may well succeed in propagating itself in Eastern Europe, on the point of a bayonet. Mandel's most recent qualification seems to suggest that the USSR is not so much a hybrid as a mutation.[51] Even more than the hybrid notion does this argument suggest that Soviet-type societies stand alone, *sui generis*. But this is exactly the argument which Trotskyism is constituted against, and precisely the logic which Trotskyism has so long resisted, for it violates the Trotskyist philosophy of history. As Hillel Ticktin has argued, Mandel here is trapped within the definition and tradition of Trotskyism. Mandel is prevented from thinking his theoretical position through to its logical conclusion by the structural constraints imposed by the concepts of the Trotskyist tradition.[52]

Transition in the West: Mandel's theory of socialist revolution

Mandel views world revolution as an objective process which has dominated the recent history of the modern world. It is a process which has detoured through the Third World: the epicentre of world revolution passed, from 1948 to 1968, from Western Europe to the East, implicitly returning to Western Europe with the May events in France and later activity in Italy. Revolution remains on the European agenda for Mandel, but has been re-routed. In the West, the situation is quite simply that the revolution has been betrayed, delayed by bad leader-

Political Economy and Transition: Mandel

ship. Yet in China, and in Yugoslavia, revolution triumphed despite bad (Stalinist) leaderships. The anomaly in such a judgement indicates the continuing tension in Trotskyism between objective and subjective views of the necessary conditions for socialist revolution, for Trotskyism simultaneously accepts the Leninist contention, that socialism is the product of an organised vanguard at the head of a 'mass' movement, *and* endorses the older marxist idea of the Second International, that socialism is written into the order of things and will out. This tension in Trotskyist thinking becomes particularly clear in Mandel's work, enabling him simultaneously to argue vanguardist and spontaneist strategies. For example, the Cuban Revolution, conducted in the absence of a Leninist Party, is nevertheless deemed socialist, at least to the extent that the standard recipe for deformed workers' states — political revolution — does not apply.[53] Such inconsistencies do not bother Mandel, who changes feet as circumstance dictates.

The situation in the West may be less immediately clear than it is in Cuba, but is nevertheless favourable for Mandel, even in the extreme. The events of 1968 demonstrated that new 'detonators' like the student movement can set off broader social explosions, but they can of course have real effectivity only if integrated into the workers' movement or at least into its aspiring leadership.[54] In the West, the subject of revolutionary change remains the working class, and its Party, the Fourth International, the piston in search of some steam. 'Spontaneous' revolutions, following the examples of Yugoslavia, China and Cuba, do not seem to be on the agenda in the West. Mandel relieves Trotsky of his task of awaiting the American Labour Party; he maintains a naïve faith in the revolutionary capacity of the American working class, for the most powerful and numerically largest proletariat in the world cannot fail to perform eventually.[55] Only then, finally, will the theory of world revolution be vindicated and the historic vocation of the Fourth International fulfilled, piston and mole united.

Mandel's political thinking is derived directly from Trotsky's. Both maintain that the situation for revolution is rotten-ripe. Some examples offered by Mandel as proof of this historic trend are even more fantastic than Trotsky's own projections. According to Mandel, conditions were being created in 1954 for a Trotskyist upsurge in the Soviet Union.[56] Similarly, the demonstrations on the attempted assassination of Togliatti after the war provided for Mandel an instinctive posing of the question of power.[57] More recently, Mandel has confessed that he and his friends seriously anticipated a German revolution as the outcome of the Second World War.[58] Such errors, which can presumably like Trotsky's be put down to bad timing, are extreme manifestations of Mandel's general perspective. It is his belief that all countries will follow the same road to socialism; it is his general prognosis that 'it is most unlikely that capitalism will survive another half century'.[59] The revolutionary telos is seeking a place to set itself: until it comes home, to the West, the epicentre of world revolution will shift as Reason dictates.

How is Mandel's faith in this revolutionary telos sustained? Its primary condition of existence is the conflation of economic and political forms of class struggle. The direct association of these forms of struggle produces the proletarian telos which breaks out sporadically until it finds its home in a situation characterised by a decayed regime and a growing Trotskyist (or Stalinist?) Party. For Mandel, economic struggles *grow* into political struggles. The strength of his belief is indicated in his endorsement of the Prussian Minister von Puttkammer's enunciation that 'every strike contains the hydra of the revolution'. Like Trotsky, but again with less justification decades later, Mandel cannot differentiate between industrial relations and socialist politics.[60] For Mandel, the trigger of socialist consciousness is the collapse of capitalism: social revolution is the outcome of world economic crisis. Mandel belongs to the tradition in marxism which takes the proletariat to be the historic bearers of socialism, though stand-ins may be accepted. The proletariat only needs its immediate consciousness shattered by capitalist crisis to break out of its present mould. The proletariat absorbs bourgeois ideology in its everyday existence, but is really revolutionary by disposition. Its real nature as the chosen class is beyond dispute: its 'revolutionary mission' is inscribed in its 'objective roots'. Capitalist society bipolarises into miniscule bourgeoisie and homogeneous, overwhelming proletariat.[61] Mandel adheres to the Trotskyist tradition in determining the status of the proletariat without, or even despite, reference to its actual consciousness. 'Late Capitalism' is held to provide an excellent school for the proletariat, says Master Mandel, for though it integrates the class into its structures, it also breeds working-class militancy.[62]

For Mandel the spontaneous strivings of the proletariat emerge fully in a situation of crisis. Normal situations produce reformist consciousness, crises produce revolutionary consciousness. These understandings in Mandel result from the combination of two maxims: that being determines consciousness, and that revolution is written into the order of things. Capitalist collapse, the objective determinant, forms subjective political will, rupturing the normal relationship between being and consciousness.[63] Social change occurs for Mandel first 'objectively', in society rather than in individuals; socialism is achieved in 'reality' before it is in consciousness, as though socialism, the social order premised on the development of consciousness, could arrive unheralded 'behind the backs' of its subjects.[64] Within so implausible an argument there is a familiar logic. In arguing that individuals can improve only after they have experienced abundance at the hands of a benevolent society, Mandel reveals the logic of Jacobinism basic to his thought. If politics in the new society does not consist of the practice of the sum of its willing participants confronting social problems, then it must be the domain of benevolent despots who act on their behalf. Mandel's image of social revolution continues the tradition of Bolshevism, where the Party leads the masses to overthrow the bourgeois state in order to inaugurate the 'new' society for the good of the people.

Mandel's theory of socialist revolution is an articulated variant of Marx's 1859 Preface, where the forces/relations formula functions as objective component, the source and determinant of social change, and the Leninist Party functions as subjective component. The maturity of objective conditions is seen as prior to the subjective moment. The latter is nevertheless held to be indispensable. The subject, the proletariat, is reduced to the Party: 'The Leninist theory of organisation. . .constitutes the *marxist science of the subjective factor*'. The 1859 Preface provides the objective basis of the subjective possibility of socialism.[65] The 'incompletion' of Marx's 1859 Preface warrants the introduction of an external factor, the Leninist Party, which crowns the work of the endogenous factor, the productive forces. Yet it is only endogenous necessity which makes this intervention possible. This is true to the extent that Mandel allows for cases in which socialism is the product of such forces alone, even in the absence of a healthy Bolshevik Party. Yet Mandel simultaneously holds that the absence of revolutionary victories (in the West) is the result of the crisis in the 'subjective factor', that is, in proletarian leadership. Mandel's theory of revolution is therefore not only a revision of the 1859 Preface, but is also a reworking of the *Transitional Program*, where objective conditions are understood to be ripe, but explained more systematically with reference to economic cycles and crises, and where the 'subjective factor' (and the Fourth International) still lags behind.[66]

As in Trotsky, so in Mandel does this argument pertain less directly to specific individual nation-states than to a world process of socialist revolution which is held to be unfolding, subject to uneven development and delays brought about by treacherous leadership. Mandel is nothing if not an internationalist. His international commitment to socialist revolution and to the Fourth International are constructed at a high level of abstraction, again eschewing specificity. The slogans of Mandel's political agitation are abstract and rhetorical; according to him, the only legitimate orientation for socialist politics today is — towards the Socialist United States of Europe![67] The sequence of logic is clear: international revolution — the necessary response to the internationalisation of capital — necessitates international organisation. Mandel defends the principle (and the practice) of a 'single centre' of world revolution. His argument, that the world concentration of revolutionary initiative is necessary in order to deal with centralised capital, recalls the arguments of the early Comintern. He argues like Trotsky after 1933, that such problems as emerge in the International are circumstantial, rather than immanent to the idea of a centralised International. Significantly, Trotsky and Mandel alike see the construction of the International as the solution to the problems faced by socialists. Their common premiss is that organisational responses can solve cultural problems, that an organised International can negate the cultural absorption of the popular masses into bourgeois society.[68] In keeping with his notion that the world system is more than the sum of its parts, Mandel invests the International with a mystique, suggesting that it is somehow more than the sum of its parts, the national Trotskyist parties. His loyalty to the Fourth International is therefore to be understood as loyalty to the idea of an International.[69] This abstract organisational loyalty corresponds with his refusal of the priority of national specificities, serving further to elide even his own principles and commitments.

This level of misplaced abstraction, so common to Mandel, is also evident in his more directly political thinking, which is always 'utopian' to some degree in that it typically presumes the achievement or establishment of the state of affairs under discussion. Mandel usually argues as though he has already arrived at some transitional point, thence moving the focus onto the consolidation and extension of gains which are presumed to have been made. In one place, for example, Mandel slips from a tactical argument about revolution into the presumption of the actual existence of dual power, moving on to considerations of the extension of this non-existent dual power situation into socialism. He proceeds to explain not how socialism arises, but how it can be protected, avoiding always the problems of its beginnings.[70] A more spectacular example of Mandel's ethereal politics can be found in his proposed solution to the contradictory problem, how to increase both accumulation and consumption in the transition period. Mandel proposes, as solution, that arms expenditure be transferred to socially useful needs — an eminently sensible suggestion, but one which is totally impracticable, in the absence of a separate demonstration as to how the world might arrive at a situation which would allow such a project of social engineering.[71] Even Mandel's more immediate proposals posit the existence of that which is yet to be achieved: he issues assurances that the workers' state *will* wither, *will* be more democratic than the bourgeois state, *will* eliminate careerism; and even guarantees that Soviet democracy *will* be exercised by workers and poor peasants.[72] Regardless of chronology in projection, Mandel's claims are based on nothing more than assurance, yet are presented as necessity.

Two levels or types of utopia can be discerned in Mandel's work: a more immediate variant approximating the 'Government of Soviets', and a more abstract variant reminiscent of Trotsky's image in *Literature and Revolution.* Mandel's immediate 'utopia' is, in a specific sense, no less utopian than his advanced variant, for its precondition is a regime of direct democracy. Mandel refuses absolutely the legitimacy of representative government, to the extent that he reduces the question of the status of parliamentary forms in the transition to socialism to the level of tactics rather than theory. According to Mandel, the citizen in a regime of representative democracy 'is neither a protagonist nor even an actor in the political drama. He can only have a walk-on part, as a spear carrier.'[73] The theatrical image is eye-catching, but misses the point: everyday politics is not an epic in bourgeois society. Mandel's image of the new society is one dear to the Trotskyist tradition, and best expressed in works like those of C.L.R. James: it is a composite of Athens and the early days of the Russian Revolution, the regime of associated producers where cooks govern, using recipes from Mandel's cookshop.

Beyond the realm of direct democracy lies another image of the future, which immediately brings to mind Trotsky's rationalist fantasies in *Literature and Revolution*. The resemblances are almost complete: Mandel anticipates in socialism the achievement of a situation of social transparency in which all men master all social relations and all develop scientific aptitudes, as 'nothing now stands in the way of progressively transforming all men into scientists and scholars'.[74] (Presumably all women will still be doing the washing up.) Unlike Lafargue's socialist hedonists, the citizens of Mandel's utopia need leisure to work, to pursue science and politics. For mankind's first task is not in responding to local or national needs, but in working out a Faustian agenda, a plan of economic development encompassing the irrigation of the Sahara and the transformation of the Amazonian jungle.[75] 'Humanity will master its geographical surroundings, the configuration of the globe, the climate and the distribution of great water reserves, at the same time preserving or restoring ecological equilibrium. It will overturn everything down to its own biological foundations.'[76] The scenario is Trotsky's, or Goethe's, with an added twinge of ecological conscience. Mandel's spear-carriers, the ordinary citizens of East and West, would very likely have difficulty raising enthusiasm for such a project.

There is also a more practical dimension to Mandel's political proposals. Practical politics does enter in Mandel's proposals concerning the *Transitional Program*. If neither of Mandel's 'utopian' proposals have much bearing on reality, then what are the effects of his transitional proposals? Much of

Mandel's earlier notoriety on the revolutionary left springs from his interpretation of the *Transitional Program*, with its proposals for 'structural reforms'. In the early formulation spear-carriers can become titans through the pursuit of such reforms. The main purpose of the strategy of structural reforms 'is to effect an integration between the immediate aims of the masses and the objectives of the struggle which effectively challenge the very existence of the capitalist system itself'.[77] Understood as an alternative to the mere juxtaposition of minimum and maximum programs, 'structural reforms' are thrown up which objectively challenge the operation of capital; in function, therefore, 'structural reforms' seem to be identical to the program of transition drawn up by Trotsky. In a more recent argument, however, Mandel presents the demands of the *Transitional Program* — the shorter working week, sliding scale of wages and so on — as defensive in character, and therefore preliminary to the transition to socialism proper. According to Mandel this defensive program must be integrated into the overall anticapitalist struggle of 'transitional demands', including nationalisation, workers' control, popular committees and a people's militia.[78] In this later definition, Mandel seems to be calling Trotsky's *Transitional Program* nothing more than a defensive strategy, reserving the label 'transition proper' for the elementary phases of the revolutionary process (the overthrow of the state). No explanation is given as to how defensive trade union struggles might grow into anticapitalist transitional struggles; no such explanatory obligation falls on Mandel's shoulders, for he believes political class struggles to be the natural outgrowth of economic class struggle. To explain, here, is nothing: to assert, is everything.

Mandel probably introduces these later qualifications into the argument in order to rectify a situation which allowed his proposals for transition to be cast as 'reformist'. Indeed his earlier calls for structural reforms bear a close resemblance to the arguments of his besworn enemies, the Eurocommunists: the fundamental goal of structural reforms is to take away the levers of command in the economy from the financial groups, trusts and monopolies and place them in the hands of the nation, to expand the public sector and workers' control.[79] Here Mandel is caught in a polemical trap. Burdened by unrealisable utopias, he must specify a practical political program. But his economic catastrophism and rationalism militate against the consideration of practical political programs. Mandel argues that to work in and against bourgeois society is impossible without integration. What policies might then be pursued by revolutionaries living in bourgeois societies? Mandel concedes that 'revolutionary vocational practice', organised radical work by teachers, doctors and others, can be of some positive effect — provided, of course, that such activity is subsumed organisationally to the Fourth International.[80] Mandel refuses the argument that socialism, if at all possible, could only be the work of consciously organised alliances and movements. He rejects social movements. The basis of his position is a kind of political ontology of labour: he argues that social movements can only fill vacuums which are created by the default of the labour movement to fulfil its historic tasks.[81] He cannot therefore allow detailed attention to the politics of contestation: revolutionary posturing and theoretical guarantees prevent Mandel from taking new political forms into earnest consideration. These forms, and their theoretical implications, simply do not register on the grid of the orthodox.

Leaving behind his earlier arguments for structural reforms, refusing other attempts to bridge the present and future, Mandel's politics seem therefore to cleave precisely into the bifurcation of minimum and maximum programs, the only 'bridge' being provided by a revolutionary class telos. Mandel's politics therefore reflect those of the heritage which he seeks to renounce. That such a bifurcation should be the outcome of Mandel's theory comes as no surprise; it is already visible in the revolutionary stand of Trotskyism. The revolution will continue to be delayed, but it can still be nurtured; in the meantime, such empirical or defensive struggles as are thrown up and deemed sound must be guarded. Mandel's Trotskyism is, as Sartre put it years ago, after all 'a waiting art'.[82] Mandel is obliged by the tradition within which he works to limit the potential in contestatory struggles or issue-movements as they relate to both state and economy. His strategic response to the state is no more sensitive than his one-dimensional view of economic struggles. If the state is nothing but the tool of the ruling class, it can belong either to the bourgeoisie or to the proletariat. If it belongs to the bourgeoisie, it can only be seized or overthrown all at once, in one decisive act: as it is monolithic and lacking contradiction, it cannot be the site of contesting groups and interests but only the exclusive spoils of the ruling class.[83] In economy it is also a case of 'all or nothing'. Mandel allows that the demand for workers' control has a place in the program of structural reforms, but no more: self-management can come only after the revolution, after the seizure of power. The state must be overthrown before self-management can be contemplated. Everything must be changed all at once, or it will not be changed at all. . .unless it is changed by Stalinists or petty-bourgeois adventurers, when the criteria are modified.

These arguments place Mandel squarely in the Bolshevik tradition, and in the Bolshevik lineage of Trotskyism, marking him off clearly from the later Pablo and other 'radical Trotskyists' who stress that practical change, however humble, is possible now. However qualified Mandel's position may be in relation to both his own heritage and his own earlier positions, the overall logic of his marxism is traditional rather than radical in nature, and imaginary rather than practical in disposition. His fundamental commitment to the inevitability of revolution and the guarantees of world history serve to prevent Mandel from undertaking a serious contemplation of transition or practical politics, for such a consideration must begin taking issues and people as they are and not as they ought to be. Mandel fails therefore not only to address problems of transition, but also avoids facing the present conjuncture. As Hussain points out with specific reference to the British case, Mandel's proposal of a transitional recipe combining soviets and nationalisation could not be less appropriate, given that parliamentary forms remain hegemonic and nationalisation discredited in England.[84] But if it is the conceptual structure and limits of his tradition which establish Mandel's politics and prevent his advance onto the terrain of contemporary struggles, his can hardly be viewed as a case of simple Bolshevism. Mandel's revolutionary telos is of a special and original kind, being theorised to a high degree of sophistication in his own technological variant of the 1859 Preface. Mandel's theory of technological revolutions and long waves is the culmination of his intellectual project, and provides the structure which ultimately encompasses and supports his revolutionary politics. It is here that this criticism of Mandel must conclude.

Mandel's theory of technological revolution and long waves

Mandel first fully articulated his argument about technological revolutions and long waves in *Late Capitalism*, revising his position in certain respects in *Long Waves of Capitalist Development. The Marxist Interpretation*. Mandel's images, if provocative, are also problematical. The combined metaphor of waves and revolutions simultaneously suggests movement of repetition and breakthrough: the synthesis of the two images might be taken to imply a repetitive but spiral motion in economy, or else to suggest that revolutions occur as waves, cyclically and automatically. Two main difficulties emerge here. First, the precise relationship between the schema of waves and that of revolutions is unclear. If waves predominate, then a repetitionist and anti-revolutionary philosophy of history is suggested, boom followed by crash *ad nauseum*. If, on the other hand, revolution or rupture is dominant, what then becomes of the cyclical trends of the economy? Second, it should be observed that the nomenclature in both its metaphorical derivations contradicts the Trotskyist program, denying the scheme of prolonged decay outlined in the *Transitional Program*. At the root of the metaphorical confusion lies the tension in Mandel's work between science and revolution. Mandel's argument is compromised by the contradiction between accurate economic analysis and his desire to see the revolutionary telos vindicated. Either economic cycles reproduce capitalism, or they do not. For Mandel, the revolutionary scientist, they must do both.

Mandel details his scheme of long waves in *Late Capitalism*. His argument is that in the history of international capitalism, cyclical movements of seven or ten years' duration exist within longer spans of approximately 50 years, of which there have so far been four, characterised respectively by handicraft made or manufacture made steam engines, machine-made steam engines, electric and combustion engines, and by electronic apparatuses and the gradual introduction of nuclear energy. Ours is the long wave of the third technological revolution.[85] According to Mandel each long wave can be divided into two parts: an initial phase of application and subsequent accelerated accumulation, followed by a phase of generalisation, bringing with it a tendency to gradually decelerating accumulation as technology is cheapened and loses its 'revolutionary' effect. According to the general contours of the scheme, 'we should today have entered into the second phase of the 'long wave' which began with the Second World War, characterised by decelerated capital accumulation'.[86] The rapid succession of recessions in the central imperialist countries is taken to confirm this hypothesis. Mandel's scheme of periodisation is the basis for his choice of the term 'late capitalism' to describe the present epoch. As the title of its French edition — *Le troisième âge du Capitalisme* — suggests, late capitalism is the third and final age of capitalism: it followed classical capitalism, analysed by Marx, and imperialism, analysed by Lenin, and it is also the third stage of the technological revolution, the stage of capitalism corresponding with automation, its highest preterminal development.

It is Mandel's argument about the decelerated phase of accumulation characteristic of the present epoch which is significant here, as it raises the question of revolution and the revolutionary status of the factor of technology. Both as regards the general theory itself and as regards the nature of the present epoch, critical attention must be focused on the character of the motor force which drives technological revolutions forward.[87] The central question can be posed as follows: are technological revolutions and their accompanying long waves endogenous or exogenous in origin? This question immediately raises another, that of the status of Mandel's forced combination of the views of Trotsky and Kondratiev. Against both logical and historical arguments, Mandel insists that the theory of long waves is marxist in parentage.[88] He combines the incompatible in order to form the basis of his theory. Trotsky's theory was constructed against Kondratiev's primarily because Kondratiev took change to be endogenous in origin. More than this, Trotsky denied even the idea of the comparison of short, ten or seven year cycles with 'long' cycles. Kondratiev's theory had, for Trotsky, to be seen for what it was — not a theory of change, but one of equilibrium. As Richard Day has it, Mandel agrees with both Kondratiev and Trotsky at the same time, 'something which is logically impossible'.[89] Mandel's procedure — contrasting the views of Kondratiev and Trotsky, only to retain the logic of the former in tandem with claims of political fidelity to the latter — is completely unconvincing. Despite claims to pluralist explanation, Mandel privileges the explanatory and historical power of waves driven by technology.[90] But if technology is the motor of history, what then becomes of human agency, or in marxist terminology, what becomes of the class struggle?

Having 'forgotten the class struggle' in *Late Capitalism*, Mandel later introduces the notion of long waves of class struggle which correspond to long waves in economic growth. He fails completely to specify the basis of construction for this more political cycle in statistical, historical or theoretical terms. The long wave of class struggle seems to be nothing more than assurance presented in diagrammatic form. The wave of class struggle functions as an effect of the long wave of development itself, as is indicated in Mandel's claim that class struggle 'intensifies' with the depressive period of the long wave.[91] There is, however, a considerable shift in the arguments involved. Mandel attempts to throw focus back onto the political within the confines of the 1859 Preface scheme, suggesting that social development is not automatic but contingent on the class struggle. He wishes to argue that the cause of the downturn is endogenous, whereas upturn, being contingent, is not endogenous.[92] Mandel's determinism is accentuated by each attempt at its public denial. His recent arguments about 'relative autonomy' do little to improve his case, as the 'relativity' given with one hand is constantly retrieved, dialectically, by the other. The overall logic of Mandel's theory remains unaltered, if qualified and more closely specified: technology remains the prime mover of social change, and automation remains the great force for socialism. There are no substantial differences between the scheme in *Late Capitalism* and that in *Long Waves*: technical change in the later version is still endogenous but exogenously triggered, externally detonated.[93] The argument of *Late Capitalism* is likewise based on the principle of endogenous development with external triggering mechanisms. The argument that the internal causation of long waves by technology is externally triggered by wars and revolutions functions as a theoretical 'last instance' of determination, while practically politics and history are reduced to economic and technological after-effects, or fuses.

Mandel's afterthought six years after the first publication of *Late Capitalism*, that class struggle rather than technology determines the course of history, is too little, too late. It serves only to shift emphasis within his modified 1859 scheme: either politics or economics is determinant, as circumstances require. This is exactly the ambiguity which is the hallmark of orthodox marxism: orthodox marxism is always correct because it cannot be proven wrong. Either the economic or political factor can always be blamed for the non-event of social revolution. Whatever the situation, whatever the outcome, all defeats and 'victories' can be explained within the existing paradigm. By this means, Trotskyism maintains its claim always to be correct, no matter how frequently it is refuted by history or by criticism.

Conclusions:
Mandel and the technological road to socialism

Ernest Mandel's economic interest and background serve to add a novel dimension to contemporary Trotskyism. Retaining from Trotsky basic philosophical principles as well as notions of impending collapse and organisation, Mandel's view of socialist transition is qualified by an intense faith in technology and automation. In this regard, and more emphatically than Trotsky, he is a 'Department I' marxist, awaiting the results of the self-development of the productive forces. Mandel modifies Lenin, defining socialism as soviets plus automation and television (the latter to be used as an instrument of direct democracy rather than privatised 'leisure').[94] Automation takes on a central role in Mandel's marxism, and one which is all the more perplexing given his stated opinion on technology. Against Mandel's dedication to technology as the prime mover of history can be placed his professed position:

> *Belief in the omnipotence of technology is the specific form of bourgeois ideology in late capitalism* . . . All bourgeois and many self-styled Marxist theorists of the omnipotence of technology elevate it into a mechanism completely independent of all human objectives and decisions, which proceeds independently of class structure and class rule in the automatic manner of a natural law.[95]

Into which category would Mandel fall were we to apply his own terms of criticism to the theory of long waves and technological revolutions?

Mandel accepts the proposition that automation and capitalism must reach a point of incompatibility, thus implying that the complete fulfilment of the third technological revolution is identical with the advent of socialism.[96] The alternative — socialism or barbarism — resolves itself, for those who operate with this technological vista, into a choice between socialist automation and capitalist decay. In its most emphatic formulation, it is Mandel's position that 'All the historical conditions of capitalism are concentrated in the twofold character of automation'.[97] Automation presents simultaneously the threat of destruction and the possibility of emancipation. Within his own variation of the 1859 Preface, socialism presents itself as the fulfilment of history, understood as the progress of technique.

With specific reference to the nature of capitalist society, Mandel's arguments reflect the least satisfactory dimension of the *Grundrisse* — its tendency to discuss socialism both as end and as process in a determinist manner. Certainly Mandel endorses the *Grundrisse's* technological utopia, if in combination with elements of the image of the regime of associated producers in the third volume of *Capital*. More fundamentally, he is committed to the notion in the *Grundrisse* that capital is immanently self-expansive, that it is an ambiguous power which, in striving for both self-emancipation and self-preservation, inevitably brings itself to the point of self-destruction. The logic at work here is analogous to that in Mandel's theory as such: despite class struggle, whether in its cyclical or immediate form, the implication is that capital somehow revolutionises itself. In his limited analyses of capitalism, and in his more extended interest in history as the unfolding of technological progress through successive modes of production, Mandel's marxism advances an 'automatic' view of history, which forecloses the discussion of problems of social change.

It has been argued in this chapter that following and modifying Trotsky, Mandel's theory of history forecloses even on the possibility of a close scrutiny of the specific political or cultural situations or formations which arise in the twentieth century. This foreclosure is no mere deficit or absence, and is more emphatically true of Mandel than of Trotsky, for Mandel produces even stronger arguments than Trotsky for the certainty of socialism, and this in an age where its likelihood seems even more remote. Indeed, it may even be the case that Mandel's arguments herald not progress but reaction. Mandel fails to understand the complications thrown up for transition by the technological theory of history. The short term replacement of labour by machines serves not to introduce socialism, but rather to prolong the crisis, increasing unemployment and extending low paid work. Automation here is the harbinger not of socialism, but of increased capitalist wealth and extended working class poverty. Mandel's 'scientific' analyses and his 'revolutionary' predictions do not mesh. For all his 'revolutionary' professions, Mandel's 'scientific' theory has more in common with the theory of capitalist equilibrium than it has with Trotsky and the 'revolutionary' tradition.

Hussain's charge that Mandel's 'science' is an exercise in astrology, stands perhaps in need of modification: it can also be usefully viewed as an exercise in astronomy. Those who deal with the circular movements of bodies, whether celestial or terrestrial, can after all only observe and not influence their movements. The notions of fate and prediction remain central to Mandel's cosmological constellation.[98] Mandel's attempts to combine science and revolution are bound to fail, for capitalism cannot simultaneously reproduce itself in theory and transform itself into socialism in rhetoric. The work of Mandel, this most innovative of Trotskyists, founders on the rocks of its claims to be simultaneously 'scientific' (in Mandel's specific sense) and 'revolutionary' (in accordance with the Trotskyist tradition). The rhetorical revolutionism of Mandel's science serves to undermine both its scientific and its political credibility. Striving after the identity of revolution and science, it ends in denying both; presuming social transition to be already under way, it serves only to work against its possibility.

Notes

1. Mandel, *Trotsky* (New Left Books, London, 1979); and see *From Stalinism to Eurocommunism: The Bitter Fruits of Socialism in One Country* (NLB, London, 1978), where quotations from Trotsky suffice to both dispatch the opponent and close the case; pp. 33, 47.
2. Mandel, *Trotsky*, p. 128.
3. Mandel, *Trotsky*, p. 53; Mandel, *On Bureaucracy. A Marxist Analysis* (IMG, London, n.d.), p. 15; Mandel, 'The Leninist Theory of

Organisation' in R. Blackburn (ed.), *Revolution and Class Struggle: A Reader in Marxist Politics* (Fontana, Glasgow, 1977), p. 93f.

4. Mandel, 'The Leninist Theory', p. 98.

5. Mandel, 'The Causes of Alienation' in Mandel and G. Novack (eds), *The Marxist Theory of Alienation* (Pathfinder, New York, 1974), pp. 23, 29.

6. Mandel, Introduction to Marx, *Capital, 3* (Penguin, Harmondsworth, 1981), p. 77.

7. Mandel, 'Workers Under Neocapitalism' in Mandel and Novack (eds), *The Revolutionary Potential of the Working Class* (Pathfinder, New York, 1974), p. 28.

8. Mandel, *On Bureaucracy*, p. 10.

9. Mandel, *Marxist Economic Theory* (Merlin, London, 1974, One Volume edn), p. 668.

10. Mandel, *On Bureaucracy*, p. 11.

11. Mandel, *Introduction to Marxism* (Ink Links, London, 1979), p. 157f.

12. Ibid., 163f.

13. Ibid., p. 164f.

14. Mandel, Introduction to *Capital, 1* (Penguin, Harmondsworth, 1976), p. 13ff.

15. *Late Capitalism* (NLB, London, 1975), p. 140.

16. See, for example, Mandel, *The Second Slump. A Marxist Analysis of the Recession in the Seventies* (NLB, London, 1978), pp. 9, 13, 62, 84.

17. Mandel, *Introduction to Marxism*, pp. 175, 183.

18. Ibid., p. 180.

19. Mandel, *Marxist Economic Theory*, Chs 1–4.

20. See, for example, *Trotsky*, pp. 56, 75; *From Stalinism to Eurocommunism*, pp. 194, 199: *Late Capitalism*, pp. 469, 486, 571; *The Revolutionary Potential of the Working Class*, p. 35; *Marxist Economic Theory*, p. 501; 'The Leninist Theory of Organisation', pp. 108, 121; *Late Capitalism*, p. 486; *The Second Slump*, p. 35.

21. Mandel's *Introduction to Marxism* presents materialist dialectics as the proletariat's epistemology: pp. 160, 169.

22. Mandel, *Late Capitalism*, p. 516.

23. Mandel, *On Bureaucracy*, p. 34.

24. Mandel, 'Report on the World Political Situation'. *1979 World Congress of the Fourth International. Major Resolutions and Reports* (Inprecor/Intercontinental Press, New York, 1980), p. 42. It was this attitude which prompted M. Kidron's criticism of *Marxist Economic Theory* as 'Maginot Marxism' (in Kidron, *Capitalism and Theory*, Pluto, London, 1974, Ch. 4).

25. Mandel, *The Inconsistencies of State Capitalism* (IMG, London, 1969), p. 4.

26. Mandel, *The Formation of the Economic Thought of Karl Marx* (Monthly Review, New York, 1971), pp. 23, 33, 44, 89, 209.

27. Ibid., pp. 83, 166.

28. Mandel, *Formation*, pp. 153, 210.

29. Mandel, *Marxist Economic Theory*, Ch. 5.

30. Mandel, *Der Spätkapitalismus, Versuch einer marxistischen*

Erklärung (Suhrkamp, Frankfurt, 1972), p. 7.

31. Mandel, *Late Capitalism*, p. 589.

32. Ibid., p. 16f.

33. B. Rowthorn, 'Late Capitalism', *New Left Review, 98*, p. 67.

34. A. Hussain, 'Crises and Tendencies of Capitalism', *Economy and Society, 6(4)* (1977), p. 443.

35. P. Mattick, 'Ernest Mandel's Late Capitalism' in *Economic Crisis and Crisis Theory* (Merlin, London, 1981).

36. 'On the Nature of the Soviet State', *New Left Review*, 108, p. 27.

37. Mandel, *Trotsky*, p. 87.

38. Mandel, *Revolutionary Marxism Today* (NLB, London, 1979) pp. 116ff.

39. Mandel, *Marxist Economic Theory*, pp. 565, 572.

40. Ibid., p. 573.

41. Mandel, 'Once Again on the Trotskyist Definition of the Social Nature of the Soviet Union', *Critique, 12*, p. 117; 'The Nature of the USSR, Socialism, Democracy', *Inprecor, 18*, 18 December 1977, p. 6f.

42. 'Ten Theses on the Social and Economic Laws Governing the Society Transitional Between Capitalism and Socialism', *Critique, 3*, p. 10.

43. 'On the Nature of the Soviet State', p. 28. Elsewhere, Mandel summons more familiar images, explaining the Soviet bureaucracy as a parasitic cancer on the proletarian body. See his exchange with Paul Sweezy, *Monthly Review, 31(3)* (1979).

44. 'On the Nature', p. 30.

45. 'Ten Theses',p. 15.

46. Mandel, 'The Rise and Decline of Stalinism' in *The Development and Disintegration of World Stalinism* (SWP Education Series, New York, 1970).

47. Mandel, *Marxist Economic Theory*, p. 621.

48. *Fifty Years of World Revolution* (Merit, New York, 1969), pp. 12, 293, 298.

49. *Formation*, p. 194; *Fifty Years of World Revolution*, p. 280.

50. Ibid., p. 275f; 'On the Nature of the Soviet State', pp. 30,34.

51. Mandel, 'Once Again on the Trotskyist Definition', p. 117.

52. H. Ticktin, 'The Ambiguities of Ernest Mandel', *Critique, 12*, pp. 128, 135.

53. Mandel, *Revolutionary Marxism Today*, p. 104.

54. Mandel, 'The New Vanguard' in T. Ali (ed.), *New Revolutionaries — Left Opposition* (Peter Owen, London, 1969), p. 51f. And see Mandel, *The Revolutionary Student Movement. Theory and Practice* (Merit, New York, 1969), and *The Changing Role of the Bourgeois University* (Spartacus League, London, n.d.).

55. Mandel, *Revolutionary Marxism Today*, pp. 200ff; Mandel, *Introduction to Marxism*, p. 82.

56. 'The Rise and Decline of Stalinism', p. 15f.

57. Mandel, *Revolutionary Marxism Today*, p. 12.

58. Ibid., p. 117.

59. Mandel, *The Second Slump*, p. 194; Mandel, 'Introduction' to *Capital* 1, p. 86.

60. Mandel, 'Workers' Control and Workers' Councils', *International, 2(1)* (1973), p. 1. This tendency is especially evident in Mandel's construction of a graph of the 'long cycle of class struggle', without any reference to political determinants. See *Long Waves of Capitalist Development. The Marxist Interpretation* (Cambridge, 1980), p. 50.

61. 'Workers Under Neocapitalism', p. 18; 'Economics' in D. McLellan (ed.), *Marx: The First Hundred Years* (Fontana, London, 1983), pp. 200ff.

62. Mandel, *Late Capitalism*, pp. 183, 498, 585.

63. 'Revolutionary Strategy in the Imperialist Countries', p. 34.

64. Mandel, *Marxist Economic Theory*, p. 655.

65. 'The Leninist Theory of Organisation', p. 81; 'Althusser corrige Marx' in J.-M. Vincent *et al.*, *Contre Althusser (10(18)*, Paris 1974), p. 278.

66. Mandel, *Introduction to Marxism*, p. 127.

67. Mandel, *From Stalinism to Eurocommunism*, p. 36; Mandel, *Late Capitalism*, p. 341.

68. Mandel, *From Stalinism to Eurocommunism*, p. 41.

69. See Mandel to G. Breitman, 9 December 1953 in C. Slaughter (ed.), *Trotskyism versus Revisionism: A Documentary History* (New Park, London, 1974), vol. 2; 'The Split in the International', p. 29; and Breitman to Mandel, 14 January 1954 in ibid., pp. 41, 43.

70. Mandel, *Revolutionary Marxism Today*, pp. 17ff.

71. Mandel, *Marxist Economic Theory*, p. 613f.

72. Mandel, *Introduction to Marxism*, pp. 101, 120.

73. Mandel, *From Stalinism to Eurocommunism*, p. 164f.

74. Mandel, *Formation*, p. 115.

75. Mandel, *Marxist Economic Theory*, p. 614.

76. Mandel, *Introduction to Marxism*, p. 187.

77. Mandel, *A Socialist Strategy for Western Europe* (Institute for Workers' Control Pamphlet 10, Nottingham, n.d.), p. 7.

78. Mandel, *The Second Slump*, p. 206f.

79. Mandel, *An Introduction to Marxist Economic Theory* (Pathfinder, New York, 1971), p. 78.

80. Mandel, *Late Capitalism*, pp.266f.

81. 'Social Democracy and Social Movements', *Thesis Eleven, 7* (1983), pp. 159–62.

82. J.-P. Sartre, *The Communists and Peace* (Hamish Hamilton, London, 1969), p. 99.

83. Mandel, *From Stalinism to Eurocommunism*, p. 178.

84. A. Hussain, 'Symptomatology of Revolution', *Economy and Society, 9(3)* (1980), p. 358.

85. Mandel, *Late Capitalism*, p. 120f.

86. Ibid., p. 121f.

87. We leave aside here other grounds of criticism. It has been argued by one critic, for example, that Mandel's theory cannot be sustained theoretically or empirically. See A. Kleinknecht, 'Innovation, Accumulation and Crisis: Long Waves in Economic Development?', *Review, 4(4)* (1981), pp. 683–711.

88. Day, *Long Waves*, p. 1.

89. Ibid., p. 82.
90. Mandel, *Late Capitalism*, p. 126ff.
91. Day, *Long Waves*, p. 48.
92. See Ibid., pp. 49, 55.
93. Ibid., p. 21.
94. Mandel, 'Self-Management — Dangers and Possibilities', *International, 2(4)* (1975), p. 6.
95. Mandel, *Late Capitalism*, pp. 501, 503.
96. Ibid., p. 206f.
97. Ibid., p. 216.
96. Hussain, 'Symptomatology of Revolution', p. 348.

7
History and Transition:
Isaac Deutscher

Scholarly politician or independent critic? Apologist for Stalinism or marxist historian *par excellence*? Isaac Deutscher's reputation falls into all these categories. Few historians have attracted such controversy or drawn such respect in their own lifetimes. Perhaps Deutscher's own biography goes some way towards explaining this. He was a unique representative of oppositional Trotskyism, one who straddled the worlds of journalism, writing and agitation through the period of the cold war and after. Unlike the many who made their choice between the alternatives of liberalism and Soviet communism, Deutscher chose to remain in the Bolshevik tradition. He remained caught for the rest of his life between Trotskyism and Stalinism, radical yet orthodox. For this reason, Deutscher attracted the young who were disillusioned with Soviet marxism, while repelling those for whom the failure of that God meant the end of any commitment to socialism. Though Deutscher was widely respected he was never accepted into the academy.[1] Fortunately, Deutscher declined offers of academic positions in the Soviet Union in 1931. Considered too radical for the English university, he became, in the eyes of some activists, too cynical and personally distanced from political organisation. Considered together, these characteristics provide some explanation for Deutscher's profound influence on the formative new left. Deutscher was a leftist without the authoritarian associations of official communism, a heretic turning 'classical marxism' (in his understanding, Bolshevism) against the Soviet bureaucracy, rejecting American imperialism yet eschewing the Trotskyist movement. His location outside the academy conferred the political legitimation of 'independence' on his work. His rejection of the existing organisational alternatives placed him in a position to assess anew the experience of the twentieth century. This detached perspective coupled with his considerable literary skills produced such monumental works as his Trotsky trilogy, *The Prophet Armed — Unarmed — Outcast.* Yet this Trotskyist outside Trotskyism owed more to Trotsky than many who remained within the movement, and influenced more Trotskyists than any other in his time. More than any other did Deutscher bring into focus the fundamental tension in Trotskyism between the opposition to Stalinism and the defence of the Soviet Union — though not, in this case, through outright defence, but rather through what came to be called apologism.

Deutscher was born near Cracow in 1907 and died in exile 60 years later. His early talents were recommended by Mann, and his interest in literature was to remain with him throughout his life. His politicisation led to participation in the Polish Communist Party from 1926 to 1932. Deutscher was an oppositionist after 1931; his expulsion the following year was the reward earned for bringing attention to the impending threat of fascism. His subsequent role in the Trotskyist movement was heretical, as his participation in the Communist Party had been. Deutscher was responsible for the authorship of the document presented by Polish delegates to the Founding Conference of the Fourth International, but did not attend himself. The Polish document provided the sole argument opposing the formation of the new International. Exile in Great Britain, where Deutscher first acquired the language in which he was to write his great works, led to a life of journalism. Into the late 1940s, journalism was to be sacrificed for the fulfilment of his personal project, a planned history of the USSR. While formally suspended, that project was to be materialised in biographies of Stalin, Trotsky, and the incomplete work on Lenin, which was cut short by Deutscher's premature death.

A striking resemblance to Trotsky's work is immediately apparent in the work of Deutscher. Deutscher's project — a history of the Russian Revolution, deferred and eventually written in the form of biographies of its central personalities — provides a mirror image of Trotsky's own relevant work. Whatever else this parallel might suggest, one implication is

151

clear. Like Trotsky, and even despite himself, Deutscher interprets history through the medium of great personalities.
Personification and dramatic device are even more fundamental to Deutscher's work than to Trotsky's; and Deutscher's
sense of necessity in history is perhaps even more compelling
than Trotsky's. The two have an intimate relationship; indeed,
it might even be said that Deutscher, in full empathy with his
subject, applies Trotsky's own approach to the 'flawed'
character of Trotsky himself, thereby also revealing his own
'flaws'.

It will be argued in this chapter that Deutscher's historiographical achievements must be measured against problems
which are similar to those in Trotsky's work, but compounded
by a real scholarly sophistication. Compelling as the Trotsky
trilogy may be (— compelling as the *History of the Russian
Revolution* might be —), there are mechanisms at work in
Deutscher's writing which establish conclusions in advance,
while leaving real problems of the transition to socialism in
abeyance. Deutscher's relevant work is more integral than that
of his contemporaries considered in previous chapters. The
analysis will follow that of Trotsky's historical work in Chapter
Three, taking a narrative chronological sequence centring first
on *Stalin* (1949) and then on the Trotsky trilogy (1954, 1959,
1963), using the lesser writings as supplementary evidence.
Deutscher's broader views on transition in east and west will
then be established, prior to the critical examination of his
theory of history. For it is in the latter that a proper understanding of Deutscher's view of politics as tragedy is made
possible.

'Stalin'

Deutscher's biography of Stalin is rather less exceptional a
work than his Trotsky trilogy, though it is without doubt a vast
improvement on Trotsky's own attempt to understand Stalin.
The sombre tone of Deutscher's study accords with its subject
matter; the grey eminence of Stalin is reflected in a grey narrative. As Deutscher comments wryly: 'What was striking in the
General Secretary was that there was nothing striking about
him.'[2] Though the early parts of the text present Stalin's
formation as one which is determined by Georgian charac-

teristics of backwardness, Deutscher does not explicitly extend Trotsky's typology of personification. He hints that Stalin in power might be understood as a Pharaoh without pyramids, but does not develop the parallel suggested between Stalinism and Oriental Despotism. Later he parallels Stalin with a whole series of great Tsars.[3]

In Deutscher's final judgement, Stalin belongs to the breed of great revolutionary despots, following Cromwell, Robespierre and Napoleon. The early implication that Stalin represents Russian backwardness (while Trotsky implicitly represents cosmopolitanism) is now qualified by the introduction of a striking Hegelian ruse of history. Deutscher views primitive accumulation and forced industrialisation as the necessary costs of civilisation.[4] Stalin here is the spirit of Soviet progress *malgré lui*. Russia's 'backward, Asiatic' condition is, for Deutscher, her tragedy rather than her fault; Stalin's historic task in this context was to undertake to 'drive barbarism out of Russia by barbaric means'.[5] On this basis, Deutscher refuses the parallel of Stalin and Hitler, on the grounds that Stalin was a revolutionary, however self-contradictory. Stalin's contradiction drives the Soviet Union forward: the effect of Stalinism was to produce an obstacle to modernisation, which would undermine Stalinism through deeds of its own initiative. On the register of history, Deutscher views both Stalin and Stalinism as forces which are progressive, despite themselves.

Portrayed even thus, synoptically and from the perspectives germane to this study, Deutscher's argument is provocative in the extreme. Deutscher presents history as the fulfilment of prescribed tasks. The ruse or irony of history dictates that roles be switched, so that the actors find themselves unwittingly playing out their enemies' parts.[6] The devices summoned to present such an argument are familiar. Generative metaphor in *Stalin* is predominantly theatrical in form; gynaecological and geological metaphor is less frequently employed.[7] In at least one place in the text, Deutscher acknowledges that his discussion of Stalin is metaphorical; in no place, however, does he set out the precise meaning of, or justification for, his dependence on theatrical imagery.[8] Theatrical imagery as applied in Deutscher's work establishes a particular kind of generative framework: each historical act or deed becomes part of a sequence or unfolding which evolves in dramatic terms. Early in the piece, for example, Deutscher puts the following interpretation on the formative dispute between the young Trotsky and the young Stalin: 'As in a Greek tragedy there was a streak of fatalistic consistency in the circumstances and accidents that created the first elements of the conflict long before the real drama'.[9] Fate, as it were, gave an early sign of the tragedy which was to come. Related to his sense of the theatrical, but rather more impressive, is Deutscher's reliance on dualistic imagery. Deutscher speaks of the two faces of the revolution, the two dimensions in Leninism (East and West, skewed East in Stalinism), the two dimensions of Lenin: as ideologue and as bureaucrat, the dualistic structure of the Bolshevik party: body and spirit.[10] Stalinism is presented as a combination of Bolshevism and Byzantium, Russia as a contradictory combination of East and West.[11] Russia and Stalinism are understood as both revolutionary and traditional; Bolshevism bifurcates into two parties, a party of revolution and one of tradition; the fate of Eastern Europe after the Second World War is seen as a combination of conquest and revolution, of retrogression and progression.[12]

In this, Deutscher draws explicitly and implicitly on Goethe's image of the duality of souls, the Janus faces of Jacobinism. The image recurs frequently in Deutscher's work, in major and minor writings alike.[13] For Deutscher, history is never simply what it seems. One significant image bears recounting here. In a reflective article upon his own practice in the writing of *Stalin*, Deutscher cites Macaulay on the Cromwellian revolution. The latter tells the story of a fairy who, by nature, was condemned to appear at certain seasons in the form of a foul and poisonous snake. Those who injured her were excluded from her blessings. Those who pitied and protected here were rewarded. 'Such a spirit is Liberty', said Macaulay. Woe to those who, in disgust, venture to crush her; happy are those who, tolerant, are at length rewarded. Deutscher adds: 'Nobody has personified the spirit of the Russian Revolution in this its dual character more fully than Stalin.'[14]

Deutscher's reliance on this dualistic imagery and the imagery of masking is also indicative of his dependence on Dialectical Materialism. Things are not simply what they are or appear, they are something else; they can be decoded in order to reveal their true nature, their symbols can be interpreted to yield their true or essential moral message. Stalin understood as Robespierre and Bonaparte, Trotsky as Danton blended with Babeuf, Russia presented as a combination of Oriental and European components or of market and plan,[15] all such couplets demonstrate the principle of the unity of opposites, in which one element will eventually come to dominate the other. Dualism in Deutscher is therefore a historical expression of the traditional marxist logic which makes a motor of contradiction. The most novel use of such imagery in *Stalin* is singularly theatrical: it is the image of masking, with its Greek as well as contemporary connotations. Actors wear masks, are unmasked, express private and public personas.[16] Thus are notions of deception and duplicity introduced into the explanation of the peculiar turns of Soviet history. This is true to the extent that, in one place, Stalin seems to re-enact Biblical parable, speaking Esau's native tongue (Georgian) in order to put forward Jacob's (Russian) interest.[17] Deutscher implies in all this that history runs in deep subcurrents, setting up appearances which have no direct relationship to essential reality (unless, perhaps, they are its inverse). The ruse selects agents to complete her tasks, switching her options without notice, mere mortals find themselves undone by the cleavage of their intentions and the outcomes of their deeds. Yet the theatrical scaffolding which supports *Stalin* is incomplete; more developed, it is fully exposed only in the Trotsky trilogy, to which we must turn in order to extend criticism to its full breadth.

The Trotsky trilogy

The Prophet Armed — Unarmed — Outcast is the pinnacle of Deutscher's achievement as historian. The product of twelve years' work, it shows Deutscher at his literary best. The trilogy represents a full development of Deutscher's theatrical orientation in historiography. Here the tragic mode is ever present, rather than occasionally summoned as it is in *Stalin*: indeed, it sets the very tenor of the opus, expanding as the story develops, for Trotsky, unlike Lenin or Stalin, is given to theatrical presentation. The Preface to *The Prophet Armed*, which is perhaps the least intense or personalised of the three volumes, explains that Trotsky's life is to be understood as a classical (Greek) tragedy, 'or rather a reproduction of classical tragedy in secular terms of modern politics'.[18] The extent to which it is secular is arguable, for in the Trotsky trilogy, God (History) speaks through its prophets. Like Stalin, Trotsky acts out the opposite of his intention, with the difference that good producing evil (as contrasted with the opposite in Stalin's case) is more deserving of human sympathy. The aura is certainly Sophoclean — like Oedipus, Trotsky strives after his object too well, ultimately achieving his own undoing in circumstances not fully known to him.[19] Trotsky is more important for Deutscher than Stalin or Lenin because only he is the fully tragic figure of the October Revolution.

Deutscher summarises his perspective in closing *The Prophet Armed*; the sense of tragedy then heightens through the successive volumes. 'At the very pinnacle of power Trotsky, like the protagonist of a classical tragedy, stumbled'[20] — Trotsky, that is to say, had been doomed to act out the practices which he earlier had damned as 'substitutionism'. This presentation of Trotsky exposes Deutscher's philosophy of history, which can for the moment be encapsulated in the contrasting titles given the chapters which close the first and last volumes. The final chapter of the first volume of the trilogy, covering the period 1879–1921, is entitled 'Defeat in Victory'. The final chapter in the last volume, 1929–40, bears the title 'Victory in Defeat'. In the interim volume, 1921–9, Trotsky's experience is also viewed as 'victory in defeat', for even though the opposition is defeated, its cause is vindicated by the mere existence of the workers' state.[21] Finally, in Deutscher's overall assessment of the period, 'Stalin's victory over Trotsky concealed a heavy element of defeat while Trotsky's defeat was pregnant with victory'.[22]

The dialectics of dualism in Deutscher indicate that, while so impressive, Trotsky's victory is yet pyrrhic; whereas his eventual defeat and murder symbolise somehow the impending victory of his ideas, both within the USSR and without. Vacating his corporeal being, his spirit lives on with the mole. Trotsky was bound to win within the USSR, for Deutscher, as Stalin was doomed to act out Trotsky's earlier economic ideas; he was bound to be victorious in the West as, having been re-routed through Asia, world revolution could now return to the West. Trotsky's historical tragedy appears in this sense as one of timing rather than casting. He was the right man, but the occasion was wrong. Trotsky had been structurally mistimed: history should have planted his seed not in Yanovka or even Odessa, but in Berlin or Vienna. Here Deutscher seems to introduce a theory of revolutionary cycles, which will be analysed later; for the present, suffice it to say that the logic of this theory is to suggest that Trotsky's fate was to act without being summoned by History. Deutscher's explanation of the failure of the Fourth International is similarly constructed to his explanation of Trotsky's own failure: it had not been summoned by a historical highpoint in struggle. Trotsky himself bravely but foolishly called History's bluff, forcing the plot. It is this fact which dooms him to the role of Bolshevism's Cassandra.[23] This image of Trotsky as Cassandra is one with which Deutscher evidently associates. Deutscher sees his own location as being in the watchtower of the modern world.[24] Like Trotsky, he sees his own fate as Cassandra's — both tell the truth, though Deutscher predicts while Trotsky prophesies, but both go unheeded. As Christopher Hill puts it, modifying Deutscher's own description of Trotsky, 'it was natural' for Deutscher 'that he should be able to see himself in history, inevitably struggling against the inevitable',[25] in his case *au dessus de la mêlée*.

Cassandra is, however, but one of the many personas in which the tragic figure of Trotsky appears. Trotsky is also cast in Deutscher's Russian tragedy as Lear, as Hamlet, as the last citizen of Atlantis, — an image which jars with that of Trotsky's utopia in *Literature and Revolution* — as well as in numerous Titanic and Homeric guises.[26] Beyond these images and even more evocative is the character of Sisyphus, already suggested in Hill's modification of Deutscher above. Speaking of Trotsky's organisational struggles in the 'stillborn' Fourth International, Deutscher portrays his character as follows: 'Thus at his sunset Trotsky watched for the last time the rock he rolled up his dreary mountain rolling down the slope again.'[27] The image is struck again, less explicitly, in Deutscher's conclusion:

> Even if it were true that it is man's fate to stagger in pain and blood from defeat to defeat and to throw off one yoke only to bend his neck beneath another — even then man's longing for a different destiny would still, like pillars of fire, relieve the darkness and gloom of the endless desert through which he has been wandering with no promised

land beyond. And no one in our age has expressed these longings as vividly and sacrificially as Trotsky . . .[28]

— sacrificially, because the Soviet Union has advanced. The picture is one in which great men are set the quest of labouring like Sisyphus in order that mankind might progress. As in Camus' retelling of the tale, Sisyphus functions as the proletarian of the gods, wretched and futile yet content. The lot of these latter-day followers of Sisyphus is, however, not only to be locked into repetition but also into rupture: for social progress is achieved through the destruction of great men and the masses who they inspire.

The development of Deutscher's sense of history as tragedy is nowhere better witnessed than in the theatrical metaphor within which the text of the trilogy is constructed. Images of tragedy, theatre, drama, overwhelm the text.[29] As elsewhere, Deutscher seems to be self-conscious in his use of metaphor but, like Trotsky, seems unaware of the dangers involved in the use of images of necessity.[30] Dualistic imagery is similarly extended in the Trotsky trilogy. The theatrical dimension of masking is given special emphasis, particularly in one passage where Deutscher suggests that Trotsky's flaw was to wear *no* mask, to be too honest.[31] Deutscher seems to apply mechanically the Hegelian distinction between essence and appearance, as a contrast between depth and surface. This tendency is especially marked in the choice of the image of clothing, an extension, as it were, of the earlier theme of Esau and Jacob to the explanation of Stalin's alleged application of Trotsky's policies: 'Popular apathy allowed Stalin to steal Trotsky's clothes with impunity. Trotsky still consoled himself with the thought that Stalin would not be able to wear them, because they would not fit him.'[32] And later: 'Under any regime allowing a modicum of political controversy, a party or faction which has the misfortune of seeing its rivals steal its clothes may be still permitted to assist with dignity at the realisation of its own program by others.'[33]

While an extensive analysis of Deutscher's historiography will be taken up later in this chapter, certain criticisms can already be advanced here. It is by no means clear how Deutscher intends his imagery to be read. The result of his art obfuscates rather than clarifies. Does the thief determine history by his action, or does he merely fulfil a part prescribed

by the ruse? If clothes make the man, then how does 'essence'
actually relate to 'appearance' in such an image? Is the theft
merely a public act, with private connotations of a quite
different kind? Should the critical view focus on the clothing,
or on the bearer? Here, as elsewhere, Deutscher shows an
affinity with writers like the Victorian prophets, especially
Carlyle. Carlyle speaks in his lectures on heroes of clothing as
form to substance:

> All substances clothe themselves in forms: but there are
> suitable true forms, and then there are untrue unsuitable
> . . . Forms which *grow* round a substance. . .will correspond
> to the real nature and purport of it, will be true, good; forms
> which are consciously *put* round a substance, bad . . . [this]
> distinguishes true from false in Ceremonial Form, earnest
> solemnity from empty pageant, in all human things.

The living man, Carlyle says, will find himself clothes;[34] but in
Deutscher, clothes seem to play the part, to seek out the actor.
Trotsky's mantle thus falls upon Stalin.

This is perhaps in accordance with Carlyle's observation,
that men pay reverence to clothes rather than their bearers.[35]
Certainly Deutscher seems to accept Carlyle's sense that the
body is the clothing of the Mind. Symbols therefore serve as
Enigma, as both clarification and obfuscation. Men function as
spirits, but clothing envelopes their deeds in mystery.[36] The
sense of enigma in Deutscher's writing is indeed pervasive.
The relationship between character and mask, essence and
immediacy in Deutscher's work remains irresolvable. While
provocative in the extreme, Deutscher's image of clothing does
not rest well with the argument about the 'dualism of souls' on
which he also relies: the former suggests a spatial contrast of
'inner' and 'outer' dimensions, while the latter implies one
compartmentalised whole characterised by internal contradiction. For Deutscher simultaneously argues that Bolshevism,
however clothed, has two souls — marxist and Jacobin, that the
Russian worker can be dichotomised into hero and slave, that
the Soviet Union be understood as a combination of bourgeois
and socialist forms. The Faustian nexus is also present in
Deutscher's view of revolutionary politics as the business of
doing deals with the devil.[37]

Shakespeare is equally present here as Faust. Deutscher says

159

of Trotsky,'If he was an actor, then he was one to whom. . .theatre and life were one',[38] thus conjuring up in the reader's mind the words of *As You Like It*: 'All the world's a stage, and all the men and women merely players. . .' Understood thus as theatre, History allots the parts, hands out the glory and disrepute; it acts as *Geist* in authoring the drama and in allocating vice and virtue. In the Preface to *The Prophet Outcast*, Deutscher argues that, 'In Trotsky's life the ideological debate is as important as the battle scene in Shakespearean tragedy; through it the protagonists' character reveals itself while he is moving towards catastrophe.'[39] Deutscher does not cite the passage in *Hamlet*, though it expresses his view of history well: 'Our wills and fates do so contrary run that our devices still are overthrown; Our thoughts are ours, their ends none of our own. . .' Tamara Deutscher relates that Bradley's *Shakespearean Tragedy* was Isaac's bedside book, along with Collingwood's *The Idea of History*.[40] This should be small surprise, for Deutscher's biography of Trotsky conforms to Bradley's characterisation of the substance of Shakespearean tragedy. For Bradley, the Shakespearean tragedy is a story of high calamity leading to the death of a man in high estate, a fate engendered through human action which itself engineers the tragic outcome, leaving a profound impression of human waste. In Deutscher's world, as in Shakespeare's, 'Everywhere. . .man's thought, translated into act, is transformed into the opposite of itself. . .whatsoever he dreams of doing, he achieves that which he least dreamed of, his own destruction.'[41]

In Deutscher's self-understanding, contemporary history is indeed identical with tragedy. According to Deutscher, 'Trotsky pointed out [in *Literature and Revolution*] that the essence of tragedy lies in the wider conflict between man's awakened mind and his constricting environment, a conflict which is inseparable from man's existence and manifests itself in different forms at different stages of history.'[42] Fate, for Deutscher as for Trotsky, here takes the form of social limits, that is to say, tragedy is identical with life under capitalism, or class society. Socialism must therefore be the end of tragedy, the transcendance of fate, the achievement of a state of social transparency and the realisation of Reason. Deutscher clearly believes that Soviet society achieved such a condition of transparency; only by *1926–1927* was it the case that 'On all sides cleavages arose or reappeared between what men thought [of themselves and others], what they willed and what they did.'[43] Yet the scope of Deutscher's canvas is such as to limit participation to heroes: everyday life under capitalism may be tragic for Deutscher, but the focus remains on great men, on the contest of the base and the sublime. Deutscher turns popular tragedy into aristocratic tragedy; his writing lacks the elements of the popular and the grotesque, the crowd and the fool. The mass suffering which is the fabric of the Soviet experience is not the centre of his focus; rather, his interest is in the fate of the heroic individuals who soil and wash this fabric fouled with blood and sweat. However, Deutscher insists that socialism, the overcoming of this tragic fate, is still possible, indeed, necessary. History therefore takes a final ruthless plunge before the 1859 Preface fulfils itself. The logic of his contemporary analysis remains deeply pessimistic. As Deutscher has it elsewhere: 'We are no longer living in the age of heroic legend — such myths as our epoch has thrown up have all been shabby and extremely short lived.'[44] And, speaking of the Holocaust, Deutscher makes clear the implication that, to modify Adorno, after Auschwitz there can be no talk of politics.[45] On occasions, then, Deutscher's objectives are relatively modest, as when he endorses Trotsky, who he says speaks of 'three basic tragedies — hunger, sex and death — besetting man. Hunger is the enemy that Marxism and the modern labour movement have taken on.'[46] On other occasions, the scenario is brighter and Deutscher, still gripping the maxim that was Trotsky's own — *Dum spiro spero* — intends to ride out the present downturn of the revolutionary cycle and await the revival of classical marxism, when the cast will at last fit the plot and the outcome is tragic only for the class enemy. Despite all, Deutscher does believe history to be on his side.

Deutscher on Russia's transition

Deutscher's analysis of elements of transition in the USSR and his positive projections of the possibility of reform after Stalin have engendered much controversy.[47] In Deutscher's understanding, the film of the Russian Revolution 'is still on', it is not running backwards to capitalist restoration as Trotsky believed, but neither has it stopped in its tracks or returned to its Tsarist roots. The Russian Revolution has, for Deutscher, actually achieved the material prerequisites of socialism *ex post facto*, opening the possibility/necessity of post-Stalin reform.[48] Deutscher accepts Trotsky's thesis in *The Revolution Betrayed* of contradiction and dualism in the Soviet regime between socialist property forms and bourgeois forms of distribution, accepting the dominance of the former over the latter and therefore advocating defence of the USSR.[49] The dualistic form of explanation summoned by Deutscher here is typically ambivalent; dialectics indicates a motor process in which one element, socialism, conquers the other, capitalism. Dualistic imagery predominates in Deutscher's definition of the USSR. In one passage, for example, the argument is put that, 'neither Russia nor China are socialist: theirs are the post capitalist societies which still carry within themselves the heritage of capitalism and contain elements of an even more backward — feudal and prefeudal — civilisation.'[50] The USSR for Deutscher is 'somewhere halfway between capitalism and socialism'; it has made only the 'very first step' on the road of the transition from capitalism, and that implicitly in form rather than substance.[51] The whole period since October has, for Deutscher, been a period of transition; the USSR is only now (1960) seen to be reaping the first benefits of socialism.[52] What are these benefits? Deutscher explains that Stalinism, which represented 'an amalgamation of Marxism with the semi-barbarous and quite barbarous traditions and the primitive magic of an essentially preindustrial, i.e. not merely presocialist but prebourgeois, society'[53] has achieved through industrialisation the degree of modernisation which Marx took to be the prerequisite of socialist revolution. In its present condition, the Soviet Union can be understood, then, as a hybrid combination of two different and opposed components, capitalism and socialism.[54] The notion of the hybrid society might seem at first to be more metaphorically consistent in Deutscher's theory than in Mandel's. But inasmuch as Deutscher, like Mandel, ascribes a teleological power to the contradictory combination, one of the two components must, by necessity, be striving to overcome the other. In Deutscher's vista, the new society must be viewed as heading toward socialism, however slowly and unsurely.

Deutscher shares the analytical premisses of Trotskyist orthodoxy on the question of the Russian transition. It is important to note here that his arguments were widely influential in the Trotskyist movement long after his departure from its organisations: indeed, Deutscher was viewed in some quarters of the movement as the *de facto* theorist of Pabloism. Pablo within, and Deutscher without the Fourth International, alike argued that Stalinism, however distasteful, was the world historic representative of socialism.[55] Deutscher's explanation of the decay of the Russian regime, then, has profoundly impacted popular Trotskyist wisdom. The decimation of the Russian working class during the civil war, the subsequent rise of the bureaucracy, the Stalinist bloodletting help to explain the Soviet Union's present condition, but do not undercut its status as the beacon, the first workers' state. Stalinism serves, however, to bring about its own destruction, for in Deutscher's view, it is the forces which bring about Soviet modernity which provide thereby the basis of Soviet democracy. Stalinist modernisation cuts the political ground of ignorance from under the regime's feet. As the 'irony of history' would have it, progress is produced by repression, by regression. 'I maintain', argued Deutscher in response to critics of his controversial views, 'that urbanisation and modernisation are "curing" the Soviet Union from Stalinism.'[56] Whether reform was to be slow and gradual, as the generative metaphor implies, was never entirely evident. In one place, for example, Deutscher, like Mandel, anticipates the Soviet peoples preparing themselves for another world-shaking historical experience. Elsewhere Deutscher argues, this time in a way reminiscent of Mandel's arguments for the West, that Soviet Stalinism will be overcome by a three or four hour working day and free higher education.[57]

The analytical compatibility of Deutscher's argument and that of orthodox Trotskyism is further witnessed in his refusal of alternative explanations of the USSR. He inveighs against the argument that the Soviet regime is a mere extension of Tsarism, and attacks E. H. Carr's stress on continuity in the Russian experience on the basis of his own claim that change (in property forms) is the dominant historical fact.[58] Earlier intimations, like those in *Stalin*, that Deutscher might follow up the Asiatic heritage into the dispute over the Asiatic mode of production, remain unfulfilled. Similarly, Deutscher refuses Djilas' argument for a new class on the traditional Trotskyist grounds, that the ruling group lacks legal property rights in the means of production.[59] Despite his traditionalism, he admits the ambiguous location of the new ruling group — over and against the workers it nevertheless professes a 'socialist' ideology.[60] Domination and suffering are, however, seen as the necessary costs of the achievement of the transition thus far. The revolution by 1967 has, for Deutscher, 'by no means come to a close. It is still on the move.'[61] Indeed, Deutscher goes so far as to predict, again like Mandel, the revival of a Trotskyist hegemony within the USSR:

> Through the forcible modernisation of the structure of society Stalinism had worked towards its own undoing and had prepared the ground for the return of classical marxism. . .The open vindication [of Trotsky] is bound to come in any case, not perhaps before Stalin's aging epigones have left the stage.[62]

For Deutscher, the Russian Revolution maintains its universal import: '*The message of 1917 remains valid for the world at large.*'[63] On this note we can turn to the discussion of Deutscher's understanding of the transition to socialism in the West, for, like Trotsky and Mandel, Deutscher's view of the West is that through the grid of the Russian experience.

Deutscher on the achievement of socialism in the West

Deutscher agrees, with Bolshevik tradition, that the Russian Revolution was a good idea misapplied. The revolution could not but be 'betrayed', occurring as it did in inappropriate conditions. In this conclusion, as in his basic premises, Deutscher's thinking is entirely orthodox. In anthropology, Deutscher seems to identify with Trotsky's claimed preference for the combination of an immediate pessimism with a long-term optimism, a position which signifies a conceived tension between 'actual' and 'potential' in history. As has been shown, however, his philosophy of history seems, at least in part, to denote the impossibility of socialism, suggesting rather an immediate optimism within a desperate pessimism.[64] In philosophy, Deutscher adhered to the tradition of Dialectical Materialism with a sophisticated turn of the dualistic notion of contradiction, where the unity of opposites produces the victory of one or other. In political economy, Deutscher follows the tradition of focusing on the labour theory of value, and restates the orthodox principle that the basic contradiction of capitalism is that between the immanent socialisation of the production process and the private character of appropriation.[65] The objective socialisation of the production process is seen by Deutscher as providing a socialist telos within capitalism; efficiency is taken to be the primary value of socialism, and in accordance with the standard explanation of Soviet backwardness, abundance is seen as its real achievement.[66] Productive forces are ascribed a determining power; planning is presumed to be definitionally expansionary.[67] Deutscher follows Trotsky in reading the 1859 Preface as proof of the obsolescence of the nation state.[68] He in a sense outdoes Trotsky here, with his economistic logic suggesting as it does that Soviet modernisation must bring with it superstructural democracy.

Deutscher's understanding of politics is similarly orthodox. His theory of class is 'old left' rather than 'new left', if such a distinction has any meaning. He argues, like Trotsky, that the working class as traditionally understood remains the privileged social actor of the socialist movement,suggesting that critics of this view should look to their own petty-bourgeois class roots in order to understand their folly.[69] The task of intellectuals for Deutscher, accords with the traditional proposal put forward by Kautsky and Lenin: intellectuals must carry the socialist idea back into the working class, for the (American) 'working class remains the decisive agency of socialism'. According to Deutscher, the working class has been bought off by the welfare state, but the sleeping giant must yet reawake.[70] In his scenario, a United Socialist States of Europe can be achieved by the year 2000.[71] In keeping with the 'automatic' logic of these arguments, Deutscher avoids any discussion of how socialism might be prefigured by the radicalising of democracy or the existing social relations or by the pursuit of social self-management. Indeed, his very philosophy of history votes against the prefigurative argument, in its presumption that good can be achieved by evil means and that fate rests in history's hands.

In terms of political projection, Deutscher endorses the theory of Permanent Revolution, in general if not always in specific terms. For Deutscher, the theory of Permanent

Revolution is proven and lived out by the revolutionary events of the twentieth century. Trotskyism proves itself, most notably, through its unlikely but unconscious representatives, Mao and Khrushchev.[72] Mao, especially, is seen by Deutscher to obey the logic of Permanent Revolution: the theory of Permanent Revolution is thus verified, contrary to Trotsky's expectations, via the East. Having shifted toward the East after the Russian Revolution, the epicentre of world revolution is now returning to the West in accordance with a general cyclical trend.[73] For Deutscher, the first cycle of revolution was initiated by 1917, to be followed by a second cycle after the Second World War. This second cycle was one of revolution from above, where revolution was installed 'on the point of a bayonet', with the exception of the Chinese experience, which Deutscher views as a revolution from below. The strategy implicit in Deutscher's argument is clear: we must await the third cycle. Ironically, therefore, Trotsky is not the man of the second cycle, yet it is he who explains why Mao is the revolutionary of the second cycle.[75] This theory of cycles in Deutscher helps explain his hostility to the formation of the Fourth International in 1938. The new International appeared too early, unprompted, in the wrong act; it proved to be, in the appropriate metaphor, a stillbirth in the absence of an international revolutionary movement to breathe life into it. What matters for Deutscher, in contrast to Mandel, is neither the existence nor the idea of the International, but the idea of internationalism.[76] The new International was premature for Deutscher, based as it was on the unrealistic expectation that the epicentre of revolution had already returned to the West. Living and thinking against the current, Deutscher sought to keep 'classical marxism' alive so that it could later ride the third revolutionary wave to socialism in the West.

Deutscher's historiography and philosophy of history

While Deutscher's practice of history has come under increasing criticism of late,[77] such criticism is conspicuous in its attention to matters of detail such as mistakes of fact (— natural blemishes on a pioneering work —) at the expense of more general considerations. Presumably this is the case not only because the dominant historiographical consciousness turns naturally to questions of empirical detail, but also because some critics (like Mandel and Broué) share the Trotskyist conception of history as the unfolding of a socialist telos. In the foregoing analysis, in contrast, Deutscher's reliance on the metaphor of theatre and tragedy has been especially emphasised. It has been argued here that Deutscher's history depends on the ideas of Goethe and Shakespeare, which he reads across into history perceived as a world stage. This criticism can now be extended in order to take up the question of Deutscher's use of an Hegelian ruse of history and the problems which this ruse engenders in his work. However, it is first appropriate to discuss as preliminary Deutscher's historical self-understanding and his specific arguments about necessity and personality in history.

Deutscher spells out his historical self-understanding in several places. He explains, for instance, in the 1961 Introduction to *Stalin* that the task of the historian in comparison to the political fighter, is to portray the irreversible, the inevitable. 'The historian. . .cannot help being a determinist, or behaving as one if he is not.'[78] Deutscher articulates his position in response to the charge of apologia for Stalinism, arguing that he rejects the inevitability of Stalinism as a partisan, but accepts it in his capacity as scholar. Scholarly judgement about inevitability is not personal for Deutscher, who holds, on the contrary, that 'Some of the proudest moments in man's history are those when he struggles against the inevitable; and this his struggle, too, is inevitable.'[79] In another reply to criticism, this time from Raymond Aron, Deutscher further clarifies his historiographical views: 'I certainly take the view that the human will is "free" only to the extent to which it acts as the promoter of "necessity", that is within limits circumscribed by conditions external to it.'[80]

Deutscher formally refuses the 'great man' argument because it undercuts the case for inevitability. Significantly, the test case here is Trotsky's explanation of Lenin's role in the October Revolution. Deutscher takes Trotsky's argument about Lenin's indispensability to be a denial of historical materialism. His alternative is to fall back on Plekhanov's monistic definition of historic forces, circumscribing analysis of the problems of accident and the reality of the Russian Party in 1917 by reinserting into the picture the telos of certainty.[81] MacIntyre suggests that the choice of authority is appropriate,

167

for Deutscher's trilogy is the kind of work we would imagine a latter-day Plekhanov writing.[82] Deutscher attempts to reinforce his case for inevitability by introducing the Chinese and Yugoslavian experiences, where 'the revolutionary trend found or created its organ in such human material as was available'[83] — a highly significant phrase which occurs again elsewhere.[84] Mankind is the material with which history works: the philosophy of history at work here is brutal.

For Deutscher, history is simply the realm of necessity. Stalinism is viewed as historically necessary, as is Trotsky's own 'optimistic tragedy'.[85] Deutscher makes clear his view that destalinisation is to be understood with reference to the historic forces at work. Great men here represent class forces.[86] The clear implication is that Stalin was chosen by History to do its bidding. As he puts it in *Russia After Stalin*: 'The trend of the time found in Stalin its "organ". If it hadn't been Stalin it would have been another.' Stalin was merely 'the vehicle of anonymous forces at work in the background'.[87] The logic involved clearly suggests that Trotsky's defeat was a happy fate: in power, his lot should have been tragically to act out Stalin's part. History here is presented as a closed and shut case. But if History seeks out and finds material adequate to its own ends, why then should socialists bother to struggle at all? Deutscher provides two variations of an argument intended to foreclose such questioning. Trotsky, he says in one place, compared marxism with Calvinism: determinism, like the doctrine of predestination, serves to strengthen will, as will is an expression of a higher necessity. Elsewhere, it is Bukharin who offers this explanation: the Leninist philosophy of historical determinism, in common with the Puritan doctrine of predestination, peculiarly, extends the dimension of moral responsibility by its sense of certainty.[88] It is the argument we have met before, in Plekhanov.

The inadequacy of Deutscher's proposed solution to the question of the role of will in history is underlined by his fascination with personality. Considering here only the case of Trotsky, it can be seen that Deutscher's position is innerly ambivalent: he denies the 'great man' argument, yet dedicates his life's work to the biography of just one such, producing a study which presents great men as creators of history in the manner of Carlyle. However much Trotsky is Bolshevism incarnate or cosmopolitanism personified, however much he be the tragic figure or victim of history, it must nevertheless be recognised that he is still Trotsky — a great individual whose historic achievements were intimately bound up with the exercise of his own *will*. More generally speaking, Deutscher's identification with personality is written into the very nature of his major works: they are all, uniformly, biographical. Deutscher turns his original plan for Soviet history 'à la Thiers'[89] into several parallel Soviet histories constructed around the medium of the revolution's great personalities. Where E. H. Carr, for example, chose to write an extensive and integral history of Soviet Russia, Deutscher instead writes three *biographical* variations on the theme — one of Lenin (incomplete), one of Stalin, one of Trotsky. Tragedy, as Deutscher understands, centres on individuals, even though they appear the playthings of History or represent classes. In few modern biographies is the sense of identification between author and subject so marked as in Deutscher's Trotsky trilogy. Deutscher himself knew, like Trotsky, what it meant to stand against the current, and both saw themselves as representing History against history itself.

The idea that one should refuse fate and stand against it did not, however, overturn Deutscher's more fundamental premiss, that History sets itself only such problems as it can solve using whatever human 'material' comes to hand. Will is a negligible factor, in Deutscher's understanding, because intention is historically ineffective. History, to invert Marx's maxim of *The Eighteenth Brumaire*, makes itself through men, even over them, just as it pleases. The Hegelian ruse of history is introduced to explain this paradox of modern times. In Soviet history, Deutscher argues:

the Hegelian *List der Geschichte*, the sly irony of history, comes into its own. Circumstances force men to move in the most unforeseen directions and give their doctrines the most unexpected contents and significance. Men and doctrines thus serve purposes sometimes diametrically opposed to those they had envisaged.[90]

The Hegelian ruse functions here as a theory of progress through barbarism. Deutscher cites Hegel to the effect that 'History is not the realm of happiness' but rather of achieve-ment.[91] As in Hegel's *Philosophy of History*, so in Deutscher's theory does history evolve from East to West, only with rather different temporality. As in Hegel, so in Deutscher do great men act out the world spirit unknowingly, finding themselves doomed to unhappiness. As in Hegel, but unconsciously so in Deutscher, is the unfolding of the *Weltgeist* a theological perspective. Present barbarism, however prolonged, remains for Deutscher the prelude to the fulfilment of world history in socialism. Deutscher seems oblivious to the apparent logic of his argument, which seems to suggest simultaneously the permanence of barbarity and the impossibility of socialism understood as the willed product of human activity, rather than its impending achievement.

For there is an abundance of images in Deutscher's work which contradict the unfolding socialist telos. Not only do Faust, Hamlet, Sisyphus and Cassandra present the image of desolation and futility. More specific images also occur, like that of the pendulum of history swinging between progress and reaction, seemingly reflecting the duality of good and evil in 'human nature'.[92] Yet the dominant image in Deutscher is that of progress through regression rather than that of the vicious circle of repetition. Deutscher's momentary insights into the possibility of repetition are cancelled out by constant references to necessity. The most notorious of these references was formulated on the occasion of the Hungarian Revolution of 1956. Here was a case, said Deutscher, in which the Hungarian rebels strove heroically but foolishly to 'wind back the clock' which had been set forward by communism.[93] Perhaps it is 'progress' rather than socialism which is written into history. As Deutscher has it: 'In art as well as in science progress is achieved by a combination of "repulsion" and "attraction" and the tension between these two forces.' He goes on to cite Hegel, to the effect that every step forward continues tradition as well as changing it.[94] In another place, he articulates his position with reference to Louis Blanc:

'What do we know, after all?' Louis Blanc once wrote in a similar context. 'In order that progress be realised, perhaps it is necessary that all evil alternatives be exhausted. The life of mankind is very long, and the number of possible solutions very limited. All revolution is useful, in this sense at least, that every revolution takes care of one dangerous alternative.'[95]

But Bolshevism has never transcended the Jacobin alternative. The lonely figure of Deutscher was still to advocate that dangerous alternative, and thereby to parody Collingwood rather than to follow him: for his argument was effectively that progress was gain *through* losses. In this regard, Deutscher managed to combine Carlyle and Macauley, vulcanising together a romantic anti-industrialism with an unrepentant modernism.

The political results of Deutscher's philosophy of history

The ruse of history does more in Deutscher's work than foreclose the political discussion about transition. It serves to travesty history, to deflect the analysis of its specificities into the contemplation of realms of duality and duplicity. Deutscher seems to develop a quasi-Hegelian spiritualism via Carlyle: Deutscher's practice of history is necessarily representational or emblematical because nothing is what it seems. Actors fuse with the scenes or forces they represent; History remains enigmatical, or rather Deutscher produces a history which is enigmatic. The ruse or irony of history in Deutscher serves to obfuscate the real problems involved in history and historiography: the language of philosophy of history, whether positive or ironical, serves to obscure the events in history, personification prevents the analysis of personality. A series of examples can be produced in order to establish more concretely this case against Deutscher.

Deutscher repeats the popular misunderstanding which sees Stalin as fulfilling the policies of Trotsky after the latter is discredited.[96] The image corresponds with Deutscher's theatrical presentation of Soviet history, where roles find bearers and the ruse uses the means available to her own ends. With reference to the specific arguments and practices of Trotsky and Stalin, Deutscher's argument is simply indefensible. Not only is Trotsky's disdain for forced collectivisation widely acknowledged, but also, as Day establishes, the early proponent of isolationist war communism later took up an integrationist position and was at least on occasion ambivalent in his attitude to the relationship between market and plan.[97] Stalin took up, extended and applied in the bloodiest way

171

possible, the policies of war communism, not the policies of Trotsky or the Left Opposition. If Stalin can be said to have 'applied' Trotsky's policies at all, then it can only be in a strictly delimited historical and not theatrical way. Nor can Preobrazhensky be legitimately cast as the *de facto* theorist of Stalinism, unless the argument about the irrelevance of intention is both strictly adhered to and justified.[98] The specific differences between Deutscher's actors are simply obliterated by such argument.

The same problem emerges in Deutscher's scenario of leadership alternatives in the young Soviet state. In his obituary of Stalin, Deutscher argues that:

> If Lenin had lived longer he would have had to become either a Stalin or a Trotsky, for these two men embodied two solutions to the dilemma of the twenties. Yet Lenin could probably become neither . . . in a sense both these characters were blended in him.[99]

The result is puzzling. Stalinism has already been decreed necessary and inevitable, regardless of whether it be applied by Trotsky or by Stalin allegedly using Trotsky's ideas. How Lenin could force back this necessity is by no means apparent. But the distortion produced by Deutscher's argument is more extensive yet. Were these absolutely the only 'alternatives'? What of a Preobrazhensky road to socialism, one of decades of competition between market and plan, or a similar Trotskyist policy? What of a Bukharinist agrarian alternative, or what of a possible policy produced by some combination of these? Deutscher ignores the existence of theoretically possible alternatives. History in its specificity and complexity simply does not fit onto Deutscher's stage.

Perhaps the most significant convenient use of the irony of history, however, relates to the treatment of the problem of Jacobinism. Deutscher employs this irony to explain Trotsky's apparently contradictory behaviour before and after October. He argues that Trotsky was doomed to act out the politics which he had earlier condemned as 'substitutionism' in *Our Political Tasks*. 'It was another of history's ironies that Trotsky, the hater of the Leviathan, should have become the first harbinger of its resurrection.'[100] The literary use of the device of irony here prevents Deutscher from confronting Trotsky's

172

Jacobinism — for Trotsky's shift after power was no 'irony of history', but a switch of orientation into the Jacobin problematic, from the necessitarian logic of the Second International into an attempt to make history do it faster. Neither Hegel nor Shakespeare, nor Dialectical Materialism, ought properly be summoned to explain this shift, which should rather be rendered in theoretical and political terms. In thus avoiding the Jacobin problematic Deutscher unwittingly portrays the dualism peculiar to Jacobinism as the dilemma of modern politics as such. For the 'duality of souls' belongs to the Jacobin tradition, not to the human condition.[101] Deutscher cannot confront the problem of Jacobinism because he is a Jacobin himself. Revolution from above for the good of humanity is his standpoint. Jacobinism in Deutscher takes precisely the form of the combination of two souls, one heretical, the other orthodox. Deutscher never experiences political power and consequently does not recognise (or act out) Bolshevism's authoritarian face. Consequently, he blames the paradoxical result of Bolshevik politics — which seeks to change the world for its own good — on History rather than on Bolshevism. But the Faustian pact is a problem not for humanity, only for those who engage it.

From his own perspective in the watchtower, neither the political realities of Bolshevism nor the historical subtleties of the Russian experience are completely visible. What remains lacking is the view from the ground. While the director has remained inside his theatre, history has continued to be made — outside.

Conclusions

Isaac Deutscher is a compelling writer, perhaps even more so than Trotsky. His biting satire of Khrushchev, the *muzhik* on world safari, his piercing criticisms of Pasternak and Ehrenburg, his pathetic portrayal of the 'half-real and half-imaginary character', the 'Polrugarian Minister', reveal a literary skill rare among political commentators.[102] His characterisations of the tragic hero, Trotsky, and the triumphant Marshal Stalin are without parallel in the English language literature on the Russian experience. His is truly a nostalgic historiography. The breadth of his learning and culture, the

173

wealth of images, biblical, theatrical and mythological, which make up his texts, all serve to carry the reader through his arguments. Deutscher sees into the minds of his subjects, above all Trotsky, but is too close to them to develop a critical perspective. As in Trotsky's best historical writing, the sympathetic reader is swept thereby into an acceptance of the author's premises and conclusions, into the acceptance of the certainty, inevitability and 'optimistic tragedy' of history.

Critical marxism has long been bound up with literature, and its best presentations have often taken literary form. Yet the distinction between literature and history is nevertheless worth maintaining. As Momigliano argues, against Hayden White, history may be rhetorical, or tragic, but it is not rhetoric or tragedy; in literature evidence is optional not compulsory.[103] There is no 'true' history, only competing interpretations of history; this means that appeals to 'History' are inherently suspect, and that, *pace* Deutscher, history can only be rewritten: it cannot be 're-enacted' in any theatrical sense. It follows from the argument in this chapter that if Deutscher does, for all his shortcomings, 'tell the truth' of modern society, then the outcome should be quiet despair rather than a sense of optimism, whether 'tragic' or not. Doubtless it is Deutscher's ability to plumb the depths of the modern 'human condition' which goes some way to explaining his influence: for the independent Bolshevik historian has produced works which sustain the interpretations of liberal scholar and marxist activist alike. His self-proclaimed political beliefs provide the independent Calvinist Bolshevik with secure reasons for continuing the struggle; while, for the scholar, the effect of Deutscher's work is to produce a speculative feeling, conducive to the contemplation of the impossibility of intentional action, of the contradictory ways and appetites of men. These are, of course, necessary and productive sources of contemplation, and no one would deny the enigmatic centrality of the characters of Faust or Hamlet in the civilisation which is called modernity, nor the legitimacy of their intellectual consideration. Presented as history, however, the effect of such matters in Deutscher's work deflects scrutiny away from the possible to the inevitable, and away from the realm of freedom to that of necessity. As Sedgwick puts it, Deutscher's 'extraordinary dramaturgical and poetic gifts led him to operate within a group of concepts that have absolutely no place in any analytical work of social history or social theory: particularly those of tragic irony, tragic destiny, tragic hero'.[104] Sedgwick's judgement may be overstated. If, alternatively, the relationship between literature and politics is to be viewed as integral, the argument shifts to the sense that Deutscher's tragic mode is less inappropriate than it is misdirected. If the quest for some kind of historiographical 'authenticity' is rejected, then it needs to be recognised that Deutscher's limit is in the aristocratic bent of his mode of tragic presentation. For if Soviet history reads ultimately as a tragedy, then it is the popular suffering which is its fabric and not the struggles of its empyrean heroes. In this regard Deutscher, like Trotsky, seems to place the people in the audience or outside the theatre rather than on the stage. Deutscher's use of aristocratic personification is simultaneously historically inaccurate and politically insulting to the Soviet people, the human 'material' who endured forced industrialisation, collectivisation and purge trials, and who perished in the war against fascism. History in Deutscher functions as fate; its outcome is a historiography which is morally indefensible, for it avoids responsibility in politics.

It might be said that Deutscher was less a political thinker than a 'man of letters'. As much else, this is a judgement which is equally true of Deutscher as of Trotsky, and this is so, even if Deutscher is the heroic man of letters to Trotsky's heroic figure as king and prophet. Deutscher accepts the injunction of Machiavelli and Carlyle, to look upon and imitate the great man. Both Trotsky and Deutscher stand as prophets, alone; happily, perhaps, Deutscher was never to become a prophet armed. Deutscher's own marxism was clearly modelled on that of Trotsky. Like Machiavelli's archers, Deutscher fires his theoretical arrows high, attempting to reach the target, but falling short of an emancipatory marxism. Deutscher's interpretation of the 1859 Preface closely resembles Trotsky's: in common with the Second International, both thought of socialism as the product of (nationalised) economic growth. Trotsky and Deutscher also share the peculiar view of history as theodicy, where human progress can be achieved over the bodies of the masses. Deutscher's premiss that negative forces could achieve positive acts, is entirely in keeping with Trotsky's position on means and ends. All that is sacred is consequently profaned, for, as Marshall Berman puts it in his analysis of

Faust, if good can be created through evil then the maxim should be reversed. 'The road to heaven is paved with bad intentions';[105] Stalin is our saviour, politics becomes demonic; the workers dig their own graves, and this is called 'socialism'. Certainly the criticism of Deutscher, of all Trotskyists, provides the best insight into the nexus between the problematics of Stalinism and Trotskyism. Its single most prominent point is the insistence on the defence of the USSR, indicating an underlying faith that its substantive achievements do after all approximate socialism. Corresponding to this premiss is another, that revolutions can be engaged 'from above': for it is the results, and not the processes, which matter in this view. Indeed, Deutscher's argument for 'revolution on the point of the bayonet' indicates a line of continuity with the late Trotsky that is rather less happy than that running between Dunayevskaya, James and the late Trotsky. Deutscher, like Trotsky, did not think through history from below, from the perspective of the actually existing, suffering masses, their everyday lives and culture, their ordinary victories and tragedies. The focus on the view from above strikes disharmonic chords in Deutscher's world view, for it should by rights be the case that his anticipated 'third wave' of revolution depends on the consciousness and action of just these masses. Deutscher showed, at least on occasions, that he understood the 'crisis of marxism' and the necessary tasks of rethinking the question of transition which follow from such a recognition. His intuitions that marxism had seen the end of its *raison d'être* in the absolute severance of theory and practice were never to be substantiated. Ordinary people will continue to live out their tragedies in bourgeois civilisation: the tragedy of Trotskyism is its inability to face or explain this situation, let alone begin to conceive of ways to alter it. Deutscher was swept away from a fresh consideration of the problem of transition by the allegedly impending third wave of the sixties. However influential his half-radicalism may have been for an earlier generation who sought an alternative road in the dark days of the fifties, his assurances that socialism would come, even through barbarism, make Deutscher sound today like a voice from the past, a misplaced M. Jourdain speaking a language known all too well to an audience which not only knows of the Gulag, but sees it in its full significance.

176

History and Transition: Deutscher

Notes

1. D. Singer, 'Armed with a Pen' in D. Horowitz (ed.), *Isaac Deutscher. The Man and His Work* (Macdonald, London, 1971), p. 49.
2. Deutscher, *Stalin, A Political Biography* (Penguin, Harmondsworth, 1970, revised edn), p. 275.
3. Deutscher, *Stalin*, pp. 327, 357. Similar images appear elsewhere, as, for example, in 'The Roots of Bureaucracy', *Socialist Register*, 1969, p. 13f.
4. Deutscher, *Stalin*, p. 340.
5. Ibid., p. 553.
6. Ibid., p. 306.
7. Perhaps the most effective image used is that of Stalin behind the scenes; Deutscher, *Stalin*, p. 145. Other examples of theatrical metaphor occur at pp. 9, 71, 81, 83, 278, 292, 343, 368, 520, 533, 556. Images of disease or gynaecology appear at pp. 280, 293, 307, 342, 611. Geology, astronomy and tidal metaphors appear at pp. 400, 529, 239; at p. 345, Deutscher uses Trotsky's image of the cooling lava. Personification is employed at pp. 82, 244 and 484 with varying degrees of persuasion.
8. Ibid., p. 288.
9. Ibid., p. 130.
10. Ibid., pp. 178, 212f, 231, 236.
11. Ibid., pp. 271, 296.
12. Ibid., pp. 358, 563, 516, 480, 540.
13. It appears in 'Three Currents in Communism' *Ironies of History. Essays On Contemporary Communism* (Oxford, 1966) in the form of Jekyll and Hyde, p. 87. In 'The Roots of Bureaucracy', state and bureaucracy are presented as the Jekyll and Hyde of human civilisation, p. 12. In 'Maoism — Its Origins and Outlook', *Ironies of History*, the peasants have two souls, p. 108. In 'The Post-Stalinist Ferment of Ideas', *Heretics and Renegades* (Bobbs-Merill, Indianapolis, 1969), there are two souls in the breast of the Malenkov Government, p. 212. In *The Unfinished Revolution. Russia 1917–1967* (Oxford, New York, 1977), Maoism has two souls, p. 94; and the figure of Janus appears in 'Vietnam in Perspective' in *Ironies*, p. 156, in 'Ideological Trends in the USSR', *Marxism in Our Time* (Ramparts, Berkeley, 1971), p. 210, and 'Reflections on the Russian Problem', *Political Quarterly, 15* (1944), January–March, p. 79.
14. 'Writing a Biography of Stalin', *Listener*, vol. 38, 25 December 1947, p. 1098.
15. 'Trotsky on Stalin', *Heretics and Renegades*, pp. 79, 66, 162ff.
16. The most effective single image here is that of Stalin in an iron mask, Deutscher, *Stalin*, p. 455. Other images of masking occur at pp. 215, 275, 332, 445, 597, 604, and see p. 239.
17. Ibid., p. 242.
18. Deutscher, *The Prophet Armed* (Oxford, University Press, 1970), p. vii.
19. The image recurs elsewhere, bringing to mind the influence not only of Oedipus, but also of Freud: 'There was thus a tragic

element in Bolshevik fortunes: all their profound and acute awareness of the danger [of corruption] did not save them from it; and all their abhorrence of the corruption did not prevent them from succumbing to it.' *The Unfinished Revolution*, p. 31.

20. Deutscher, *The Prophet Armed*, p. 486.

21. Deutscher, *The Prophet Unarmed* (Oxford, University Press, 1970), p. 467.

22. Deutscher, *The Prophet Outcast* (Oxford, Oxford University Press, 1970), p. 515.

23. Deutscher, Introduction to *The Age of Permanent Revolution. A Trotsky Anthology* (Dell, New York, 1973), p. 13; 'Trotsky at his Nadir' in *Ironies of History*, p. 175.

24. See 'The Ex-Communist's Conscience', *Heretics and Renegades*, p. 20.

25. C. Hill, 'The Theory of Revolutions' in Horowitz, *Isaac Deutscher*, p. 130.

26. *The Prophet Outcast*, pp. 435, 480, 512; 'Russia in Transition' in *Ironies of History*, p. 29.

27. Deutscher, *The Prophet Outcast*, p. 477.

28. Ibid., p. 510f. Sisyphean imagery appears *inter alia* in *The Prophet Armed*, p. 439; *The Prophet Unarmed*, p. 2,; *The Prophet Outcast*, pp. 207, 212; *Stalin*, p. 548; 'Mid-Century Russia' in *Heretics and Renegades*, p. 114. Images of fate occur *inter alia* in *The Prophet Armed*, p. 7; *The Prophet Unarmed*, pp. ix, 131, 312, 229.

29. Images of theatre, drama, tragedy occur at *The Prophet Armed*, pp. v, viii, 17, 35, 62, 71, 75, 95–7, 144, 177, 202, 230, 292, 304, 346ff, 486f, 489, 495, 522; *The Prophet Unarmed*, pp. xii, 27, 93, 217, 270, 284, 290, 304, 316, 318, 377, 393, 422, 435, 469; *The Prophet Outcast*, pp. vii, xiii, 10, 12, 125, 158, 175, 176, 189, 221, 222, 229, 274, 292, 318, 321, 333, 384, 410, 450, 457, 519, 520, 522. Examples of personification in the trilogy include those at *The Prophet Armed* pp. 293, 322, 306, 314, and *The Prophet Outcast*, p. 516. (Metaphors of disease, anatomy, gynaecology appear rarely in comparison: *Prophet Armed*, pp. 32, 338, 451, 521; *Prophet Unarmed*, p. 148; *Prophet Outcast*, pp. 285, 515, 519.) Images of eruption, tidal and geological movement occur at *PA*, pp. 130, 267, 270, 320, 342, 451; *PU*, pp. 136, 167, 204f, 368, 377, 421; *PO*, pp. 69, 112, 165, 168, 211, 231, 233, 316, 394, 520f.

30. See *The Prophet Outcast*, p. 253.

31. *The Prophet Armed*, p. 516, and see p. 418; *The Prophet Unarmed*, pp. 94, 195, 220; *The Prophet Outcast*, pp. 83, 171.

32. *The Prophet Unarmed*, p. 454.

33. *The Prophet Outcast*, p. 63. The image of clothing also appears at p. 169. (One of Deutscher's oft-quoted images is that of the 'washing of dirty linen' as the task of Khrushchevism: the linen is soaked in popular sweat and blood. See 'Khrushchev on Stalin' in *Ironies of History*, p. 17.)

34. Carlyle, *On Heroes, Hero-Worship and the Heroic in History* (Chapman and Hall, London, 1896), p. 189f.

35. Carlyle, *Sartor Resartus* (Ward, Lock, London, n.d.).

36. K. Burke, *A Rhetoric of Motives* (California, University Press, 1969), pp. 118ff.

37. *The Prophet Armed*, pp. 95, 321, 329; *The Prophet Unarmed*, p. 347; *The Prophet Outcast*, p. 304.

38. *The Prophet Unarmed* p. 27.

39. *The Prophet Outcast*, p. vii.

40. T. Deutscher, 'Work in Progress' in Horowitz, *Isaac Deutscher*, p. 80.

41. A.C. Bradley, *Shakespearean Tragedy* (Macmillan, London 1929), p. 28; and see Bradley's 'Hegel's Theory of Tragedy', *Oxford Lectures on Poetry* (Macmillan, London, 1955), pp. 69–95.

42. *The Prophet Unarmed*, p. 192.

43. Ibid., p. 313.

44. 'Israel's Tenth Birthday' in *The Non-Jewish Jew* (Oxford, Oxford University Press, 1968), p. 119.

45. 'The Jewish Tragedy and the Historian' in ibid., p. 163f.

46. 'On Socialist Man', *Marxism in Our Time*, p. 238.

47. J. Jacobson, 'Isaac Deutscher: The Anatomy of an Apologist' in Jacobson (ed.), *Soviet Communism and the Socialist Vision* (Transaction, New Jersey, 1972), pp. 86–162; and L. Labedz, 'Deutscher as Historian and Prophet', *Survey, 41* (1962), pp. 120–44. Related criticisms are A. MacIntyre, 'Trotsky in Exile', *Encounter, 21(6)* (1963), pp. 73–8; and G. Lichtheim, 'Reflections on Trotsky', *The Concept of Ideology and Other Essays* (Vintage, New York, 1967), pp. 204–24. Related criticisms from the left include M. Shachtman, 'Four Portraits of Stalinism', *New International*, September-October 1950, pp. 293ff; and 'The End of Socialism', *New International*, March-April 1954, pp. 67–83, May-June 1954, pp. 145–58, July-August 1954, pp. 170–83; T. Cliff, 'The End of the Road: Deutscher's Capitulation to Stalinism', *International Socialism, 15*, pp. 10–20; J. P. Cannon, 'Trotsky or Deutscher?' *Fourth International*, Winter 1954, pp. 9–16; J. G. Wright, 'The Soviet Union Under Malenkov', ibid., pp. 23–8.

48. *The Prophet Unarmed*, p. 462.

49. *The Prophet Outcast*, p. 303f; and see 'Was the Revolution Betrayed?' in *Marxism in Our Time*, pp. 265–71.

50. 'On Internationals and Internationalism', *Marxism in Our Time*, p. 111.

51. Introduction to *The Age of Permanent Revolution*, p. 22; 'The Roots of Bureaucracy', p. 24. In 'Russia and Transition: Reply to Critics', *Dissent*, Winter 1955, Deutscher's image of Soviet insubstantiality is that of the amoeba, without backbone, p. 35.

52. Deutscher, *The Great Contest. Russia and the West* (Oxford, 1960), p. 68.

53. 'The Meaning of Destalinisation', *Ironies of History*, p. 21.

54. *Marxism in Our Time*, p. 23; *Stalin*, p. 587.

55. See, for example, J.-J. Marie, *Trotsky, le trotskyisme et la Quatrième International* (PUF, Paris, 1980), p. 114f.

56. 'A Reply to Critics'. *Heretics*, pp. 193, 196; 'The Soviet Union Enters the Second Decade After Stalin' in *Russia, China and the West 1953–66*, (Penguin, Harmondsworth, 1970), p. 253.

57. 'Germany and Marxism', *Marxism In Our Time*, p. 179.
58. *The Unfinished Revolution*, p. 10; 'The Irony of History in Stalinism', *Ironies of History*, p. 234.
59. *The Unfinished Revolution*, p. 54.
60. 'The Roots of Bureaucracy', p. 25f.
61. *The Unfinished Revolution*, p. 3.
62. *The Prophet Outcast*, p. 521f.
63. *The Unfinished Revolution*, p. 113. Emphasis added.
64. *Marxism in Our Time*, p. 18.
65. Ibid., p. 26.
66. *The Unfinished Revolution*, pp. 28, 29, 37; *The Great Contest*, p. 57; *Soviet Trade Unions. Their Place in Soviet Labour Policy* (Oxford/RIIA, 1950), Ch. 7.
67. 'A Reply to Critics', p. 197f.
68. See, for example, *Marxism in Our Time*, p. 29; 'Israel's Tenth Birthday', p. 123.
69. 'Marxism and the New Left' in *Marxism in Our Time*, p. 73.
70. 'On Socialist Man', p. 244, and see pp. 250, 254, 251f, 249, 253.
71. 'Germany and Marxism', p. 179.
72. Introduction to *The Age of Permanent Revolution*, p. 36; *The Prophet Outcast*, p. 311f; 'Maoism — Its Origins and Outlook' in *Ironies*, p. 104.
73. *The Unfinished Revolution*, p. 20.
74. *The Prophet Outcast*, p. 517.
75. Ibid., p. 519f.
76. 'On Internationals and Internationalism', pp. 108, 112.
77. See especially Van Heijenoort, *With Trotsky in Exile*, p. 154; Marie, *Trotsky, le trotskyisme*, p. 127; P. Broué, 'Les derniers secrets des archives de Trotski', *Le Monde Dimanche*, 4 May 1980, p. xvii.
78. *Stalin*, p. 13.
79. Ibid., p. 14.
80. 'A Reply to Critics', p. 198.
81. *The Prophet Outcast*, pp. 242ff.
82. 'Trotsky in Exile', p. 77.
83. *The Prophet Outcast*, p. 245f.
84. See, for example, 'The Meaning of Destalinisation', p. 23; 'Russia in Transition', *Ironies*, p. 42; *Russia After Stalin* (Hamish Hamilton, London, 1953), Ch. 3.
85. *The Prophet Unarmed*, p. xii.
86. *Russia After Stalin*, p. 13.
87. *Russia After Stalin*, Ch. 3; p. 41f.
88. *The Prophet Armed*, p. 27; 'The Moral Dilemmas of Lenin', in *Ironies*, p. 7f.
89. T. Deutscher, 'Work in Progress', p. 58.
90. 'The Irony of History in Stalinism', p. 236.
91. *The Unfinished Revolution*, p. 97.
92. 'Roots of Bureaucracy', p. 25.
93. 'Russia in Transition', in *Ironies*, p. 45f; and see 'The Polish and Hungarian Revolts', p. 88f and p. 90f and 'The Causes of the Crisis in Eastern Europe', pp. 92ff, both in *Russia, China and the West*.

94. 'Pasternak and the Calendar of the Revolution' in *Ironies*, p. 258.
95. 'Two Revolutions' in *Heretics*, p. 67.
96. See, for example, *The Prophet Armed*, p. 515.
97. See Day, *Leon Trotsky and the Politics of Economic Isolation*, p. 182.
98. 'Mid-Century Russia', p. 118.
99. 'Obituary on Stalin', *Ironies*, p. 182f.
100. *The Prophet Armed*, pp. 486, 521.
101. But see the exceptional analysis of Jacobin duality in Robespierre executed in *The Prophet Outcast*, p. 318.
102. See 'Khrushchev at Home', *Ironies*, pp. 60–7, and 'Khrushchev Goes to Washington', *Russia, China and the West*, pp. 179–84. See 'Pasternak and the Calendar of the Revolution', and 'Two Autobiographies', both in *Ironies*, pp. 248ff; and 'The Tragic Life of a Polrugarian Minister', *Heretics*, pp. 23ff.
103. A. Momigliano, 'The Rhetoric of History and the History of Rhetoric' in E. S. Shaffer (ed.), *Comparative Criticism: A Yearbook, 3* (Cambridge, Cambridge University Press, 1981), pp. 259–61.
104. Sedgwick, 'Tragedy of the Tragedian', *International Socialism, 31* (1967), p. 15f. Sedgwick also indicates that the decline across the volumes of the Trotsky trilogy is related to this personalisation of the tragic.
105. M. Berman, *All That Is Solid Melts Into Air*, p. 48.

8
Conclusion:
Trotskyism and its Outcome

Trotskyism is reconciled with 'actually existing' socialism as the epicentre of the world revolution moves East. Transition in the West is forsaken. The mass audience of Trotskyism shrinks as that of Stalinism expands; the bazaar shifts eastward, following business. Yet this logic, popularised by Deutscher and widely influential throughout the Fourth International, is ultimately self-defeating, if not dangerous outright, because self-destructive. 'Socialism' can now be introduced from above by unconscious agents, Mao, Tito, Castro, the Sandinistas, chosen by Permanent Revolution or by History itself. The necessitarian philosophy of history developed by Trotsky and extended by Deutscher explains the tragic spectacle in which Trotskyists must themselves defend their own mortal enemies. If Stalinism is revolutionary, then Trotskyists must kneel before History. Orthodox Trotskyists thus defend to this day the regime which murdered their leader, as they defend regimes like Castro's which suppressed the Cuban Trotskyists, seizing their printing press and smashing, ironically, the type of the local edition of *Permanent Revolution*.[1] If the conscious enemies of Trotskyism can thus become its unconscious world executors, so then can Trotskyists become obstacles in history's way. If, as Pablo and Deutscher argued, there were two major camps, communism and imperialism, then there was always the risk that Trotskyists might become the indirect instruments of other classes.[2] Such is the outcome of Trotskyism. The Trotskyist philosophy of history allows no option: if History chooses an agent other than the Fourth International to do its bidding, then this chosen agent must ultimately represent the best interests of the theory of Permanent Revolution. Trotskyists must accept and celebrate the judgement of History, even be it against them. Not all Trotskyists have followed this position through to its liquidationist conclusions; those who have empathised more with the wilful Jacobinism of the Bolshevik tradition have refused the ruse. Trotskyism remains a variegated discourse, held together by notions of necessity, whether Bolshevik or not. But all Trotskyists accept the Hegelian principle, that History is the world's court of judgement. Those closer to the Bolshevik tradition are simply waiting for more Petrograds. Those who view the proletariat as inessential to the plot see Permanent Revolution as being vindicated throughout the world, using other 'materials'. Modern Trotskyism is a pathetic spectacle: contemporary Trotskyists argue endlessly about the new form Jacobinism might take while they are frogmarched away by the carnal representatives of Behemoth. This is a qualitatively new form of tragedy for the movement. Trotsky's own trajectory was certainly tragic; his personal suffering and integrity ought never be forgotten.[3] Yet Trotsky submitted to the process of tragedy; the role of will in this emplotment remains unrecognised. Marxists seem to need tragic figures; but can they afford mass suicides?

Trotsky, at least, was prepared to stand against History. He believed, after 1917, that history could only make contact via the Party; his hyperbolshevism mediated the theory of Permanent Revolution, while the latter ultimately made the Party obsolete. His ambivalence towards the Soviet Union meant that Stalin had to destroy him. Modern Trotskyists are more obliging: they are prepared to open the process themselves, if it helps History work out. The language of necessity in Trotskyism turns the theory of Permanent Revolution into a language of reconciliation. In contemporary Trotskyism the rhetoric of revolution in the West coexists with the language of reconciliation in the East. Trotsky's work was dominated by the language of Jacobin revolution; the elements of a language of reconciliation in his work were related only to the Soviet experience. In contemporary Trotskyism the priorities have been reversed. Trotsky, by comparison, did at least allow the possibility that the socialist experiences of the twentieth century may have been mere experiments. Trotsky also indicated that if his view of the epoch was mistaken, he would call for a new minimum program defending not the regimes, but their victims. The dominance of the language of necessity in the Fourth International threatens to eclipse not only the libertarian, but even the humanist dimension of Trotsky's thinking. Trotskyist orthodoxy today lacks the contradiction characteristic of Trotsky's own work; it also lacks the sincerity of revolutionary conviction which led Trotsky to dedicate his life to the cause of socialism.

Yet the continuity of the Trotskyist tradition remains substantial. Trotskyism functions as theodicy or eschatology, the purpose of which is the intellectual recruitment of the audience through language. The transition to socialism, presumed by Trotskyism in its very vocabulary, has simply been re-routed. This vocabulary, it has been argued here, is, as Arendt observed, the vocabulary of Jacobinism: flow, necessity, masking, gangrene, the lawful and irresistable, the power of necessity.[4] As Arendt observes, the Jacobin notion of the popular movement, *le peuple*, indicates a multi-headed monster, a mass that moves as one body and acts as though possessed by one will; and as Furet adds, *le peuple* is not only an amoebic but also a carnivorous concept, devouring individuals, identifying enemies as those who remain concealed.[5] In the marxist tradition *le peuple* becomes *le proletariat*. In its Trotskyist caricature *le proletariat* becomes, in organisational terms *le parti*, while the image of 'mass' activity becomes rhetoric, a principle of historiography. The language and message of Trotskyism can thus be seen as an extension of Jacobinism, if with a technological twist, for Trotskyist images of the future are not only naturalistic, but also technological. Trotskyist orthodoxy combines claims to the recovery of naturalism with claims for the desirability of social engineering, veritably, as Deutscher had it, Trotskyism is the Jekyll and Hyde of the socialist tradition. Jacobinism is here modified by Dialectical Materialism: mediated by technical rationality, the unity of opposites makes everything possible, provided the mole eventually gets it right.

The tension between will and necessity absent from Lenin, in Arendt's understanding, remains constant in Trotskyism, though later Trotskyist arguments minimise it. Trotskyism highlights its internal tension between will and necessity in the periodic divisions in the movement over different historical developments. Jacobinism draws it toward necessity. The *Transitional Program*, which remains the basic orienting device of Trotskyism, identifies the main problem as that of will, but within the context of necessity. Developments after the Second World War produce debates within Trotskyism over questions such as the nature of Eastern Europe and the Chinese, Cuban, Algerian, Vietnamese and Central American revolutions, all of which prompt divided responses: either workers' states have been brought into objective existence despite the intentions of Stalinist leaderships, or else these sociological mutants are viewed as the result of an absence of will, the working class or the Trotskyist Party. Theorists like Deutscher, Rizzi, Burnham and the early Pablo epitomise the first response, as they raise objectivism to the level of a first principle, viewing socialism or collectivism as an inner principle of an evolving universal history. Others like James and Dunayevskaya, Shachtman and Cliff advanced the argument that socialism could only be viewed as a consciously willed process. The source of this tension between subjective and objective dimensions is to be found in Trotsky's own work. Trotskyism as a tradition has never reconciled this dualism, because it is its motivating force, providing the mechanism which allows Trotskyists always to be correct, blaming or accrediting subjective or objective factors as circumstances necessitate. It is this dualism which underlies the Trotskyist proclivity to combine the irreconcilable and to engage constant acts of *volte face*. This dualism continues to structure the debate in the Fourth International, even if its power is muted. Contemporary Trotskyism becomes a language of reconciliation to the extent that it fails to maintain this dualism.

Necessity, then, has a powerful appeal for Trotskyism. In this regard it can be said that Trotskyism is more directly formed by the Second International than by Marx's own theory. Trotskyists typically espouse some variant of the 1859 Preface, productive forces being viewed as the motor of history. Evolutionary arguments like those of Mandel clearly privilege 'objective' developments in the manner of Kautsky, and this despite the separate argument about the need for a proletarian vanguard. Other arguments like those of Dunayevskaya or James subscribe to an epistemological automatism, viewing the maturity of the age or the self-development of the proletariat as the condition for socialism, while people like Deutscher view progress as something inscribed into industrialisation and enculturation. Regardless of whether they privilege 'subjective' or 'objective' tendencies, all these Trotskyist arguments remain fundamentally teleological: they tell us something about the desire for socialism, but little of its conditions of possibility.

Trotskyism develops within intellectual parameters which allow it the structural and linguistic scope to elaborate an associational logic and a vocabulary appropriate to it, so that associations are constantly generated in a cosmological or historiosophical manner. This is as true of libertarians like James and Dunayevskaya as it is of Jacobins like Mandel and Deutscher. The constellations of association struck up by James and Dunayevskaya refer to the subjective component in Trotskyism, to the element of mass spontaneous will-formation and organisation and to the philosophical expression of this dialectic of freedom, understood as manifesting the inner self-movement of things in the sense that History is the actualisation of (*menschlicher*) *Geist*. James and Dunayevskaya add to history a philosophical layer of myth, effectively ascribing everyday life a profound philosophical significance: texts become analogs for the commonplace, the commonplace becomes cosmological (houses become dialectical for James, philosophical texts become anticipations of third world leaders or union bureaucrats for Dunayevskaya).

The constellations of association set up by Mandel and Deutscher are complex in different ways. Mandel's language is structured by the vocabulary of necessity, understood as the objective evolution of world history through successive modes of production or technological revolutions. Like the later Trotsky, Mandel interprets the subjective factor as identical with the Party and views the Party as the ethereal component of will injected into this objective process. Deutscher's constellation of language is even more strictly circumscribed by a sense of necessity, which is geared to a sense of progress understood less as a theory of successive modes than as a theorem that human and industrial progress is achieved through barbarism. Of all the Trotskyist arguments considered in this study, Deutscher's seems to be the most complex, and arguably the most persuasive, for the layers of meaning in his constellation are referenced to signification in classical tragedy and mythology as well as Shakespearean and Faustian notions of action, and Victorian senses of progress and pessimism in the manner of Macaulay and Carlyle. Deutscher remains intriguing to the extent that he actually combines Macaulay and Carlyle, Prometheus and Sisyphus. Mandel's associations are unimpressive compared to Deutscher's, relating mainly to cruder images of geological or anthropological evolution, to senses of crisis and intervention and subterranean action. Mandel's vocabulary is reminiscent of Trotsky at his worst, while Deutscher's resembles, perhaps even surpasses, Trotsky at his historical best. The constant tension between subjective and objective elements in Mandel's work mirrors Trotsky's own position more directly than any other argument considered here: for the scope given to freedom rather than necessity is sufficient to justify the existence of the Fourth International while simultaneously allowing support of each and any 'progressive' development in the emergence of new deformed 'workers' states'. Deutscher's thought, however, remains more influential because of the extent to which the Fourth International is now increasingly tied to these regimes.

The constellations struck up by Mandel and Deutscher throw considerable light on the intricacies and contradiction of Trotsky's own work. The philosophical cosmology established by James and Dunayevskaya, like their libertarian politics, shows only a passing relation to what is conventionally called Trotskyism; it is their interpretation of East European societies which reveals the stronger point of contact with Trotsky and the tradition. In this regard, it can be observed that if the state capitalist argument produces better results than arguments like those of Mandel or Deutscher, it is because the associations invoked are more appropriate, addressing not the historic vocation of the proletariat or the superior value of central planning, but the more earthly question of what it means to be a 'worker in a workers' state'. Mandel and Deutscher also modify Trotsky, but they do so in a way which is more substantively reflective of the inner dynamic of Trotsky's thought. This development is particularly evident in their extension of Trotsky's Jacobinism. Probably neither Deutscher nor Mandel would concede the point; Lenin seems to have been the only marxist who was prepared to publicly view Jacobinism as a virtue, and then only in passing. A defining characteristic of Trotskyist Jacobinism is its self-refusal. Trotskyist Jacobinsm cannot recognise itself as Jacobin: it is itself tragic, in political terms, because it refuses to recognise the inner contradiction between the project of human perfectibility and the practice of social engineering conducted from above. It refuses to accept that within its own language the tension in Jacobinism is that between freedom and necessity.

While Bolshevism has proven to be an historically tragic project of action, Social Democracy has meantime proven to be an historically indecisive project of inaction. Though bankrupt, revolutionary and reformist languages still remain dominant in radical discourse, perhaps the more so because they share some basic articles of vocabulary, allegiance to central planning from above chief among them. The problem of social change or transition in the West needs to be faced in the light of this situation. Marx argued more than a century ago that the poetry of revolution had to be created from the future, not the past; he did not explain how this might be possible, nor did he develop a political language adequate to its discussion. Jacobinism has filled the void. As a result, marxism today has no practical language for a transition to socialism. In the twentieth century there are simply too many dead for the dead to bury. Trotskyism, however noble, however defiant, is part of the past; the traditions of its dead generations continue to weigh like a nightmare on the minds of the living.

Notes

1. R. J. Alexander, *Trotskyism in Latin America* (Hoover, Stanford, 1973), pp. 228ff.
2. Pablo, 'From the Third to the Fourth World Congress', *Towards a History of the Fourth International* (SWP Education for Socialists Series), Part 4, vol. 3, p. 146.
3. See especially G. Steiner, 'Trotsky and the Tragic Imagination' in *Language and Silence* (Atheneum, New York, 1982).
4. H. Arendt, *On Revolution* (Viking, New York, 1963). See also E. Pankoke, 'Social Movement', *Economy and Society, 11(3)* (1982).
5. Arendt, *On Revolution*, p. 89f; Furet, *Interpreting the French Revolution*, p. 27.

Bibliographical Note

Materials on Trotskyism are abundant. They are as diverse as the Fourth Internationals themselves, and frequently as ephemeral in nature. This note refers only to materials consulted for this study, and especially to those which were found more useful. More exhaustive lists can be found in the bibliographies produced by L. Sinclair, *Leon Trotsky: A Bibliography* (Hoover, Stanford, 1972) and by W. Lubitz, *Trotsky Bibliography* (K. G. Saur, Munich, 1982); Sinclair covers Trotsky alone, while Lubitz covers Trotskyism as well. Saur will publish a new, expanded and revised edition of Lubitz in 1987. Both are immensely useful, and indispensable for those interested in Trotskyism.

Trotsky and his era

There is no complete or standard edition of Trotsky's writings in English. The 14 volumes of his exile writings (twelve volumes, two volumes supplement) are published by Pathfinder of New York; his classics are available in different prints, primarily from Pathfinder and New Park (London). The different Trotskyist sects have capitalised on their own favoured Trotsky; thus, for example, the American SWP (Pathfinder) have published the three volume *Challenge of the Left Opposition*, while the British WRP have produced Trotsky's military writings, *How the Revolution Armed* (New Park, 5 vols.).

Beyond the efforts of Trotsky's partisans, a significant collection is *The Trotsky Papers*, edited by J. M. Meijer (Mouton, The Hague, 2 vols., 1964, 1971). Other titles such as *My Life*

Bibliographical Note

and *1905* have been published by Penguin. As observed above, the vitally important early writings remain unavailable in English to this day. Trotsky's Archives at Harvard received considerable publicity recently when the closed section, sealed from 1940 to 1980, was made publicly accessible. A microfilm guide to the new and old sections is available from the Houghton Library at Harvard. The Archives have been publicised by the Paris-based Trotsky Institute in their excellent journal, *Cahiers Léon Trotsky*; see also, for example, L. and N. Trotsky, *Correspondance 1933–1938* (Gallimard, Paris, 1980). It is difficult not to imagine that it will be the historians of the inner-party debates who will most benefit from the new archive, which contains extensive correspondence to and from Burnham, Ciliga, Rizzi, Shachtman, and Cannon.

Writings which frame Trotsky's formation have recently become a little more accessible in English; see for example L. Kolakowski, *Main Currents in Marxism* (Oxford, University Press, 1978, 3 vols.); T. Bottomore and P. Goode (eds), *Austro-Marxism* (Oxford, 1978); K. Kautsky, *Political Writings* (Macmillan, London, 1983); M. Blum, *The Austro-Marxists* (University Press, Kentucky,1985); M. Salvadori, *Karl Kautsky* (New Left Books, London, 1979); G. P. Steenson, *Karl Kautsky* (University Press, Pittsburgh, 1978); I. Getzler, *Martov* (University Press, Melbourne, 1967); A. Ascher, *Pavel Axelrod and the Development of Menshevism* (Harvard University Press, Cambridge, 1972).

For the post-1917 period, E. H. Carr's *History of Soviet Russia* (Macmillan, London, 14 vols., several editions) is indispensable; also most useful are R. W. Davies, *The Industrialisation of Soviet Russia* (Macmillan, London, 1980, 2 vols.), A. Erlich, *The Soviet Industrialisation Debate* (Harvard, Cambridge, 1960) and M. Lewin, *Political Undercurrents in Soviet Economic Debates* (Pluto, London, 1975). For Preobrazhensky, see particularly his *New Economics* (Oxford, 1965), and see D. Filtzer (ed.), *E. A. Preobrazhensky. The Crisis in Soviet Industrialisation* (Macmillan, 1980). On Bukharin, see S. F. Cohen, *Bukharin and the Bolshevik Revolution* (Vintage, New York,1975), M. Haynes, *Nikolai Bukharin and the Transition from Capitalism to Socialism* (Croom Helm, London, 1985), and R. B. Day (ed.), *N. I. Bukharin. Selected Writings on the State and the Transition to Socialism* (Sharpe, Armonk, 1982); these and related issues have been widely canvassed in the excellent Glasgow-based journal,

Bibliographical Note

Critique. Also worth consulting are C. Rakovsky, *Selected Writings on the Opposition in the USSR 1923–30* (Allison and Busby, London, 1980), and *Theses, Resolutions and Manifestoes of the First Four Congresses of the Third International* (Ink Links, London, 1980).

Special issues of journals given to the analysis of Trotskyism include *Studies in Comparative Communism, 10(1–2)* (1977) and *Survey, 24(1)* (1979). A contribution of great importance is the two-volume collection of papers given at the Follonica Feltrinelli Conference on Trotsky: see F. Gori (ed.), *Pensiero e azione politica di Lev Trockij* (Olschki, Florence, 1982), which contains papers by most significant Trotsky-scholars. The best surveys of Trotsky's thought are those by Knei-Paz, *The Social and Political Thought of Leon Trotsky* (Oxford, 1978) and Day, *Leon Trotsky and the Politics of Economic Isolation* (Cambridge, 1973). Most readable as introductions are I. Howe, *Trotsky* (Vintage, New York, 1978), R. Segal, *The Tragedy of Leon Trotsky* (Hutchinson, London, 1979); R. Warth, *Leon Trotsky* (Twayne, Boston, 1977); and D. Wyndham and J. King, *Trotsky, A Documentary* (Penguin, 1972). See also Van Heijenoort's memoirs, *With Trotsky in Exile* (Harvard, 1978). Closer to the Trotskyist tradition, in different ways, are A. Brossat, *Aux origines de la révolution permanente* (Maspéro, Paris, 1974) and M. Löwy, *The Politics of Combined and Uneven Development* (Verso, London, 1981); Brossat and D. Avenas, *De l'antit-rotskysme*, (Maspéro, Paris, 1971); Avenas, 'Trotsky's Marxism', *International* (IMG, London), *3(2)* (1976), *3(3)* (1977); J. Molyneux, *Leon Trotsky's Theory of Revolution* (Harvester, Brighton, 1981); D. Hallas, *Trotsky's Marxism* (Pluto, London, 1979). Also worth consulting are L. Comby, *Léon Trotsky* (Masson, Paris, 1976) and P. Naville, *Trotsky Vivant* (Maurice Nadeau, Paris, 1979). The work of J.-J. Marie is especially important: see particularly his *Trotsky, le trotskysme* (PUF, Paris, 1980). Good English-language criticisms include J. Callaghan, *British Trotskyism: Theory and Practice* (Blackwell, Oxford, 1984); G. Hodgson, *Trotsky and Fatalistic Marxism* (Spokesman, Nottingham, 1975); P. Thompson and G. Lewis, *The Revolution Unfinished? A Critique of Trotskyism* (Big Flame, London, 1977); and P. Corrigan, H. Ramsay, D. Sayer, *Socialist Construction and Marxist Theory* (Macmillan, London, 1978), Ch. 3. Other contributions include N. Krasso (ed.), *Trotsky — The Great Debate Renewed* (New Critics, St Louis, 1972) and Projekt

Bibliographical Note

Klassenanalyse, *Leo Trotzki: Alternative zum Leninismus?* (VSA, Westberlin, 1975). Dissertations on Trotsky include C. Stokes, 'On the Evolution of Trotsky's Theory of Revolution', PhD thesis, Michigan, 1978; T. F. Egan, 'Leon Trotsky: His Political Philosophy in Opposition', PhD thesis, Florida State, 1978; D.K. Rowney, 'The Generation of October: The Politics of Twentieth Century Social Revolution in the View of L. D. Trotsky', PhD thesis, Indiana, 1965; N. Heyman, 'Leon Trotsky as a Military Thinker', PhD thesis, Stanford, 1972; H. Nelson, 'Leon Trotsky and the Art of Insurrection, 1905–1917', PhD thesis, Michigan, 1978; T. R. Poole, 'Counter-Trial: Leon Trotsky and the Soviet Purge Trials', PhD thesis, Massachusetts, 1974, 2 vols.; P. Beilharz, 'From Marx to Trotsky: The Theory of Degeneration and the Degeneration of Theory', M. A. Preliminary, Monash, 1978; Beilharz, 'Trotsky, Trotskyism and the Theory of the Transition to Socialism', PhD thesis, Monash, 1983.

Much scholarly attention has been given to Trotsky's historical interests and to specific national traditions and problems. See, for example, F. Rosengarten, 'The Gramsci-Trotsky Question (1922–1932)', *Social Text, 11* (1984/5); B. Bayerlein, 'Trockij und seine Auseinandersetzung mit dem Faschismus' in *Pensiero e azione politica di Lev Trockij*, vol. 2, pp 667–92; S. Corvisieri, *Trockij e il communismo italiano* (Samonà e Savelli, Rome, 1969); J. Pluet-Despatin, *La presse trotskiste en France de 1926 a 1968* (Editions de la maison des sciences de l'homme, Presses universitaires de Grenoble, Paris, 1978), *Les trotskistes et la guerre 1940–1944* (Anthropos, Paris, 1980), and *Trotsky et le Trotskisme* (Armand Colin, Paris, 1971).Other related materials are listed in the next section.

Trotskyism after Trotsky

There is no full or complete history of the Fourth Internationals. Most useful are A. Westoby, *Communism Since World War Two* (Harvester, Brighton, 1981) and Westoby and T. Wohlforth, *'Communists' Against Revolution: The Theory of Structural Assimilation* (Folrose, London, 1978) and two surveys by Workers Power: *The Degenerated Revolution* (Workers Power, London, 1982) and *The Death Agony of the Fourth International* (Workers Power, London, 1983) as well as Callaghan, *British*

Bibliographical Note

Trotskyism. Other works include P. Bellis, *Marxism and the USSR* (Macmillan, London 1979); P. Frank, *The Fourth International* (Ink Links, London, 1979); J. P. Cannon, *The History of American Trotskyism* (Pathfinder, 1974); T. Wohlforth, *The Struggle for Marxism in the United States: A History of American Trotskyism* (Bulletin, New York, 1971); M. Fisk, *Socialism From Below in the U.S.* (ISO, Cleveland, 1977); R. J. Alexander, *Trotskyism in Latin America* (Hoover, Stanford, 1973); P. Shipley, *Revolutionaries in Modern Britain* (Bodley Head, London, 1976); C. A. Myers, *The Prophet's Army: Trotskyists in America 1928–1941* (Greenwood, Westport, 1977); G. Lerski, *Origins of Trotskyism in Ceylon* (Hoover, Stanford, 1968); G.Lora, *A History of the Bolivian Labour Movement* (Cambridge, 1977); J. Roussel, *Les enfants du prophète. Histoire du mouvement trotskiste en France* (Spartacus, Paris, 1970); Y. Craipeau, *Le mouvement trotskyste en France* (Syros, Paris, 1971); W. Reisner (ed.), *Documents of the Fourth International* (Pathfinder, 1973); G. Healy, *Problems of the Fourth International* (SLL, Sydney, n.d.); P. Jenkins, *Where Trotskyism Got Lost* (Spokesman Pamphlet 59,Nottingham); D. Widgery, *The Left in Britain* (Penguin, Harmondsworth, 1976); B. Bongiovanni, 'The Dissolution of Trotskyism', *Telos*, *52* (1982); B. Cartosio, Introduction to M. Glaberman, *Classe Operaia, imperialismo e rivoluzione negli USA* (Musolini, Turin, 1976).

Much of the American Trotskyist press, including *New International* and *International Socialist Review* is available in microfilm or fiche from Greenwood. See also J. Conlin (ed.), *The American Radical Press* (Greenwood, 1974, 2 vols). Also useful is the Harvester fiche collection, *The Left in Britain*. Most valuable is the *Education for Socialists* series published by the US SWP; see also C. Slaughter (ed.) *Marxism Versus Revisionism* (New Park, 1974, 5 vols.). Dunayevskaya's Archives are available on film from the Walter Reuther Library, Wayne State University, Detroit. A new collection has just been published by Dunayevskaya, *Women's Liberation and the Dialectics of Revolution* (Humanities, New York,1985); Mandel's recent forays into the outer limits of historical materialism have issued in a study of crime novels, *Delightful Murder* (Pluto, London, 1984). Two additions to Deutscher's writings are *Marxism, Wars and Revolutions* (Verso, London, 1984) and *The Great Purges* (Blackwell, Oxford, 1985). James's collected writings have been extended by the publication of *At the*

Bibliographical Note

Rendezvous of Victory (Allison and Busby, London, 1984).
Further background on some of the figures analysed here can
be found in D. Horowitz (ed.) *Isaac Deutscher. The Man and His
Work* (Macdonald, London, 1971); P. Buhle (ed.), *C. L. R.
James: His Life and Work* (Urgent Tasks 12, Chicago, 1981), C.
Robinson, 'C. L. R. James and the Black Radical Tradition',
Review, 6(3) (1983) and in the special issue of *Intervention: 3.
Contributions to Marxist Studies. Critical Reviews: Ernest Mandel in
Focus* (London, 1979). Broader context again might be found
in the work of T. Cliff, *State Capitalism in Russia* (Pluto, London,
1974) and *Neither Washington Nor Moscow* (Bookmarks,
London, 1982); J. Burnham, *The Managerial Revolution*
(Penguin, Harmondsworth, 1945); M. Shachtman, *The
Bureaucratic Revolution* (Donald, New York, 1962), B. Rizzi, *La
bureaucratisation du monde* (published by the author, Paris 1939)
and especially C. Castoriadis, *La société bureaucratique* (10/18,
Paris, 1973, 2 vols.). Relatively few English-language theses
have been written on Trotskyism; see A. Binstock, 'Socialisme
ou Barbarie: Examination of a Revolutionary Project', MA
thesis, Wisconsin, 1971; J. Burnett, 'American Trotskyism and
the Russian Question', PhD thesis, California at Berkeley,
1968; B. Fatheree, 'Trotskyism in Spain 1931–1937', PhD
thesis, Mississippi, 1978; A. Meyer, 'Deradicalisation: The
Case of Former Trotskyists', PhD thesis, New York at Albany,
1977.

Index

Index

Ghana 97
Goethe, J. 14, 136, 154, 175–6
Gouldner, A. 14, 109
Gramsci, A. 31

Healyites 94, 113n.38
Hegel, G. 23, 30, 42, 71, 88–94,
  100–3, 113n.19, 153,
  169–70, 183
Heidegger, M. 93
Hilferding, R. 46, 120, 125
Hill, C. 157
Hook, S. 92, 113n.31
Humanist Marxism 9–10,
  87–112
Hungarian Revolution (1956)
  170
Hussain, A. 125, 139, 145

Jackson, G. 102
Jacobinism 9–15, 21, 24, 40, 48,
  72, 75, 79, 159, 171–3, 182–8
James, C.L.R
  and Hegel 91–4
  on socialism 96–8
  on Soviet Union 94–6
  on Trotsky and Lenin
  88–91
Johnson, J.R.
  See James, C.L.R.

Kamenev, L. 44, 50, 53
Kant, I. 21
Kautsky, K. 10, 19, 20–1, 46,
  125
Kerensky, A. 44, 46
Khrushchev, N. 30, 166
Knei-Paz, B. 27, 70
Kojève, A. 102
Kondratiev, N.D. 28, 29, 141
Kornilov, General 44, 46
Korsch, K. 120
Kosik, K. 106

Labriola, A. 19, 20
Lafargue, P. 20, 136
League for the Revolutionary
  Party 73–4
Lenin, V.I. 9–10, 42, 44, 45, 52,
  64, 89–91, 98–9, 112, 143,

167, 187
Leontiev, W. 95
Lessing, G. 46
Lukács, G. 75, 112
Lunacharsky, A. 41, 45
Luxemburg, R. 9, 100

Macaulay, T. 154, 171, 186f
MacDonald, D. 24
Machiavelli, N. 175
MacIntyre, A. 167
McNeal, R. 51
Malamuth, C. 48
Mandel, E. 28, 162, 167
  and 1859 Preface 133–4
  on Marx 122–6
  on Soviet Union 126–30
  and technology 140–5
  and Trotsky 118–22
Manuilsky, D. 47
Mao 102, 166
Markus, G. 66
Martin, K. 36
Martov, J. 44
Marx, K.
  and class 20, 30, 103
  1859 Preface 25–6, 28–9,
  75, 101, 133, 161, 165, 175,
  185
  on history 14–15, 169, 188
  and socialism 66–7, 188
Mattick, P. 125
Mehring, F. 19
Metaphor, 15, 41–8, 57n.51,
  65, 68–70, 121, 127–9,
  153–76
Michels, R. 79
Miliukov 44
Momigliano, A. 174
Morgan, L.H. 23

New Deal 77
New International
  See Fourth International
News and Letters 87
Nkrumah, K. 97

Pablo, M. 117, 139, 163, 182,
  185
Paris Commune 81, 103

196

Index

Parvus, A. 38
Permanent Revolution 20,
27–8, 97–9, 130–5, 165–6,
182–3
Planning 66–8, 95, 105, 127
Plekhanov, G. 19, 20, 21, 38, 45,
94, 167–8
Poland 71
Popular Front (France) 77
Poulantzas, N. 1
Preobrazhensky, E. 26, 66, 67,
127, 172

Rakovsky, K. 26
Raptis, M.
See Pablo, M.
Reed, J. 41
Ricardo, D. 26
Ricoeur, P. 15–16
Rizzi, B. 60, 94, 121, 185
Robespierre, M. 10, 153–4
Rostow, W. 28
Rousseau, J-J. 15, 102
Rowthorn, B. 125
Rühle, O. 25–6

Sartre, J-P 138
Schachtman, M. 10, 24, 88, 185
Second International 9, 19, 20,
23, 25, 31, 39, 41, 43, 66, 98,
131, 175, 185
See also Hilferding, Kautsky,
Plekhanov, Social
Democracy
Sedgwick, P. 174
Shakespeare, W. 14, 159–60
Shaw, G.B. 46
Social Democracy 10, 12, 16n.1,
19, 79, 188
See also Second International
Socialist Workers Party (US) 74,
78
Soltz 13
Sombart, W. 26
Sontag, S. 15, 42, 43
Sophocles, 44, 156
Sorel, G. 48
Souvarine, B. 50

Stakhanovism 61, 94, 105
Stalin, J. 22, 24, 44, 45, 48–53,
57n.66, 105
State Capitalism 94–6, 104–9,
111
Sternberg, F. 26
Substitutionism 10–11, 14, 172
Sweezy, P. 37

Thiers, A. 169
Thomas, N. 52
Ticktin, H. 130
Togliatti, P. 132
Trade Unions 77
Transitional Program 71–6
Trotsky, L.D.
on America 63, 76–7
Americanism 29–30
on Bureaucracy 52, 63–6
and Class 30–2
and History 36–54
Morality 11, 21–2, 24
Theory of Permanent
Revolution 27–8
on Philosophy 19–20
and Planning 66–8
Political Economy 25–32
and Soviet Union 59–71
on Stalin 48–53, 57n.66
on Transition in West 71–80
Utopianism 12, 20, 30, 110,
135–6, 157

Uneven Development 37–8,
55n.23, 90

Van Heijenoort, J. 26

Webb, B. and S. 60
Weber, M. 63–4
White, H. 14, 174
Workers Party (US) 88, 114n.45
World System 27–9

Yugoslavian Revolution 131,
168

Zinoviev, G. 44, 50, 53

197

For Product Safety Concerns and Information please contact our EU
representative GPSR@taylorandfrancis.com
Taylor & Francis Verlag GmbH, Kaufingerstraße 24, 80331 München, Germany